Praise for

MOLLY IVINS CAN'T SAY THAT, CAN SHE?

★ ★ ★ ★ ★ ★ ★ ★ ★ ★ ★

"Three cheers for Molly Ivins . . . [She] is H. L. Mencken without the cruelty, Will Rogers with an agenda, and should never have been fired from *The New York Times* for calling a chicken-killing festival 'a gang-pluck.' "
— *L.A. Times Book Review*

"A delight from start to finish . . . all by herself, Molly Ivins proves that keen intelligence and a Southern accent are real good buddies. She is a canny observer of the political and cultural scene at both the local level and the national level."
— *The New York Times Book Review*

"If you're a liberal, you'll finish this book wanting Molly Ivins to keep on writing as long as she can breathe. If you're a conservative, you'll wish you had someone of her talent and humor in your ranks."
— *Christian Science Monitor*

"Has so many laugh-out-loud, memorable lines it's tempting to simply list them . . . for posterity, and for a darn good read."
— *Dallas Morning News*

"Molly Ivins is one of the funniest political columnists currently covering the national scene. . . . Ivins's wit does not quit."
— *St. Louis Post-Dispatch*

"Her writing is so wickedly funny . . . she's fresh in every sense of the word."
— *Detroit Free Press*

Molly Ivins

MOLLY IVINS CAN'T SAY THAT, CAN SHE?

Molly Ivins was born and raised in Texas. She has been a journalist for more than twenty years and has written for the *Texas Observer, The New York Times, Time,* and many other national magazines. She has appeared on the *MacNeil/Lehrer NewsHour, Nightline, The Tonight Show,* and *Today.* She currently lives in Austin, Texas, and writes a nationally syndicated column for the *Fort Worth Star.*

MOLLY IVINS CAN'T SAY THAT, CAN SHE?

★ ★ ★ ★ ★ ★ ★ ★ ★ ★ ★ ★

Molly Ivins

Vintage Books ★ A Division of Random House, Inc. ★ New York

Riverside Community College
Library
4800 Magnolia Avenue
Riverside, CA 92506

DEC '02

First Vintage Books Edition, October 1992

Copyright © 1991 by Molly Ivins

All rights reserved under International and Pan-American
Copyright Conventions. Published in the United States by
Vintage Books, a division of Random House, Inc., New
York, and simultaneously in Canada by Random House of
Canada Limited, Toronto. Originally published in hardcover
by Random House, Inc., New York, in 1991.

Owing to limitations of space,
this copyright page is continued on page 285.

Library of Congress Cataloging-in-Publication Data
Ivins, Molly.
Molly Ivins can't say that, can she?/Molly Ivins.
p. cm.
ISBN 0-679-74183-6
1. Texas—Politics and government—1951– —Humor. I. Title.
[F391.2.I95 1992]
976.4—dc20   92-50107
CIP

Manufactured in the United States of America
3579C8642

To Robert P. Moore,
the best teacher

ACKNOWLEDGMENTS

I love this bit where you get to say thanks. Hell, I could go on for hours and still forget half of them. Moore, my high school English teacher, I already dedicated the book to; Mel Mencher at Columbia J. School; Dick Cunningham and the late Frank Premack at the *Minneapolis Tribune*; Ronnie Dugger, publisher of the *Texas Observer*, still and always a hero; Kaye Northcott, best editor I ever had; David Jones, God bless you, and the Usual Suspects at *The New York Times*; Ken Johnson, Roy Bode, and Gaylord Shaw, who talked me into it, and a cast of hundreds at the *Herald,* especially the Austin bureau over the years, not excluding Eve McCullar in the Morgue, which they keep reminding us is now called the Library. Victor Navasky, Erwin Knoll, and Doug "Sweetpea" Foster, that splendid trio of lefty editors who have given me so much low-paying employment.

How to count the friends? Luckiest thing that ever happened to me in life was being adopted by Ida and Jesse Frankel of New York City. Kay and Michael Vickers of Boulder, the Albachs and the Andersons of Dallas, the entire Horses' ASSociation of Austin—my love to you all.

Eden Lipson, Liz Faulk, Richard Aregood, Myra MacPherson, Marlyn Schwartz, Bob and Mary Sherrill, the Sher clan—no one ever had better friends. To my mother, and my father, for whom it has never been easy to be related to me, love and gratitude.

I'd also like to thank the material—Texas politicians over a quarter of a century. From the Goober to the Gibber, from Poor Ol' Preston to Dollar Bill Clements, from Goodtime Charlie Wilson to the Wrong Don Yarbrough, from the Unspeakable Hollowell to Mad Dog Mengden, from the Bull of the Brazos to Goose Finnell, to that whole fabulous cast of characters in the Texas Legislature over the years: God love you, guys, I couldn't have done it without you. And my thanks to the heroes, too—Ralph Yarborough, Bob Eckhardt, the late John Henry Faulk, Sissy Farenthold, and all the Old Forts (membership requirements are you have to have been a freedom fighter in the Lege, over fifty, and not able to spell real well.)

And then, of course, there are those folks who account for the book. Dan Green, the agent, and Peter Osnos, the editor. And me 'cause I wrote it, what the hell.

CONTENTS

THE DISCREET SMARM OF THE BUSHWAZEE: CAMPAIGN NOTES AND THE FIRST YEAR

WIMMIN, AND ANCILLARY MATTERS

WORDS AND HEROES

INTRODUCTION

I n my youth, I aspired to be a great journalist. George Orwell, Albert Camus, and
I. F. Stone were my heroes. Great writers
and intellectuals who helped illuminate
their times. But look, God gave those guys
fascism, communism, colonialism, and
McCarthyism to struggle against. All I got was
Lubbock. It's not my fault.

Sometimes readers come up to me to say
they think I'm an awfully funny writer. I have
perfected this routine where I shuffle my feet,
say "Aw shucks," and then allow, "It's all in
the material." This has the dual virtue of allowing me to appear unconceited and also of being
perfectly truthful.

I suppose I could claim I did my best with
what I had. Lord knows, Texas politics is a rich
vein. Politics here is like everything in Texas,
just like it is everywhere else—only more so.

Twenty-five years of reporting on the place and I still can't account for that lunatic quality of exaggeration, of being slightly larger than life, in a pie-eyed way, that afflicts the entire state. I just know it's there, and I'd be lying if I tried to pretend it isn't.

Being used to it has advantages. Expecting things to make no sense gave me a great leg up during the Reagan years. As for George Bush of Kennebunkport, Maine—personally I think he's further evidence that the Great Scriptwriter in the Sky has an overdeveloped sense of irony.

I'm supposed to explain myself in this introduction—specifically, how come I came out so strange. Having been properly reared by a right-wing family in East Texas, how'd I turn out this peculiar? I believe all Southern liberals come from the same starting point—race. Once you figure out they are lying to you about race, you start to question everything.

If you grew up white before the civil rights movement anywhere in the South, all grown-ups lied. They'd tell you stuff like, "Don't drink out of the colored fountain, dear, it's dirty." In the white part of town, the white fountain was always covered with chewing gum and the marks of grubby kids' paws, and the colored fountain was always clean. Children can be horribly logical.

The first great political movement to come along in my lifetime was the civil rights movement, and I was for it. The second great question was the war in Vietnam, and I was against it. So they told me I was a double-dyed liberal. I said, "O.K." What did I know? Later on, people took to claiming it meant I was for big government, high taxes, and communism. That's when I learned never to let anyone else define my politics.

I suspect there are a couple of other factors accounting for the odd hitch in my getalong. Being female, for starters. Can't say I've ever come to any particularly cosmic conclusions about gender, but when you start out in a culture that defines your role as standing on the sidelines with pom-poms to cheer while the guys get to play the game, it will raise a few questions in your mind. Another problem is my size. It wasn't that I ever rejected the norms of Southern womanhood. I was just ineligible. I was the Too Tall Jones of my time. I grew up a St. Bernard among greyhounds. It's hard to be cute if you're six feet tall.

The other problem is that I was a reader. No one's talking Junior Intellectual here. It's true I went through every book in the public library, but where I grew up that meant entire shelves of Frances Parkinson Keyes, and other lady novelists with three names.

Like everyone I ever knew who grew up reading in The Provinces, I yearned for nothing so much as to get the hell out of there. I wanted to go somewhere Up North or Back East or somewhere where people talked about books and ideas, or something besides the weather and football all the time. So I did. I went from Austin to Boston, from Alice to Dallas, Par-REE twice, and Minnesota once. And all I learned is that folks everywhere mostly talk about the weather and football. So I came home.

Came back to edit the *Texas Observer,* a spunky little liberal magazine, so poor that the business manager slept under the Addressograph and the reporters stole pencils from the governor's office. For six years I lived below the poverty level and had more fun than the law allows.

From the first moment I saw the Texas Legislature, I adored it. Opening day, 61st session, 1971, I walked onto the floor of the Texas House, saw one ol' boy dig another in the ribs with his elbow, wink, and announce, "Hey, boy! Yew should see whut Ah found mahself last night! An' she don't talk, neither!" It was reporter-heaven. Some sensitive souls are sickened by it, a few find it merely distasteful, and others persist in reporting on it in a way that squeezes all the juice and life out of it: "House Bill 327 was passed out of subcommittee by unanimous vote on Tuesday."

One of my heroes is William Brann, the great populist, who edited a paper called *The Iconoclast* in Waco before the turn of the century. Brann, a fearless man, loathed three things above all others: cant, hypocrisy, and the Baptists. "The trouble with our Texas Baptists," he once observed, "is that we do not hold them under water long enough." But there he was in the Vatican City of the Baptists, and for his pains, one fine day in 1898, on a wooden sidewalk, an irate Baptist shot him in the back. Right where his galluses crossed. But the story has a happy ending, on account of, as he lay dying on the sidewalk, William Brann drew his own gun and shot his murderer to death. Me, I hoped to go like Brann. A martyr to honest journalism.

So in my early days at the *Observer,* when I would denounce some sorry sumbitch in the Lege as an egg-suckin' child-molester who ran on all fours and had the brains of an adolescent pissant, I would courageously prepare myself to be horse-whipped at the least. All that ever happened was, I'd see the sumbitch in the capitol the next day, he'd beam, spread his arms, and say, "Baby! Yew put mah name in yore paper!" Twenty years, and I've never been able to permanently piss off a single one of them. I have finally had to admit, Texas politicians are unusually civilized people.

For reasons no longer clear to me, I quit the *Observer* in 1976 and went to work for *The New York Times*. Naturally, I was miserable, at five times my previous salary. *The New York Times* is a great newspaper: it is also No Fun. Happily, they sent me out West for three years so I didn't have to mess with 'em much. I loped around the Rockies havin' a fine time despite the peculiar editing of that institution. (I once described a fella as havin' "a beergut that belongs in the Smithsonian"; he turned up in the pages of the *Times* as "a man with a protuberant abdomen.") Finally got fired for describing a community chicken-killing festival as "a gang-pluck." As a lady at Harvard University once said to an applicant who had killed both his parents, "Well, these things do happen."

The *Dallas Times-Herald* made me an offer I could not refuse; said, "Come home, and we will let you write about whatever you want to, and say whatever you want to." And through more editors than I care to remember, the *Herald* has been as good as its word. So I've been home again (home being where you understand the sumbitches) for the past ten years. I am grateful and always will be to the *Herald,* which has taken substantial heat for publishing my column. The title of this book stems from an early *Herald* effort to defuse protests over the column. I had written of a local congressman, "If his IQ slips any lower, we'll have to water him twice a day." This observation touched off an advertiser boycott and many subscription cancellations, to which the *Herald* made a gutsy response. It rented billboards around Dallas that said, MOLLY IVINS CAN'T SAY THAT, CAN SHE?

According to Texas legend, in 1836, when Sam Houston, master of the strategic retreat, and the Texan Army finally allowed Santa Anna and the Mexicans to catch up with them, the Texans waded into the sleeping Mexicans at San Jacinto yelling, "Remember the Alamo! Remember Goliad!" while filleting Mexicans left and right with their bayonets. The panicked Mexicans tried to scramble away, screaming, "Me no Alamo, me no Goliad!" It has come to mean, "Hey, don't blame me. I didn't do it."

All the stuff I report in this book happened. I didn't make up any of it. Me no Alamo.

Molly Ivins
Austin, Texas
January 1991

TEXAS BIDNESS

★ ★

"Texas politicians aren't crooks: it's just that they tend to have an overdeveloped sense of the extenuatin' circumstance. As they say around the Legislature, if you can't drink their whiskey, screw their women, take their money, and vote against 'em anyway, you don't belong in office."

—MOLLY IVINS,
The Progressive

TEXAS OBSERVED

Seems to me I wrote this piece a million years ago. First and only time I've ever tried to explain Texas to non-Texans. That learned me. It's weird to tell, but the more a body tries to explode all the foolish myths that have grown up about Texas by telling the truth, the more a body will wind up adding to the mythology.

THE CLEAN CRAPPER BILL

The rest of the country is in future shock and in Texas we can't get Curtis's Clean Crapper bill through the Legislature. Curtis Graves is a state representative from Houston who introduced a bill to provide minimum standards of cleanliness for public restrooms in this state. It was defeated. Solons rose on the floor of the House to defend dirty johns. The delights of peein' against the back wall after a good whiskey drank were limned in excruciating detail. In New York City, Zero Mostel gets up on a stage and prances around singing "Tradition!" while the audience wets itself with nostalgia. In America, the rate of change shifts from arithmetic to geometric progression. In Texas, where ain't nothin' sanitized for your protection, we still peein' against the back wall.

What this country really needs, along with a new government, is a stiff dose of Texas. Things still are the way they used to be down here, and anybody who thinks that's quaint is welcome to come dip into the state's premier product. Like Johnny Winter sings, "They's so much shit in Texas/you bound to step in some."

WHY THE SKY IS BIGGER IN TEXAS

I love the state of Texas, but I regard that as a harmless perversion on my part and would not, in the name of common humanity, try to foist my pathology off on anyone else. Texas is a dandy place, in short spells, for anyone suffering from nauseé de Thruway Hot Shoppe. It is resistant to Howard Johnson, plastic, interstate highways, and Standard Television American English. But the reason it's resistant to such phenomena is because it's cantankerous, ignorant, and repulsive.

The reason the sky is bigger here is because there aren't any trees. The reason folks here eat grits is because they ain't got no taste. Cowboys mostly stink and it's hot, oh God, it is hot. We gave the world Lyndon Johnson and you cowards gave him right back. There are two major cities in Texas: Houston is Los Angeles with the climate of Calcutta; to define Dallas is to add a whole new humongous dimension to bad.

Texas is a mosaic of cultures, which overlap in several parts of the state and form layers, with the darker layers on the bottom. The cultures are black, Chicano, Southern, freak, suburban, and shitkicker. (Shitkicker is dominant.) They are all rotten for women. Humanism is not alive and well in Texas. Different colors and types of Texans do not like one another, nor do they pretend to.

Shitkicker is pickup trucks with guns slung across the racks on the back and chicken-fried steaks and machismo and "D-I-V-O-R-C-E" on the radio and cheap, pink, nylon slips, and gettin' drunk on Saturday night and goin' to church on Sunday morning, and drivin' down the highway throwin' beer cans out the window, and Rastusan'-Liza jokes and high school football, and family reunions where the in-laws of your second cousins show up.

You can eat chili, barbecue, Meskin food, hush puppies, catfish, collard greens, red beans, pink grapefruit, and watermelon with Dr Pepper, Pearl, Lone Star, Carta Blanca, or Shiner's, which tastes a lot like paint thinner but don't have no preservatives in it. People who eat soul food here eat it because they can't afford hamburger. Since last year, you can buy a drink in some bars, but a lot of folks still brown-bag it 'cause it's cheaper, and Chivas and Four Roses look alike comin' out of a brown bag.

WHAT TO WATCH IN TEXAS

The frontier is what John Wayne lived on. Most Texans are Baptists. Baptists are civilized people. Beware of Church of Christers.

Once when Ronnie Dugger was being poetic he said, "To a Texan, a car is like wings to a seagull: our places are far apart and we must dip into them driving . . . the junctions in the highways and the towns are like turns in a city well known." It's true, Texans are accustomed to driving three hours to see a football game or 150 miles for a movie.

Texas is an un-self-conscious place. Nobody here is embarrassed about being who he is. Reactionaries aren't embarrassed. Rich folks aren't embarrassed. Rednecks aren't embarrassed. Liberals aren't embarrassed. And when did black folks or brown folks ever have time to worry about existential questions? Lobbyists, loan sharks, slumlords, war profiteers, chiropractors, and KKKers are all proud of their callings. Only Dallas is self-conscious; Dallas deserves it.

Texas is not a civilized place. Texans shoot one another a lot. They also knife, razor, and stomp one another to death with some frequency. And they fight in bars all the time. You can get five years for murder and 99 for pot possession in this state—watch your ass.

ENVIRONMENTAL ADVANCES

The only thing that smells worse than an oil refinery is a feedlot. Texas has a lot of both. Ecology in Texas started with a feedlot. So many people in Lubbock got upset with the smell of a feedlot there that they complained to the city council all the time. The city council members didn't act like yahoos; they took it serious. After a lot of hearings, it was decided to put up an Air-wick bottle on every fencepost around the feedlot. Ecology in Texas has gone uphill since then.

The two newest members of the Air Pollution Control Board were up for a hearing before a state senate committee this June. E. W. Robinson of Amarillo told the committee that he was against allowin' any pollution that would prove to be very harmful to people's health. A senator asked him how harmful was very harmful. Oh, lead poisonin' and such would be unacceptable, said Robinson. What about pollution that causes allergies and asthma? Well, you don't die of it, said Robinson. While the air of Texas is entrusted to this watchdog, the water is in good hands, too. Not long ago, the director of the Texas Water Quality Board was trying to defend what the Armco Steel Company is dumping into the Houston Ship Channel. "Cyanide," he said, "is a scare word."

THEY SAID IT WAS TEXAS KULCHER/BUT IT WAS ONLY RAILROAD GIN

Art is paintings of bluebonnets and broncos, done on velvet. Music is mariachis, blues, and country. Eddie Wilson, who used to be a beer lobbyist, started a place in Austin, in an old National Guard armory, called Armadillo World Headquarters. Willie Nelson, Freddie King, Leon Russell, Ravi Shankar, the Austin Ballet, the AFL-CIO Christmas Party, the Mahavishnu Band, and several basketball teams have held forth in this, the southwest's largest country-western bohemian nightclub.

Kinky Friedman and the Texas Jewboys cut a single recently with "The Ballad of Charles Whitman" on the one side and "Get Your Biscuits in the Oven and Your Buns in the Bed" on the flip. Part of the lyrics of "The Ballad" go like this: "There was rumor/Of a tumor/nestled at the base of his brain . . ." Kinky lives on a ranch in Central Texas called Rio Duckworth, reportedly in a garbage can.

There is a radio station just across the border from Del Rio, Texas. It plays hymns during the day and broadcasts religious advertisements at night. They sell autographed pictures of Jesus to all you friends in radioland. Also prayer rugs as a special gift for all your travellin' salesmen friends with a picture of the face of Jesus on the prayer rug that glows in the dark. And underneath the picture is a legend that also glows in the dark; it's written, "Thou Shalt Not Commit Adultery."

Texas is not full of rich people. Texas is full of poor people. The latest count is 22 percent of the folks here under the federal poverty line—and the feds don't set the line high. The rest of the country, they tell us, has 13 percent poor folks, including such no-account states as Mississippi. Because Texas is racist, 45 percent of the black folks and the brown folks are poor.

Onliest foreign thang that approaches Texas politics is Illinois politics. We ain't never left it lyin' around in shoeboxes, elsewise, we got the jump on everybody.

Texans do not talk like other Americans. They drawl, twang, or sound like the Frito Bandito, only not jolly. *Shit* is a three-syllable word with a *y* in it.

Texans invent their own metaphors and similes, often of a scatological nature, which is kind of fun. As a group, they tell good stories well. The reason they are good at stories is because this is what anthropologists call an oral culture. That means people here don't read and write much. Neither would you if the *Dallas Morning News* was all you had to read.

Texas—I believe it has been noted elsewhere—is a big state. Someone else can tell you about the symphony orchestras and the experimental theaters and those Texans who are writing their Ph.D. theses on U.S. imperialism in Paraguay and seventeenth-century Sanskrit literature. I'm just talking about what makes Texas Texas.

Place, 1972

INSIDE THE
AUSTIN FUN HOUSE

Here's another piece that's almost twenty years old; at that time, it was semidefinitive concernin' the Texas Lege. I wish I could report that the Lege has improved since. But it's only become more entertaining.

The Texas Legislature consists of 181 people who meet for 140 days once every two years. This catastrophe has now occurred sixty-three times. The Legislature is, among other things, the finest free entertainment in Texas. Better than the zoo. Better than the circus.

In 1971, the Citizens Conference on State Legislatures produced a comparative study entitled "The Sometime Governments." It ranked the Texas Legislature thirty-eighth out of fifty, leading to stunned reactions among connoisseurs of the local peculiar institution, such as,

"My God! You mean there are twelve worse than *this*?" Since fans of the Texas Lege share the state mania for being Number One, even in inverse fashion, we gave serious consideration to firing off a hot letter to the C.C.S.L. explaining just why the Texas Lege is more outstandingly awful than any other. While the New Jersey state government might boast more Mafia ties, and Illinois did have that wonderful old fellow who stashed his loot in shoeboxes, nonetheless, the Texas Lege just has more . . . well, style. Class, you could call it. Panache, perhaps.

Take the last all-House duke-out. It was, distressingly enough, over ten years ago. Although there have been a fair number of fistfights in the capitol since, none has qualified as total Fist City. On the last such occasion (the cause long forgotten), over half of the 150 House members were actively engaged in slugging their colleagues, insulting the wives and mothers of same, knocking over desks, and throwing chairs. Now any legislature can have a mass duke-out, but where else would there be musical accompaniment? In mid-melee, four members mounted the speaker's dais and held forth, in barber-shop-quartet harmony, with "I Had a Dream, Dear."

Every two years, one of the most hotly contested elections in Texas is the poll taken among members of the capitol press corps to determine who are actually *the* ten stupidest members of the Legislature. Two years ago, there were thirty-seven official nominees and several write-ins. For the last three sessions, the title of Number One Dumb has been captured by a Republican, leading to no small degree of ill feeling among loyal Democrats. Another consistent source of complaint has been that the poll fails to take into account those members who are suspected of spectacular stupidity but are incapable of standing up and talking so they might be judged. This breed of legislator has led to the creation of a new subcategory in the press-corps poll, the Top Ten Pieces of Furniture.

And what manner of work is produced by this wondrous assembly? Well, in 1971, the House passed a resolution honoring Albert DeSalvo for his efforts in the field of population control.* Last session, Representative Jim Kaster of El Paso introduced a bill requiring felons to submit twenty-four-hour advance notice of what crimes they planned to commit and where. After an epic battle, the late

---

*DeSalvo was convicted of the "Boston Strangler" murders. The resolution was introduced on April 1, by a liberal who wanted to make a point about how much consideration the House gives the material it votes for.

Hawkins Menefee managed to pass a bill permitting retailers to sell bread by the half-loaf. But former Representative Curtis Graves was less successful in the 61st session with his chicken-by-the-piece bill.

Many bills are passed by the Legislature after consideration lasting one minute. During the traditional end-of-the-session logjam, this bill-a-minute pace is sometimes sustained for four or five days. The House's all-time record was passing the state's first sales tax at eight minutes to midnight on the last night of the 1961 session. The House then took four of the remaining minutes to consider and pass the entire $388 million biennial appropriations bill. Still other bills are passed without being given any consideration. To do this, a legislator gets a bill placed on what is called the local-and-consent calendar, which is reserved for those bills affecting only one legislative district. Water district bills, a notorious boon to real-estate developers, are thus passed.

State Comptroller Bob Bullock, who served in the House from 1954 to 1958, described the thoughtful process by which he came to vote Yea or Nay on many a bill. "I'd be settin' there of a mornin', hung over as hell, probably been to some lobby party the night before, and a friend would stop by my desk and ask, 'Yuh heard about ol' Joe's bill?'

"I never wanted to let on that I knew no more about ol' Joe's bill than I do about quantum physics, so I'd nod, lookin' as wise as a treeful of owls, and he'd say, 'Bad bill, bad bill.' And I'd nod some more.

"Two minutes later, some freshman'd come by and ask me what I thought of ol' Joe's bill. I'd say, 'Bad bill. Bad bill.' And the two of us would vote against it without ever knowin' what was in it. It was done that way, y'see. It's all done on friendship."

OK, OK, that was back in the 1950s. Surely, folks always insist, things have changed. It's 1975, and *The New York Review of Books,* which apparently thinks it should know, is always saying that the South ain't like it used to be. Whole books have been written about the decline of the Good Ol' Boy.

Well, sure, some things have changed. Hattie's whorehouse burned down in 1960. That was a blow to a lot of the boys, it having been so convenient to the capitol and all. One notoriously horny legislator had a charge account at Hattie's, and that was considered the height of prestige. Even the Chicken Ranch, a LaGrange whorehouse favored by lawmakers and Aggies, was closed by the state laws last summer. (The Chicken Ranch laid claim to being the oldest continuously operated business establishment in Texas. There are now a lot of bumper stickers around Central Texas that read BRING BACK THE CHICKEN RANCH—KEEP ON PLUCKING!)

Oh, there've been some other changes. The lobbyists are more subtle these days. They used to operate with what was called the Three B's—beef, bourbon, and blondes. "Get me two sweathogs for tonight," I once heard a legislator command a lobbyist. The first two B's are still In, and no one is sure the new lobby-reporting laws cover all the checks that are picked up at the Caravel Club and the Deck Club and the Headliners and the Quorum.

The chief reason legislators allow lobbyists to pick up tabs for them is that Texas legislators are underpaid. They get $4,800 a year and a $12 per diem (that's pronounced *purr dime* in legislative circles) for the first 120 days of a regular session. Last year, Representative Paul Ragsdale of Dallas successfully applied for food stamps on his legislative salary.

There are almost no full-time Texas legislators, but regular sessions get extended, and special sessions run on and on, and then new special sessions get called. In the meantime, the legislators' law practices and funeral parlors and pharmacies and ranches and jewelry stores and insurance companies and real-estate businesses are all going to hell. Their family lives frequently aren't in great shape, either. It would take a constitutional amendment approved by the voters to get Texas legislators a pay raise. Since Texans are generally, with cause, ticked off at the Lege, they stubbornly refuse to vote such a pay raise. Thus they continue to get approximately what they pay for in terms of a legislature.

Lots of folks thought the Lege would change for sure after Gus Mutscher, Jr., bit the dust. Mutscher was the Speaker of the House from January 1967, until March 1972, at which time he and two associates were convicted of conspiracy to accept a bribe. The conviction was one result of our late, great Sharpstown Scandal, a sort of Texas Watergate that broke open in early 1971. Almost everybody who was anybody in state government turned out to be involved with Frank Sharp, a Houston wheeler-dealer. At his instigation, a couple of very suspicious bills went flying through the Lege during a late-session logjam. After Mutscher's conviction, the pols were hot for ree-form. No fewer than eighty head of freshman legislators were elected, and every blessed one of them on a platform of ree-form. An actual liberal of sorts named Price Daniel, Jr., son of a former governor and U.S. senator, was elected speaker.

The 63rd session cleaned up the House rules and passed a campaign-reporting law with teeth in it and some species of ethics legislation, and that exhausted ree-form for the year. Ree-form expired totally about halfway through the session on Apache Belle Day. The Apache Belles are a female drill and baton-twirling team that performs during halftime at college football games. They are real famous in their field, so the House set aside a special day to honor them for their contributions to the cultural life of Texas. Representative Billy Williamson, a political troglodyte from Tyler, hometown of the Apache Belles, served as master of ceremonies.

The Belles, all encased in tight gold lamé pants with matching vests and wearing white cowboy boots and hats, strutted up the center aisle of the House with their tails twitching in close-order drill. They presented the speaker's wife with a bouquet of Tyler roses, and made the speaker an honorary Apache Beau for the day. Then Williamson commenced his address by noting that not all the Apache Belles were on the floor of the House.

Upon Williamson's instruction, everyone craned his neck to look up at the House gallery, where, sure enough, six extra Belles were standing. At a signal from Williamson, the six turned and pertly perched their gold-laméed derrières over the brass rail of the gallery. Upon each posterior was a letter, and they spelled out R*E*F*O*R*M.

Then, in 1974, the Legislature convened as a constitutional convention. The voters had agreed that the state's 100-year-old, barnacle-encrusted constitution (the governor can still call out the militia in case of an Indian uprising) needed a rewrite job. The Lege turned itself into a con-con to do the deed, and the voters were to be given final say on whether their handiwork was an improvement or not. But the voters never got a chance to say. The Lege spent six months and $6 million of the taxpayers' money, but never could agree on how a new constitution should go, so they just gave up and went home. As the con-con was expiring amid general bitterness, around midnight last July 30, a barbershop quartet of representatives sang "Nearer My God to Thee" in the members' lounge.

Daniel, the reform speaker and president of the unproductive con-con, stepped down after one term, and the new speaker is Billy Wayne Clayton of Spring Lake. Clayton, a superior specimen of

West Texas conservative, is opposed to abortion, the equal rights amendment, labor unions, and so on. And so forth. He is, however, determined to improve decorum in the House. He plans to do so by keeping the press off the House floor.

A columnist for the *Dallas Morning News,* a paper with an editorial policy to the right of Ethelred the Unready, descended one day on the ill-fated con-con and was appalled by the lack of decorum.* Why, he reported, when one state senator rose to speak, all the other legislators began to bark and howl! The columnist thought it unseemly. Shucks, that was just for ol' Mad Dog. Senator Walter ("Mad Dog") Mengden is a Republican from Houston, and that explains a lot right there. You should understand that Texas Republicans come in two flavors: conservative and extraordinary. Most of the extraordinary ones are from Houston. "Mad Dog" Mengden is against all the normal stuff, such as outlawing the death penalty, reducing the penalties for pot possession (until last year, first-offense possession of any amount was a two-to-life felony), and the like. But Mengden also crusades against sex education and the distressing modernist-socialist trends in the public schools. Last session, Mengden began one of his finer speeches by announcing, "This is the way I see the problem, if there is a problem, which I deny." This year his legislative program includes prison reform—he wants female convicts to be more ladylike.

Sometimes Texas Republicans take firm stands. On November 23, 1974, Representative Larry Vick of Houston told the Women Who Want to Be Women, an antifeminist group: "The women's rights movement is the most vicious, conniving, deceiving movement this country has ever seen next to communism."

Sometimes they do not. Paul Eggers, Republican candidate for governor in 1968 and 1970, on what to do about fat in the state budget: "I plan to stand up and be counted. And the thing I'm gonna do is, I'm gonna do what we're gonna do right now. I'm going to the people and say, 'Now this is what I'm trying to do.' And I'm going to do this because I believe the people need representation."

Texas legislators are practical. A House member from San Antonio to a reporter during a debate on whether the state should garnishee the wages of fathers delinquent in child-support payments:

---

*The *News* is the state's most conservative big-city daily but not its most conservative paper. When last I saw the papers in the Freedom chain, which operates in several small cities in the Rio Grande Valley, they were still capitalizing *Pinko.*

"There's only one solution for Those People. Clip 'em and spade 'em. Clip the men and spade the women."

Texas legislators are profound thinkers. Representative Joe Salem of Corpus Christi, speaking on an amendment requiring that all state revenues go into the state treasury: "It just makes good sense to put all your eggs in one basket."

Texas legislators can be cutups. When the speaker leaves the chair to go off and twist arms in the back hall, he picks on some hapless member to preside during the interminable periods when the House is "at ease." The members enjoy trying to embarrass the temporary chairman. One gambit is to inquire, "Are you, sir, a member of the Turtle Club?" To which a "true turtle" must respond, despite the presence in the gallery of the fourth-grade class from his hometown elementary school, "You bet your ass I am."

Texas legislators are sound on the environment and ecology. Tyler not only boasts the Apache Belles, but also harbored an asbestos plant until it was shut down in 1972. Asbestos fibers have been proved to be carcinogenic. According to statistical projections, a large proportion of that plant's employees will develop cancer in the next twenty years, and many others will suffer from asbestosis, a drastic reduction of lung capacity. Billy Williamson, the elected representative of those folks, had this to say about that: "I think we are all willing to have a little bit of crud in our lungs and a full stomach rather than a whole lot of clean air and nothing to eat. And I don't want a bunch of environmentalists and communists telling me what's good for me and my family."*

Texas legislators are natty dressers and careful about their attire. One West Texas legislator who was possessed of the appropriate committee chairmanship had the Highway Department build a rest stop at the exact edge of his district on the highway leading to Austin. The brick structure, which cost the taxpayers several thou, was not erected so motorists would have a place to relieve themselves. It was put up so the legislator would have a place to stop and change his gators (alligator shoes) as he drove back into his district from the capital. He feared the home folks would think he was gettin' too toney if they saw him in his gators 'stead of his boots.

Texas legislators are known aesthetes. The Lege never has managed to get a firm grip on the principle of one man, one vote.

---

*Billy Williamson died of lung cancer on May 25, 1982.

Until the mid-1960s, the Lege was normally described as "rural dominated," a classic understatement. One cow, one vote was the approximate operating principle in the days when the country boys drew the redistricting maps. After the Big Nine in D.C. handed down their one-one edict (locally regarded as a further advance of communism), the Lege's periodic plans for redistricting were unfailingly declared unconstitutional by state and federal courts. One splendid effort in 1971 featured districts that looked like giant chickens, districts that looked like coiled snakes, and districts with remarkable pimples in their boundary lines, zits that popped up to include the home of one liberal incumbent in the district of another liberal incumbent.

Representative Guy Floyd of San Antonio, a good ol' boy who had been shafted by the bill, rose to remonstrate with the chairman of the Redistricting Committee, Representative Delwin Jones of Lubbock. "Lookahere, Dell-win," said Floyd, much aggrieved, "look at this district here. You've got a great big ball at the one end and then a little bitty ol' strip a' land goes for about 300 miles, and then a great big ol' ball at the other end. It looks like a dumbbell. Now the courts say the districts have to be com-pact and contiguous. Is that your idea a' com-pact and con-tiguous?"

Delwin Jones meditated at some length before replying, "Wha-ell, in a artistic sense, it is."

An actual speech I heard delivered on the House floor during the 62nd session (at issue was whether or not to raise liquor taxes by about ten cents a bottle; the speaker was in favor):

"Gennlemun," he began, "imagine to yourselfs that yew are goin' into the booze shop to buy yourselfs a bottle a' booze. An' on yur way into the booze shop, yew pass a little chi-el standin' on the sidewalk. An' he sez to yew, 'Mister,' he sez, 'kin yew buy me a lollipop?' An' yew sez, 'Naw, son, Ah cain't buy yew no lollipop.' An' yew go on into the booze shop. An' yew buy yourself a bottle a' booze. An' yew pay yur extra ten cents tax. Ain't nobody yet never paid whut it's worth. An' on your way out of the booze shop, yew see that little chi-el again, still standin' on the sidewalk. An' yew sez to yourself, 'If Ah kin afford a extra ten cents for a bottle a' booze, Ah kin afford to buy that little chi-el a lollipop.' An' so, gennlemun, Ah ask fer yur vote on this bill fer the sake of the cheeldrun of Texas!"

The Texas Legislature does harbor some excellent orators,

though it's doubtful that their earthy style would make them the toast of the Oxford Union. Senator Babe Schwartz, a white-maned pixie from Galveston, scored telling points against a proposed version of a new constitution with the following peroration: "Fellow delegates, this new constitution they are offering us for a vote today reminds me of the time the seeing-eye dog peed on his master's leg. The blind man stood still for a moment and then reached into his pocket for a doggie biscuit. He fished out that biscuit and leaned down and gave it to the dog. And when the dog took it, he patted its head. A bystander observed this and was most touched. 'Why, sir,' he said to the blind man, 'I see you've given that dog a biscuit even though he peed on your leg. You clearly recognize how much you depend on that dog, how much he does for you even though he's made this mistake, and you are treating him kindly anyway. Sir, that's wonderful.'

"And the blind man said, 'Listen, you jackleg, I gave the damn dog the biscuit so I could figure out where his head is so I can kick the hmm-hmm out of his tail, and that's just what I'm fixing to do.'

"Gentlemen, I suggest to you that you are being offered a doggie biscuit today, and if you're dumb enough to take it, you know what they're fixing to do."

There are some clichés in legislative debate that are used so frequently that they take on the quality of magical incantations. If a bill won't help keep "a healthy bidness climate" in Texas, then it will "open Pandora's box," "let the head of the camel into the tent," "open loopholes big enough to drive a truck through," and is only "the tip of the iceberg."

But normally Texas political debate is conducted in highly flavored language, both on and off the chamber floors. Of a loony person: "Crazy as a peach-orchard boar." Of a normally indolent colleague, suddenly invigorated: "Who put Tabasco sauce in *his* oatmeal?" Of a cautious man: "He wears a two-inch belt and Big Jim suspenders." Of a homely man: "He's so ugly that when he was a little boy his momma had to tie a pork chop around his neck before the dog would play with him." If a Texas pol is tripped up in a lie, he confesses, "You caught me speedin'." And a saying of Darrell Royal, University of Texas football coach, has become a classic explanation for why a legislator will never vote against a lobbyist who helped him get elected: "You dance with them what brung you." Former Representative Renal Rosson of Snyder used to say to his colleagues, "Lemme give ya' a hypothetic."

The untoward advent last session of a startlingly large contingent of female legislators (five out of 150 in the House) precipitated an effort to clean up the verbal act. Several great minds listed forty-one of the filthiest expressions they knew and assigned them code numbers between 801 and 913. Thus lawmakers were able to holler "832 you" at one another without giving offense.

But the Lege is considerably more than a motley collection of clowns, crooks, racists, and fools. There have lived and worked therein many men and women of honor and decency who are committed to the people's interests as they perceive them. They range from John Birchers and members of the White Citizens Council to populists, liberal Democrats, and socialists. Conservatives have controlled the Lege since its inception, and still do. Some observers believe this is because Texas conservatives are congenitally smarter than Texas liberals. Their camp boasts such skilled parliamentarians as Representative Jim ("Supersnake") Nugent of Kerrville. The liberal *Texas Observer* once complimented Nugent on a session-long performance that combined the best elements of "Dracula, the King of the Nazgul and the Eggplant That Ate Chicago." In the Senate, Bill ("the Bull of the Brazos") Moore of Bryan is a noted manipulator. Moore once admitted that he was likely to experience personal economic benefit from a bill he was sponsoring. But, he added winningly, he'd only make a little profit, not a whole lot.

Those legislators who have fought the huge economic special interests, the racism, and the know-nothingism of Texas are possessed of a special kind of courage. It is not the courage of flashy deeds done against drear and deadly enemies, but a courage that often consists chiefly of just hanging in there. It is the courage of those who outstay boredom, pettiness, mean-mindedness, and stupidity. They stick through the subcommittee meetings and the committee meetings and the first readings and the second readings and the conference committee meetings to the final, inevitable screwing. Their courage holds up through the countless failures and frustrations, and enables them to laugh and get drunk and laugh some more, and then to try again next session. And there is a Texas legislative tradition that allows them to respect publicly, and yes, even love, those canny country bastards who always beat them.

For many years the Texas Senate was famed chiefly as a soporific. It was ruled by men of such dreadful, unrelieved racist and reactionary tendencies (not to mention one or two of your basic slimy money-takers) as to make one despair of democracy. But even there, the Texas legislative style can overcome all else—racism, ideology, and even self-interest. It is a style that places first value on loyalty and friendship. Barbara Jordan is a black lawyer from Houston now in the U.S. Congress. Her speech during the televised hearings of the Judiciary Committee on the impeachment of President Nixon jolted most of the nation out of its socks and into respectful attention. When Jordan first came to the Texas Senate in 1966, there was one senator who referred to her as "that nigger bitch," and a couple of others who called her "the nigger mammy washerwoman." But they came to develop a unanimous respect for her and something more than that.

She made her impeachment speech during the last hours of the ill-fated con-con, but most of her old Senate colleagues, liberal and conservative alike, broke off their frantic horse trading to go to a television set and hear her. "Give 'em hell, Barbara!" they crowed. As she lit into Richard Nixon, they cheered and hoo-rahed and pounded their beer bottles on the table as though they were watching U.T. pound hell out of Notre Dame in the Cotton Bowl.

For the past twenty years, the House has harbored a liberal opposition numbering somewhere between twenty and forty. They boast the longest unbroken string of defeats this side of the Philadelphia Phillies, but are *toujours gai*.

The first such group dates back to 1951, and was known as the Gashouse Gang. They never did succeed in getting a tax on natural gas. A few years later, that group, together with recruits, was christened the Shithouse Liberals by Maury Maverick, Sr., the populist, onetime New Deal congressman from San Antonio. Maverick's son Maury, Jr., was then in the Legislature, and he and his fellow liberals were serving in the Texas House when it went on a McCarthyite rampage. Unable to take the incredible political pressure to vote for some of the witch-hunting bills, the libs took refuge in the men's room to avoid voting. The Shithousers hung on grimly for a couple of years, supporting that notorious commie document, the Bill of Rights. The Gashouse Gang II emerged in the later 1950s, led by Bob Eckhardt of Houston, now a U.S. congressman. That group actually passed a tax on gas pipelines, but lobbyists managed to put unconstitutional amendments on it, to ensure that it would later be nullified. It was. Eckhardt, a peerless parliamentarian, and his troops had an occasional success in foiling the Neanderthals.

Perhaps the most famous such victory concerns the time the Russian Embassy stole the appropriations bill. The Russian Embassy, a.k.a. the Little Kremlin, had nothing to do with the Soviets. It was a big ol' house on West Avenue in Austin, rented for a couple of sessions in the late 1950s by a group of madcap liberal House members. Chief among them were Don Kennard, later a state senator from Fort Worth; "Whiskey Bob" Wheeler, the only man in Tilden, Texas, who subscribed to *The New York Review of Books*; Malcolm McGregor, now a respected attorney in El Paso; Jamie Clements, Charlie Hughes, Tony Korioth, and others. (Some conservatives ran a similarly cheerful house called the Boar's Nest. The Russians and the Nesters played poker together every Friday night.)

Late in the 56th regular session, the House-Senate Appropriations Conference Committee was meeting daily in closed session and apparently making no progress. At the close of each meeting, Bill Heatly, who headed the House conferees, and Bill Fly, who headed the Senate conferees, would emerge and sadly announce to the waiting press that there was still no agreement. In fact, the conferees had not only already agreed on how to settle everybody's hash, but they had the bill printed and ready to go. They were stalling so they could introduce the bill late in the last day of the session and get it passed without debate under the pressure of the midnight deadline.

A conservative named Jim Cotton, who was as cantankerous as he was conservative, found out about this plot. Cotton was miffed anyway, because he'd been left off the Conference Committee, so he told the liberals at the Embassy what was up. The printed bills were locked in a room on the third floor of the state capitol. The liberals plotted like Eisenhower planning D-Day. On the appointed night, Cotton stayed late in the House, reading, and at the appointed hour, with studied casualness, he called the night guards over and engaged them in a bull session. In the meantime, Wheeler was stationed by the second-floor elevators with instructions to whistle if a guard came near. His companions in crime allege that "Whiskey Bob" was so full of Dutch courage he couldn't have whistled "Dixie." Kennard and McGregor, decked out in full burglar gear, including gloves, made the actual assault on the locked room. They unscrewed the transom over the door, but since they are both hefty guys, possessed of not inconsiderable beer-guts, they got stuck trying to squirm through it. They called off the effort for the night. Next night, the same program went into effect. This time Kennard and McGregor managed to unscrew a ventilator panel at the bottom of the door, crawl through, and heist six copies of the bill.

The Embassy started leaking parts of the bill to those institutions that were most unfairly treated by it—for example, junior colleges, which had been given a pittance. Junior college presidents from all over the state started calling in to Heatly and Fly, yowling with rage. Next the Embassy gave sections of the bill to Frank Manitzas, a favorite AP reporter. Manitzas started a series that ran on front pages all over the state for a week. Meantime, the state police were called in to find the burglars. The scene of the crime was dusted for fingerprints. Heatly thought Fly was leaking the stuff to Manitzas and Fly thought Heatly was. The two of them went to Fist City.

The late Colonel Homer Garrison, a tough old buzzard, was then head of the Department of Public Safety. Garrison had Manitzas hauled into his office and grilled him unmercifully about his sources on the appropriations bill. Manitzas refused to spill, and when he got back to his office, he received a call from a suddenly accommodating Garrison. Garrison assured Manitzas that he'd meant nothing personal by the grilling, he'd been ordered to try it, hoped Manitzas would understand. And by the way, would Manitzas mind telling him how much was in that bill for the Department of Public Safety? "Colonel," said Manitzas, "if you'll send a messenger over here, I'll give him your section of the bill." Garrison sent a Texas Ranger.

The whole flap forced the governor to call a special session so that the appropriations bill could, for the first time, go through the full process of debate and amendment.

The most famous of all the opposition groups was the Dirty Thirty, a coalition of liberals and Republicans who fought Gus Mutscher in 1971. Mutscher had extraordinary power as a three-term speaker. Through his power to name committees and committee chairmen, he could see to it that no bill sponsored by anyone who opposed him ever got out of subcommittee. It is somewhat difficult to get reelected if you can't pass legislation. Nonetheless, an unlikely group, featuring, among others, Frances ("Sissy") Farenthold, who later became a liberal candidate for governor, and "Mad Dog" Mengden, hammered away at Mutscher's involvement with Frank Sharp. The session became so bitter that on the last day, Mutscher called out the state police, who stood around with their guns at the ready while shouting and shoving matches took place on the floor.

Perhaps the chief reason the Texas Lege is as baroque as it is is that no one cares much about it. Like most other Americans, not more than one or two Texans out of ten can even name their state senators and representatives. It is perhaps unfair to blame the state's media for this situation, although the Texas press has a tendency to reduce the whole Big Top bizarre-o quality of the Lege to driest business-as-usual reportage. A committee meeting that runs hip deep in betrayals, sellouts, up-against-the-wall compromises, and good-guy-*versus*-bad-guy action not infrequently turns up in the next morning's papers as "the House Agriculture subcommittee took no action on Tuesday." Most Texans who are interested in public affairs (not counting those who represent special interests anxious to avoid taxation) pay more attention to what goes on in Washington. In the meantime, how deep they will be buried, whether they can buy booze, who can install their lawn sprinklers, the size of the cells in Stripe City, whether their kids' schools are decent, what textbooks the kids use, the qualifications of people who prescribe their eyeglasses, and a thousand other matters are decided in Austin.

The quality of the lives of Texans is daily affected by the Legislature's sense of priorities. In the Lege, that's pronounced "pry-roar-ities."

The state of Texas is Number One among the fifty states in oil production. It is Number One in gas production, Number One in cattle, and Number One in cotton. In mohair, pecans, citrus fruits, wheat, sorghum, soybeans, spinach, lumber, sulphur, and petrochemical products, Texas ranks top or near the top. And that is only the tip of the iceberg, as it were, of the state's natural and man-made wealth. It was the proud boast of our last governor that he had moved Texas from forty-fifth to forty-seventh among the states in per capita taxation. It is the proudest boast of our incumbent governor that he has not raised taxes. Yet in no area of social service does the state of Texas come anywhere near the national average. It is one of seventeen states that do not supplement federal aid to the aged, the blind, or the disabled. It is thirty-seventh in expenditure per public school pupil, and thirty-seventh in average teacher salaries. On the other hand, we're right up there in infant mortality, and according to a publication called *Texas Morbidity Week,* we're contributing well over our fair share of the nation's diptheria and tetanus. In 1969, we were Number One in infectious syphilis, but have since fallen to a mere fourteenth.

What is even more surprising in a state so wealthy is that Texas is rife with poor people. Nineteen percent of the people of Texas fall below the poverty level. The national average is 13 percent below the federal poverty line. The figures are worse in parts of East Texas, which harbors most of the state's blacks. In much of South Texas, where the brown folks live (pronounced *Meskins*), the poverty level approaches 50 percent.

The Legislature's pry-roar-ities are most clearly seen in its biannual appropriations bill. Compare $400,000 for a moss-cutter on Lake Caddo with nothing for bilingual education. A healthy chunk of money for an old folks' home in the district of the chairman of the House Appropriations Committee, but nothing for the state's only black law school. Money to air-condition a National Guard armory, but no money to air-condition the state school for the mentally retarded. When it's a question of malnutrition, hookworm, or illiteracy against new equipment for the Texas Rangers, the Rangers always get what they need. In a state with no corporate income tax, no corporate profits tax, no natural resources severance tax, wellhead taxes on natural gas and oil that fall below the national average, and a light corporate franchise tax, where does the largest chunk of Texas's money come from? From a regressive 4 percent state sales tax. In 1969, when more revenue was needed, the Lege's first thought was to extend the state sales tax to food and drugs. It's one helluva healthy bidness climate.

The Atlantic, May 1975

H. ROSS WENT SEVEN BUBBLES OFF PLUMB (AND OTHER TALES)

All writers write differently for different audiences. As a "pro," I sometimes claim I can slice it any way an editor wants it sliced. One month, my byline appeared simultaneously in *TV Guide*, the *Reader's Digest*, *Playboy*, and *The Progressive*. But the fact is, I do my best work where I feel most at home—in my own newspaper column or in small, lefty publications that remind me of my old home at the *Texas Observer*. I like to write for folks who laugh at the same things I do.

Victor Navasky, the world's cheapest editor, several years ago talked me into writing "Letters From Texas" for the incurably progressive *Nation* magazine. Calvin Trillin does not lie: Navasky pays in the high two figures. Damned if I know why I still consider it an honor to write for his silly old magazine—maybe because *The Nation* is still consistently the most provocative political journal in America.

Well, our attorney general is under indictment. He ran as "the people's lawyer"; now we call him "the people's felon." But it's just a commercial bribery charge; he should get shed of it. We all know there's nothing wrong with Jim Mattox but rotten personality. Meantime, over in the Legislature, the latest incumbent indicted was Senator Carl Parker of Port Arthur, brought up two weeks ago on charges of pushing pornography, running prostitutes, and perjury. We feel this is the best indictment of a sitting legislator since last year, when Representative Bubba London of Bonham got sent up for cattle rustling. It's rare to find a good case of cattle rustling in the Lege anymore, so we're real proud of London. Happily, Senator Parker is unopposed, so we expect this to be the finest case of reelection-despite-trying-circumstances since 1982, when Senator John Wilson of LaGrange was reelected although seriously dead. Several distinguished former members have been indicted of late on charges ranging from misappropriation of funds to child abuse. We're running about normal on that front.

On matters cultural, when the World's Fair in New Orleans had Texas Week recently, they invited two of our biggest stars, Willie Nelson and Ralph the Diving Pig from San Marcos. Willie has been galaxy-famous for years now, but this was Ralph's first shot at international exposure, so we were all real thrilled for him. Ralph's the Greg Louganis of porkerdom.

We're having another bingo crackdown: we are big on busting grannies for bingo. If you bingo bad enough in this state, they'll put you in the Texas Department of Corrections, the Lone Star Gulag. Texas and California are running about even to see which state can put the most human beings in Stripe City. We got a three-strikes law here—three felonies and it's life—so we got guys doing terminal stretches for passing two bad checks and aggravated mopery.

T.D.C. is so overcrowded they were like berserk rats in there in the vicious summer heat. There have been more than 270 stabbings in T.D.C. this year. Judge William Wayne Justice, who, in my opinion, is a great American hero and, in everybody's opinion, is the most hated man in Texas, has declared the conditions in the system unconstitutional. Judge Justice continues to labor under the illusion that the U.S. Constitution applies in Texas. Just last year he de-segged a public housing project in Clarksville—almost twenty years after the Civil Rights Act—so the citizens started threatening to kill him again. Anyway, the prisons are being worked on; the Legislature passed some reforms because they knew if they didn't, Judge Justice would. He already made them clean up the whole juvenile corrections system. So now it's just a question of whether the reforms can beat the riot in under the wire.

We have also had educational reform, and it come a gullywasher. First off, our new governor, Mark White, shows signs of intelligence above vegetable level, which means he will never make the list of truly great governors, such as Dolph Briscoe, the living Pet Rock. So Marko Blanco appointed H. Ross Perot to head up this committee to figure out what's wrong with the public schools. H. Ross took off like an unguided missile. I keep having to explain to foreigners that some loopy right-wing Dallas billionaires are a lot better than others, and H. Ross happens to be one of our better right-wing billionaires. This is assuming you don't make him so mad that he goes out and buys an army and invades your country with it. But he mostly does that to no-account countries full of tacky ragheads, so no one minds. Anyway, H. Ross decided everything was wrong with the schools—teachers, courses, books. The Board of Education had ruled that no one could teach evolution as fact in Texas schools, and H. Ross said it was making us look dumber than the Luzbuddy debate team. Actually, he said "laughingstock." Then H. Ross went seven bubbles off plumb, crazy as a peach-orchard boar, and announced the trouble with the schools is *too much football*. That's when we all realized H. Ross Perot is secretly an agent of the Kremlin; yes, a commie, out to destroy the foundation of the entire Texan way of life.

The Legislature had a fit of creeping socialism and passed nearly every one of H. Ross's reforms, so now a kid can't play football unless he's passing *all* his courses, and he has to take stuff like math and English. Probably means the end of the world is close at hand. The Legislature even raised some taxes to pay for all this school stuff; first time they've raised taxes in thirteen years, so you see how serious it is.

Economically speaking, Texas is a very big state. (It's real embarrassing to have to say that, but they make us learn it in school here.) Most economists break it into six zones to report on what's going on. It's not unusual for Texas to be declared a disaster area for drought and flood simultaneously, and our economy is like that, too. In the Metroplex, which was called Dallas/Fort Worth back before chairs became "ergonomically designed seating systems," there is just a flat-out boom. The area has technically achieved full employment, 3.5 percent un-. Its building boom should crap out before long, but its economy is almost recessionproof—insurance, banking, merchandising, and defense contracts. The Centex Corridor (a.k.a. Austin and San Antone) is also Fat City; lot of high-tech firms coming in, supposed to be the new Silicon Valley. But Austin and San Antone are both mellow ol' towns, never wanted to be like Dallas or Houston. Fair amount of no-growth sentiment there, for Texas. But we reckon it's too late: both towns about ruint; gonna need separate books for the White Pages and Yellow Pages before long. The land sharks are in a greed frenzy, turning over sections every couple months for another $1 million, building all over the aquifer. There never was much around Houston or Dallas to crud up, but the limestone hills and fast rivers of Central Texas—that's a shame.

Contrarywise, the Rio Grande Valley's a disaster area. It's truck-farming country, mainly citrus, and also the most Third World place you can find in the U.S. of A. In fact, it's still feudal in some ways. The Valley was already reeling from the peso devaluation last year—we're talking as high as 50 percent unemployment in some Valley counties—when the big freeze hit right after Christmas and just wiped out the whole crop. Now the question's not how widespread unemployment is; it's how widespread hunger is, how bad malnutrition is. A real mess. The governor and the churches have been great; the Reagan administration, zero.

Also hurting real bad is most of West Texas. This drought has cut so deep the ranchers have even had to sell off their starter herds.

Just nothing left. The Panhandle, the Plains, even in Central Texas, there's no pasture. A goddamn drought is just the sorriest kind of calamity. A flood, a hurricane, or a tornado hits and then it's over, but a drought takes a long, long time to kill your cattle and your spirit, and gives you so many, many chances to get your hopes up again—in vain. You folks back East, your beef's going up considerable; we got nothing to start over with when this does break. Our farmers are bleeding to death. Mark White carried every rural (we pronounce that *rule*) area in this state in 1982 against a Republican incumbent with more money than God. But one of the laws of politics is It Ain't a Trend Till You've Seen It Twice. The polls show Reagan winning Texas with 75 percent of the vote.

Politically, we've got more talent in statewide office now than in living memory: not a certified Neanderthal in the bunch, and the treasurer, Ann Richards, is one of the smartest, funniest people in politics anywhere. Our populist Ag Commish, Jim Hightower, keeps us amused with his observations: "Why would I want to be a middle-of-the-road politician? Ain't nothin' in the middle of the road but yellow stripes and dead armadillos." (Tell the truth, I also had a great fondness for Hightower's predecessor, an entertaining linthead named Reagan V. Brown, who wanted to nuke the fire ants. Brown probably lost because he called Booker T. Washington a nigger, but there were extenuating circumstances: he called him a *great* nigger.)

Our congressional delegation still boasts enough wood to start a lumberyard. We've got a helluva U.S. Senate race. In one corner is Phil Gramm, the former Boll Weevil Democrat, now a full-fledged Republican, named the most right-wing member of Congress by the *National Journal*. And in the other corner, a thirty-eight-year-old liberal State Senator from Austin named Lloyd Doggett: smart, clean, hard-working Mr. Integrity, actually looks like the young Abe Lincoln. If you could jack up Doggett and run a sense of humor in under him, he'd be about perfect.

Doggett's a long shot because there is an ungodly amount of right-wing money in this state, and no decent newspapers, except for the *Dallas Times Herald*. (I'd say that even if I didn't work for it.) Gramm is running a charming campaign, accusing Doggett of being soft on queers and commies. That usually sells well down here. Doggett can get pretty nasty his own self, in down-populist fashion. Right now he seems to be concentrating on convincing the corporate types that Gramm's so far gone in ideology he doesn't have enough sense to protect the state's economic interests. We used to have a congressman like that from Dallas named Jim Collins. The rest of the guys would be trying to sneak gas deregulation past the Yankees, and Collins would go into a diatribe about school busing. He didn't just miss the play; he never understood what *game* it was.

People always try to tell you how much Texas is changing. Hordes of Yankee yuppies have moved in, and we have herpes bars, roller discos, and other symptoms of civilization. I think, though, maybe Texas is in a permanent state of *plus ça change.* While it is true that there are Texans who play polo and eat pasta salad, the place is still reactionary, cantankerous, and hilarious.

The Nation, October 14, 1984

THE GIBBER WINS ONE
AND OTHER NEWS

Summer's going to end any week now, as South Texas temperatures dwindle slowly out of the nineties, and none too soon, let me add, because it's been a real bastard. You could tell as far back as April it would be brutal: the Legislature ran more than usually amok, passing all manner of anti-Bubba laws. Bubba has to buckle up now and all this other bushwa. Thank God it's still legal to drink while driving.

By May the Lege had screwed things up so bad they had to be called back in special session. The most depressing thing about the Lege these days is that it has Republicans in it. Most of them are mean-mouth Republicans, too. Warren Burnett, the distinguished legal counselor from Odessa, always advises you should never let anyone on a jury whose mouth puckers smaller than a chicken's asshole. You look at those statehouse Republicans and near every one is mean-mouthed like that—mean-dispositioned, too. They had a snit because the Democrats came up with an indigents' health care plan, which means we're not going to let poor folks die in the streets anymore. The Republicans and the mean Democrats almost defeated the bill; it came down to a tie vote in the House and Speaker Gib Lewis, a man we seldom think of as a hero of the people, had to break the tie.

It's possible that the Speaker is smarter than we think he is, but it's hard to tell because he can't speak English. Sometimes you listen to him fighting to express himself—valiantly trying to battle his way out of a sentence while surrounded by dangling modifiers, mismatched predicates, and loose clauses—and you have to feel compassion. The Gibber's greatest moment this session came on Disability Day, which we have every year to honor the handicapped folks for their efforts to get better access to public buildings. We never give them any money for this, but we honor their efforts to get it. Anyway, the Guv issued a proclamation, both houses just resoluted up a storm, and Gib Lewis read all of it without making hardly any mistakes. We were so proud. Then he looked up at all the handicapped folks who had wedged their wheelchairs into the gallery and said, "And now, will y'all stand and be recognized?"

After the session, the Gibber thanked all the members for extinguishing themselves and left for South Africa. This had nothing to do with politics. Gibber likes to shoot harmless animals, preferably rare ones, for fun. It's his major passion in life. Some nit-pickers criticized him for letting the South African government pay for the trip, but he came back and said out loud, clear as anything, "Those people over there have a lot of problems," which made everything jake.

Texas Democrats are enough trouble. Why the hell anyone ever thought we needed two political parties down here is beyond me. Over in the First Congressional District, much of July was devoted to proving that we don't. Thanks to Senator Phil Gramm, who is always busier than an anthill what just been stepped on, the last congressman from the First is now on the federal bench, so we had to elect a new one. The Republicans decided this was a test run for 1986 and sent platoons of consultants, image-makers, fund-raisers, and assorted experts down to Texarkana—which serves them right. Their headquarters looked like I.B.M., all shiny and telephones with lots of buttons and such. The Democrats were working on card tables again in back rooms where the ceilings were falling down. How come Democrats keep thinking they can win when they're being outspent three to one? It's dumb.

Anyway, the Republicans had a terrific candidate, name of Edd Hargett. (One of those experts discovered that people with double letters in their names are considered more reliable by voters.) Edd Hargett has great hair and he not only played football, he was quarterback for Texas A & M. The Democrat was Jim Chapman, who is seriously bald and otherwise just your average Texas D.A., a guy who has devoted the best years of his life to making sure that perps who stick up liquor stores do life in prison. (Which reminds me, a perp in Lubbock got seventy-five years this summer for stealing sixteen frozen turkeys, which is fairly strong gargle given that all sixteen turkeys were recovered, still frozen. Not only no damage but no defrost and the guy still bought 4.7 years a bird. Don't ever steal a turkey in Lubbock.) The Republicans put up billboards all over saying, VOTE FOR EDD HARGETT, A CONGRESSMAN IN THE EAST TEXAS TRADITION. This annoyed the Democrats: never been a Republican elected in East Texas before. So the Chapman people went around putting bumper stickers that said REPUBLICAN on Hargett's billboards. The Hargetts called the Chapmans to complain their billboards were being "defaced." This made the Chapmans very happy.

Chapman is the guy who discovered that trade policy is an issue, which is why you, too, are now being bored to hives over it. Actually no one in East Texas gives a rat's ass about it either, but Hargett was dumb enough to say he didn't see what trade policy had to do with jobs in East Texas. (This view can be easily explained: he went to A & M when Phil Gramm taught economics there.) When Lone Star Steel shut down its plant two years ago, it threw 4,000 people out of work. When Hargett and Chapman had their big television debate, Chapman brought along a VOTE FOR EDD HARGETT gimme cap and showed the audience the tag on it—said "Made in Taiwan." Them Republicans may have a lot of buttons on they phones, but they are still asleep at the wheel. Chapman won with 51 percent.

August brought a wondrous event, a peace demonstration in the Panhandle. It's not easy to be for peace in Texas. A while back there was an article in *The New York Times Magazine* about New York intellectuals, which was one of the funniest things I ever read. An intellectual named Norman Podhoretz was quoted complaining about the "dominant liberal culture." To prove that liberal culture is indeed dominant, Podhoretz inquired indignantly, "Have you ever met *anyone* who was against a nuclear freeze?" Lord, I haven't laughed that hard since the governor held a press conference to announce he wasn't crazy. I love New Yorkers, they're so provincial. Bubba's pickup has a bumper sticker that says, FREEZE NOW, FRY LATER.

Anyway, all the pinko peace lovers of Texas—that's about seventy people out of 16.4 million and most of 'em from decadent places like Houston and Dallas—went up to Borger on the occasion of the fortieth anniversary of the bombing of Hiroshima. Borger is near Amarillo, and Amarillo is near what looks like a girdle factory but is actually the place where nuclear warheads are manufactured. So here's a bunch of peace lovers camped in a ditch outside a nuke factory in the middle of August in the middle of the Panhandle. And the good people of Carson County already figured peace lovers were crazy.

The chief thing about peace people is that they're earnest. For three days they prayed a lot, sang folk songs, and held seminars on nonviolence in order to prevent nuclear war. Local fundamentalists came by in a truck with a bullhorn every day to tell the peace lovers that peace does not come through disarmament; it only comes when you let Jesus into your heart. One peace lover, Dr. Larry Egbert of Dallas, thought it would be nice for all the peace folk to give blood to the local blood bank. Blood banks are always desperate for donors and this would show that the peace folk are just against nukes, not against the people who make their livings building the bombs. Well, it would have been a cordial gesture, but the Amarillo blood bank rejected their blood. The director told Egbert, "We don't want to get involved in politics."

At the end of the camp-out, the most hard-core nonviolents of them all—a menacing horde of nine vegetarians, Unitarians, and Quakers—went to sit on the railroad track to stop the "white train" from coming out of the nuke factory. That was Against the Law. Trespass, in fact. There's not that much excitement in law-enforcement work around Borger, so we had the entire Carson County Sheriff's Department, Borger City Police Department, Highway Patrol, and Santa Fe Railroad security guards gathered there to see that the Quakers didn't commit mayhem. We all standin' around in the blazin' hot sun in the middle of your typical Panhandle scene—flat as a griddle, not a tree for 600 miles, and everything is one color: dry. Suddenly from out of the nuke factory come two black four-wheel-drive vehicles, racing across the prairie, bouncing into the air, whip antennas a-lashin' behind 'em; it is the nuke plant security force. They screech to a halt by the tracks and all hop out. They are wearing jungle camouflage. They are ready to Rambo, lookin' to kill communist revolutionary terrorists. But there's only nine Quakers sittin' on the railroad tracks and none of them has seen *Rambo.* They all went to *Gandhi* instead. That's the trouble with this country, people keep messin' up each other's movies.

What else is new?

• It's illegal to be gay in Texas again, thanks to the Fifth Circuit. They reinstated our sodomy statute, so people can legally screw pigs in public but not each other in private.

• Mad Eddie Chiles, one of our better loopy oil zillionaires, is mad again and has taken to the airwaves to tell us about it. All he wants is for the government to *leave him alone*; he does not want anything from gummint—except the depletion allowance and the write-off for intangible drilling costs.

• We're having a football scandal that's so rank it might slop over into politics, which is real embarrassing.

• Waco, the Vatican City of the Baptists, has hired a P.R. firm for a quarter of a million bucks to "give Waco a more glamorous image." More?

The *dernier cri* for rich Texans is giving money to the *contras* so they can overthrow the Sandinista government of Nicaragua. And it's tax deductible, too. Ms. St. John Garwood of Austin gave $50,000 to buy a chopper for the *contras,* but they're only going to use it for humanitarian stuff, like on *M*A*S*H,* says Ms. Garwood. Buy your own little battalion of freedom fighters; it's a lot kickier than the Cattle Barons' Ball. Why give money to cure cancer when you can kill commies with it instead? Major General John Singlaub, retired, who now heads the U.S. Council for World Freedom, the outfit that channels money to the *contras,* says he gets about half his gelt from Texas. Bunkie Hunt was at the general's last do in Dallas. It's a bizarre concept: the Pentagon, a United Way agency. What can I tell you? We just have a lot of tacky billionaires.

The Nation, November 23, 1985

HELLO FROM BOOSTERVILLE

In Dallas, no one walks when it says, DON'T WALK. If you walk when it says, DON'T WALK, they arrest you. In 1980, Dallas cops shot a jaywalker. To death. Although we do like to point out to people who consider this peculiar that the man was an armed jaywalker. He was also crazier than a peach-orchard boar and wounded the cop who tried to stop him five times before he was dispatched to the Orderly Traffic Pattern in the Sky. Granted, the shorter version makes a better story, but that is often true of Dallas stories.

If Dallas has a soul—and Dallas is just as entitled to one as anyplace else—it is Dutch. Dan Wiser, a student of the city, observed years ago that the chief virtues of Dallas are orderliness and cleanliness. Dallasites not only do not jaywalk, they also do not litter. These are not sexy virtues. On the other hand, they beat dirt and disorder. The soul of Dallas is located at the Tomb of the Unknown Shopper, a monument that has not yet been built, but it will be as soon as Dallas acquires a municipal sense of humor. Dallas will acquire a municipal sense of humor as soon as:

1. The Dallas Citizens Council decides a municipal sense of humor is necessary and desirable.
2. The mayor appoints a Blue Ribbon Task Force on Municipal Humor.
3. The task force holds many prayer breakfasts: the prayer breakfast is critical to all Dallas activities.
4. The task force travels to many other cities, especially Toronto, to study their municipal senses of humor; compares and contrasts them; selects the best; and learns how said humor was instituted.
5. A referendum is put on the ballot, endorsed by both newspapers, all the television stations, the Chamber of Commerce, the Junior League, the League of Women Voters, the neighborhood associations, the Dallas Police Association, the John Birch Society, the Gay Alliance, and Citizens for Responsible Growth because everybody in Dallas supports everything that will Help Make Dallas Great(er).
6. All this must be done very earnestly. Earnestness is the civic style of Dallas.

Dallas, in case you haven't noticed, is now the premier city of Texas. I don't know what its size is in relation to Houston, but I do know it is now the state's major power center. Because Dallas is where the money is. (Houston is an oil town and oil is dying. There are 254 counties in Texas and only one of them has no oil at all under it—Dallas.) Look at who was in on the high-level meetings this month to settle the state's budget problems: the three top state officials (Dallas, Houston, Fort Worth) and Peter O'Donnell, Jess Hay, Ross Perot, and Tom Luce. All Dallas. Of course it takes that many powerful Dallasites to convince the moron we elected governor that he has to raise taxes, but that's a different discussion.

For those of you who are depressed by the thought of a Dallas-dominated Texas, take heart. It is possible to come to love Dallas. Or at least to be mildly fond of it. The least-known fact about Dallas is that it's wildly funny. No one in Dallas has ever noticed this, but it's true. What a cast of characters! Bunkie Hunt, Ross Perot, Eddie Chiles, Mary Kay Ash, the Rev. W. A. Criswell—you couldn't make up people that improbable if you tried. You understand that in Dallas all these people are considered normal. Dallas believes it has no eccentrics.

What Dallas really is is just another ol' East Texas town that happens to be real big. Folks in Dallas get up early, they work hard, they eat dinner at noon and supper at six, and they go to the Baptist Church on Sunday. Let's face it, it's a white-bread town, but there is, as in the case of the armed jaywalker, more to it. In many ways, it's much more Texan than Houston, which is to say, less cosmopolitan, less sophisticated. People move to Houston from Kansas and Connecticut and Saudi Arabia and Ethiopia. People move to Dallas from Waxahachie and Tyler and Dalhart and Weatherford. That's why you never see anyone downtown wearing cowboy boots or a cowboy hat—because they're all from Texas towns and they know that when you go to town, you should get dressed up.

The most un-Texas thing about Dallas is that it's self-conscious. The Texas of beer-drinking, hell-raising Bubbas who don't give a rat's ass what anyone else thinks of them does not exist in Dallas. It's an uptight town. Dallas is almost entirely middle class and worries obsessively about what other people think. Practically no one in Dallas makes a living pissanting heavy objects about—not many hog-butchers, toolmakers, or stackers of wheat here. Dallas is built on paper industries—primarily insurance and banking. It is also a merchandising center, wholesale and retail. Dave Hickey of Fort Worth has observed, "Dallas has more sheer mercantile energy than any place outside New York's garment district." Stanley Marsh III of Amarillo has observed that in Houston people make money by getting stuff out of the ground, in El Paso they make money off the sweat of other people, and in Dallas they make money by using their brains. That's why it hustles, Dallas does, always a little insecure, always trying too hard.

The place was founded in 1846 by John Neely Bryan, a real-estate developer, and named after a particularly undistinguished vice-president. It's not a port, not even on a river, was never a fort, never a cattle or railroad center. It took generations of boosters all hustling hard to make Dallas the largest commercial distribution center in this part of the world. And every day Dallas is still out there, selling itself. Trying too hard is rather an endearing fault. Only Dallas could try too hard too hard. Here is an excerpt from a 1982 Dallas Police Department rape report: "After sexual intercourse actor sat on edge of bed and told complainant to 'Come here.' Actor was very calm and told her not to ask any questions, not to notify the police. Actor was very apologetic, saying, 'I know I'm a sick person, I know I need help. I hope this does not turn you off to Dallas, 'cause Dallas is a great, nice city.' "

There is a black Dallas, there is a Chicano Dallas, there is a Vietnamese Dallas, there is a gay Dallas, there is even a funky-Bohemian Dallas. But mostly there is North Dallas. A place so materialistic and so Republican it makes your teeth hurt to contemplate it. You move to North Dallas with a perfectly good '72 Chevy and within two weeks you have *car embarrassment.* You need a Benz, you gotta have a Merc, it's gotta be silver-gray. North Dallas. Your trendy couple in the herpes bar, both wearing $250-from-Neiman-Marcus plush-velour jogging suits and working on their Bible study course. Ten-year-olds comparing designer jeans and Rolexes. The colorful native costume includes Izod shirts and tassle loafers, and the native food is pasta salad. In North Dallas they hold mustard tastings and play polo. Dallas women dress to the teeth. It is the make-up capital of the universe. In West Texas, when a woman is looking really knockout, her friends tell her, "Honey, you just look so *Dallas.* "

The weight of conformity is heavier in Dallas than anywhere else I have ever been—conformity of dress, thought, politics, religion, attitude. It is not terribly difficult to be a nonconformist in Dallas, but it is harder. Dallas is oppressive only when the famous Dallas earnestness turns into smugness and arrogance, something that has tended to happen rather frequently in the vicinity of Southern Methodist University. A few years ago at the SMU-UT game, SMU students held up a banner in the stands that read, "Our Maids Went to UT." Since SMU no longer has a football team, thanks to the most classic case of Dallas arrogance yet uncovered, it can be hoped that even SMU is capable of acquiring humility. During the recent festivities on campus, the students held protest rallies, chanting over and over, "No more cheating, no more lying."

Dallas prides itself on The Arts. Dallas is earnest about Art. Also competitive. We just built a dandy new museum on the grounds that both Houston and Fort Worth were outdoing us. A. C. Greene, the Dallas historian, says, "Dallas salutes a person who can buy a piece of art, not a person who can create one." At the corner of Federal and Bryan is my favorite piece of Dallas art—a bronze statue of two bidnessmen shaking hands on a deal.

The unnatural streak in Dallas's boosterism stems from the Kennedy assassination. This terribly self-conscious town found itself billed around the world as "The City of Hate"—the only place where such a dreadful thing could have occurred. Several assassinations later, we know the nuts and the guns are everywhere, but Dallas took the full brunt of the country's rage over the Kennedy assassination and it was grim. It has taken the city a full generation to recover, and even so, scars remain. The city is still defensive and touchy about it. Southfork, the mythical home of television's J. R. Ewing, recently surpassed the assassination site as the city's top tourist attraction. Poor Dallas was grateful.

There was something terribly wrong with Dallas twenty-four years ago. You can go back and read the *Dallas Morning News* of that era and smell it still, the nasty, self-righteous anger and paranoia screaming up off the curling yellow pages. Dallas at the time was no more bizarre than Waco or Phoenix or L.A.—it was the heyday of the John Birch Society and all Southwestern cities were infected by this lunacy: if Dallas was different, it was only by slight degree. The death of John Kennedy cured Dallas—no one has been able to preach hate publicly there since. I speak with some authority on the current state of Dallas's right wing: for several years now I have written a column for the *Times Herald* that is, by Dallas standards, to the left of Lenin. I am still un-hanged. Dallas is a tolerant town. For those of you whose opinion of Dallas is still unchanged from the early sixties, I recommend shock treatment: try a champagne brunch on the grassy knoll and let it go.

The disgrace of Dallas today is that it is probably the most segregated city this side of Johannesburg. Dallas was, typically, de-segged from the top down. According to Warren Leslie's book on Dallas, then-Mayor R. L. (Bob) Thornton called the Citizens Council (the big bidnessmen) together and announced, "We don't want any Birmingham or any Little Rock here—it would be bad for bidness." And so the signs came down, the city was de-segged, but not integrated. One result is that black Dallas remains curiously leaderless and largely quiet. There are a lot of middle-class blacks in Dallas bustling about the noonday streets, but none to be found in the Greenville Avenue nightclubs and the West End of downtown, where Dallas swings, as it were.

Dallas doesn't actually swing, of course. What you can do in Dallas is shop. Also, many good eats, especially upscale eats. Dallas has its full share of human folly, lunacy, and wonderfully ludicrous absurdity and wouldn't be half as funny as it is if it didn't keep trying so hard to be straight. So here's this whole city of pitch-in, can-do painfully earnest boosters. The result is that Dallas Works. It's not beautiful or even especially interesting, it's just funny. And everything there works. And it's clean. It's a nice place to live, actually.

Texas Observer, May 29, 1987

TOUGH AS BOB WAR
AND OTHER STUFF

We've just survived another political season largely unscathed. I voted for Bobby Locke for governor: he's the one who challenged Col. Muammar el-Qaddafi to hand-to-hand combat. In the Gulf of Sidra. On the Line of Death. At high noon. Next Fourth of July. "Only one of us will come out of the water alive," said Locke. Locke thinks the trouble with America is that we've lost respect for our leaders and this would be a good way to restore same. Me too. Besides, you should have seen the other guys.

The Republicans had a congressman running who thinks you get AIDS through your feet. That's Representative Tom Loeffler of Hunt, who is smarter than a box of rocks. His television advertisements proudly claimed,

"He's tough as bob war" (bob war is what you make fences with), and also that in his youth Loeffler played football with two broken wrists. This caused uncharitable persons to question the man's good sense, so he explained he didn't know his wrists were broken at the time. Loeffler went to San Francisco during the campaign to make a speech. While there, he wore shower caps on his feet while showering lest he get AIDS from the tile in the tub. He later denied that he had spent the entire trip in his hotel room. He said: "I did walk around the hotel. I did see people who do have abnormal tendencies. I'd just as soon not be associated with abnormal people." If that's true, what was he doing running for governor of Texas?

Perhaps Loeffler's most enduring contribution to Texas political lore was a thought that seemed to him so profound he took to repeating it at every campaign stop and during televised debates as well: "As I have traveled around this state, many people have said to me, 'Texas will never be Texas again.' But I say they are wrong. I say Texas will *always* be Texas." Hard to add anything to that.

On the Democratic side, the nerd issue was dominant. The ugly specter of nerditude was raised by A. Don Crowder, a candidate from Dallas. Crowder's platform consisted of vowing to repeal the no-pass, no-play rule on account of it has seriously damaged high school football and is un-American, un-Texan, and probably communist inspired. No pass, no play was part of the education reform package enacted last year by Governor Mark White and the State Legislature. If you don't pass all your school subjects, you can't participate in any extracurricular activities—including football. Quite naturally, this has caused considerable resentment and could cost White the governorship. So A. Don Crowder holds this press conference in which he says the reason Mark White favors no pass, no play is because White was "one of the first nerds in Texas." As evidence, Crowder produces White's high school annual, and there it was: the guy was zip in extracurricular activities in his school days. We're talking not even Booster Club. Not Glee Club or Stage Crew. Not even the Prom Poster Committee. According to Crowder, this explains "the psychological reasoning behind White's dislike of football."

There were headlines all over the state: "Gov. White Called 'Nerd' By Yearbook Wielding Foe." "Nerd Charge Merits Scrutiny." Meanwhile, we tracked down Donnie Crowder's high school annual and guess what? He was captain of the football team. Played baseball. Ran track. And was in the French Club. French Club! Need I say more? *Quel fromage.*

White's initial response to this slanderous aspersion was to whine about how tacky it was for Crowder to be so ugly right after the explosion of the *Challenger* shuttle. Nerd City. Then his campaign manager tries to pull it out by saying, So the guy was not real active in high school—but he was super-involved in after-school activities at the Baptist Church. Nerd! Nerd! Finally White gets his act together, comes out, and says, "Look, I grew up poor. My daddy had an accident when I was just a sophomore and he couldn't work after that, so I spent my high school years working summers and after school." While A. Don Crowder was in French Club, doubtlessly conjugating highly irregular verbs with busty cheerleaders over the pâté and vin rouge, our governor was out mowing lawns, frying burgers, and pumping gas to help his dear old silver-haired mother. Great stuff. Besides, Bubba never joined no French Club.

Marko Blanco, as we call him in South Texas, will meet former Governor Bill Clements for a rematch in November. Clements was defeated by White four years ago on account of he's an awful grouch. Grumpy versus the Nerd—what a match-up.

Also contributing to the political festivities of late is that peerless, fearless commie-hater Charlie Wilson of Lufkin. It's possible to get used to Charlie. He has a certain charm. When I called him to verify some of the more bloodthirsty quotations attributed to him in the *Houston Post*'s account of his latest trip to the Afghanistan border, the first thing he said was, "The only thing those cocksuckers understand is hot lead and cold steel." I was especially pleased that he took his lady friend, Annelise Ilschenko, a former Miss World U.S.A., along on the Afghan jaunt. According to the *Houston Post,* she is a "dark-haired and sloe-eyed beauty," and you hardly ever find a good case of sloe-eyed beauty in the newspapers anymore. The *Post* said, "[She] went everywhere with Wilson, not even flinching as she sank her high-heeled white leather boots into the thick brown ooze of Darra's main street." No sacrifice is too great when you're fighting for freedom.

Charlie told the *Post* reporter he went over there hoping to "kill Russians, as painfully as possible." Myself, I think it had more to do with an observation he made after he got back: "Hell, they're still lining up to see *Rambo* in Lufkin." Patriotism is always in good smell in East Texas. The night El Presidente started bombing Libya, the deejay at Benny B's, a honky-tonk in Lufkin, made all the patrons stand on their chairs and sing "The Star-Spangled Banner." He said if anybody refused to do it, "We'll know you're a commie faggot." Of course, they do the same thing at Benny B's for David Allan Coe's song "You Never Even Called Me By My Name." Living in East Texas can be a real challenge.

Living anywhere in Texas is getting to be a challenge as the price of oil slides gracefully toward single digits. Texas-bashing seems to be a popular new national pastime. "Let 'Em Rot in the Sun," said a cordial headline in the *New Republic.* Some Northern papers ran stories on our oil woes with heads the likes of "Sorry About That, J. R." I don't see that we've got any cause to whine about this vein of snottiness: some of the Bubbas did put bumper stickers on their pickups a few years back that said, "Let the Yankee Bastards Freeze in the Dark." Somehow I forebode that Yankees going and doing likewise is not going to teach Bubba any manners. The rest of us down here been having poor luck at it for a long time.

I would point out, though, that Texas is not a rich state, never has been. Never even made it up to the national average in per capita income until the tail end of the oil boom, and then we slid right down again. Poverty level here is always among the nation's highest and, according to a recent study by a team from Harvard University, Texas has more counties beset by hunger and malnutrition than any other state. Our second-biggest industry after oil is agriculture, and you've maybe read something about how it's going for farmers these days. Citrus crop in the Rio Grande Valley was wiped out by a freeze three years ago. Now they got drought and 40 percent unemployment, and the peso is still going down. Our banks had their money in oil, agriculture, and Mexico. We're losing a lot of banks.

There is no social support system for the poor in Texas. Adults get nothing; children get $57.50 a month. Bubba's got a beer-gut he can let shrink some and not be hurting, but almost half the children in this state are black or brown and they have no cushion. If Eddie Chiles goes broke, it's Don't Cry for Me Texarkana; John Connally and Ben Barnes on hard times, search me for sympathy; and I could give a shit about J.R. But that's not who's hurting.

Good thing we've still got politics in Texas—finest form of free entertainment ever invented.

The Nation, June 7, 1986

PRACTICING NUANCE
DOWN AT LUBY'S

Texans will be voting with their feet on November 4 in what is predicted to be the most poorly attended gubernatorial election on record. "None of the Above" is the candidate of choice for the great majority of Texans, and who can blame them? The incumbent adds new dimensions to the concept of "unimpressive," and the challenger is the guy we threw out last time we had a chance.

Governor Mark White is in deep sludge, the economy has gone to hell, and the state faces a massive budget deficit. While no one except Bill Clements, the once and future governor, blames this on White, the man's peerless imitation of a weather vane has helped spread the impression that he can't go to the bathroom without consulting the polls. According to *The*

Almanac of American Politics for 1986, "Mark White is a man with no clear philosophy." I'd say so myself. It's hard to look up to a fellow who always has his ear to the ground. Still, White is guilty mainly of bad luck—he was governor when the price of oil went from $32 a barrel to $9. His chief claim to fame is education reform, a tremendous effort from Texas, under which it was finally agreed that football is not the raison d'être of our public school system. But if Ronald Reagan is the Teflon politician, Mark White is Velcro. Part of the reform package was a competency test for teachers, who like to had a wall-eyed fit over it and now refuse to vote for White.

Dollar Bill Clements, sixty-nine, is one of those people born with a burr up his butt. He lost to White in 1982 because people thought he was mean, a well-founded impression. His political philosophy is, "If you don't have an oil well, git one." Clements made several units—which is what we used to call a hundred million dollars back when we had money down here—in the "awl bidness," which he considered made him fit to be governor and so did 50 percent of the Texans who voted in 1978. When the largest oil spill in history—caused by a rig from Clements's company—was headed for the Texas Gulf Coast, Governor Clements advised the citizenry, "Pray for a hurricane." When he disagreed with a Mexican scholar on immigration, Clements said, "He's just another Meskin with an opinion." His advice to the unemployed is that they should quit settin' around suckin' their thumbs.

There is a large collection of these sayings from Chairman Clements, many of which are being reprised in Mark White's campaign advertisements. They generally combine ignorance with arrogance, two of Clements's most salient traits, but the man's bluntness can also be endearing. You will notice this in the unlikely event you should ever agree with him. He was once confronted by a fundamentalist at a Republican convention, who demanded to know if Clements had been born again. "No thanks," said Clements, "once was enough." He is running hard on the utterly loony pledge that he will never raise our taxes: we face a $5 billion deficit on an $11 billion budget that was tighter than a tick to begin with. We could elect Jesus governor and he'd still have to raise our taxes. But you know Texans—you can always tell 'em, you just can't tell 'em much.

Clements went through the spring primaries smiling like Dale Carnegie himself. The consultants had told him he had to overcome his "mean problem," so he tried to convince voters that in addition to having a bad hip joint replaced, he'd had a complete personality transplant as well. We thought Bill Clements was running for governor, but all spring we got Mr. Chips. Fortunately, that didn't last. Clements now goes about nastily accusing White of "practicing nuance."

Among political consultants, when the candidate is a dog the preferred euphemism is, "We don't want to overexpose the candidate." Clements's people are so determined not to overexpose him, they'd like to send him out of state till it's over. He sometimes gets to campaign at the Casden's filling station near Wink, and they let him out for an occasional hand-shaking at Luby's in Longview. Meanwhile, he's all over the airwaves, blaming the state's fiscal problems on "Mark White's wild overspending."

Clements and White had one debate. Political debates are sort of like stock-car races—no one really cares who wins, they just want to see the crashes. If there aren't any crashes, everyone votes the event a total bore. Clements managed not to say anything too outrageous, just the normal political lies, and then trotted out his patented pore-boy routine. "I started out just a pore boy. . . ." When Clements was governor, *The New York Times* kept describing him as "a brash, self-made veteran of the oilfields." What nuance. Bill Clements grew up in Highland Park, the wealthiest suburb of Dallas; he went to Highland Park High School and then Southern Methodist University, where he pledged Kappa Alpha. He did work as a roughneck: a lot of college kids still do, or at least they did until last November.

Clements started this race twenty points ahead of White last spring. By mid-September, White had pulled almost even. But the most recent polls show Clements's lead holding, and most of us think he has the edge. In a small-turnout election, almost anything could swing it. Facing the oil crash and four more years of Bill Clements would have been enough to depress Hubert Humphrey. But Clements, although a miserable governor, makes a wonderful target. When told Clements had been studying Spanish, Agriculture Commissioner Jim Hightower was moved to comment, "Oh good. Now he'll be bi-ignorant."

We are having an equally swell time with the lesser races. The Republicans are quite taken with themselves for having nominated an actual Hispanic for statewide office. Roy Barrera, Jr., Republican candidate for attorney general, is the son of one of John Connally's old henchmen and is thus fated to stalk through life known to all as

Roy Junior. He accuses the incumbent, Jim Mattox, of having brought "disgrace, fiscal irresponsibility and scandal to the office." But Roy Junior says he's not mudslinging: "It's very appropriate for candidates to bring out the facts." And it is a fact that Attorney General Mattox got himself indicted for commercial bribery while in office—also acquitted.

But Roy Junior is just piddling when it comes to Mattox-bashing. The man you want for that purpose is the Rev. W. N. Otwell, who says that Mattox is ungodly, a tyrant, homosexual, a communist, and a wicked man who does not love God.

Of course, the Reverend Otwell calls everyone who doesn't agree with him a communist, homosexual God-hater, so it's not that much of an honor. Actually, Mattox is a full-blooded Southern Baptist. Otwell is mad because the attorney general is trying to shut down his home for wayward boys. The general is trying to shut it down because it doesn't meet the state's licensing requirements. The reverend claims that's a violation of church and state and also Satan at work. Right now Otwell is on the lam, ducking the law, a fugitive; but he appears at press conferences. Via videotape. Wearing burlap sackcloth. And answers questions on a speaker-phone. Just another one of those episodes that add such *je ne sais quoi* to life in the Greatest State. Otwell ankled on out of Forth Worth to avoid a court appearance at which the state was set to close down the home for troubled youth. He said, "God didn't tell me to go to jail," which is probably true, but getting the Lord to sign off on these things is damned complicated.

Perhaps you wonder why the state of Texas is persecuting a dippy preacher. Goes back to the early 1970s, when the state simply failed to enforce its licensing requirements for private schools. This legal lacuna led to the growth of a Dickensian industry; all manner of persons set up "homes" for delinquent youth. Delinquents from other states were regularly consigned to Texas—the reformatories in places like Illinois were overcrowded and their authorities saved money by shipping the little darlings here. An early example of the beauty of privatization. The homes advertised they could reform delinquents. To that end, many innovative instructional techniques were brought to bear on the wayward children, such as putting them in cages, dousing them with ice water, and making them scrub themselves with wire brushes. In November 1972, a fourteen-year-old girl at Artesia Hall, a school in Liberty County, was forced to swallow lye and left without medical care for three days. It probably would have reformed her if she hadn't died instead.

This caused some stink, so the state took to inspecting and licensing those schools and homes, over the objections of the fundamentalists, which continue to this day.

The land commissioner is in a tight race against a hospital. Garry Mauro, the commissioner, has a Republican opponent named M. D. Anderson, which also happens to be a fine cancer hospital in Houston. The M. D. Anderson on the ballot is a bartender from Seven Points and no kin to the guy who founded the hospital, but such details seldom trouble our Texas voters, a carefree lot. Mauro is running very scared.

An avalanche of apathy is the safest bet for election day. Students of politics from around the country keep wanting to know what the Texas election portends, being as the oil patch is in big trouble. Who will we blame for this mess—the Republicans in Washington or the Democrats in Austin? What will it mean? Does a victory for Clements signal continuing realignment in the South? Does it mean Reagan still has coattails? Or will a White win prove that moderate Democrats shall inherit the earth? Do yourselves a favor, friends, and seek no straws in the wind from Texas. If folks down here can bring themselves to vote at all, it'll be by holding their noses and pushing the lever against the candidate they can't stand the most.

The Nation, November 8, 1986

OIL ON THE ROCKS

I've been writing a monthly column for *The Progressive* magazine since 1986. It's the most down-home, old-shoe publication in the universe. I am considered a scintillating wit by *The Progressive*'s standards, a veritable Dorothy Parker in a monthly chiefly noted for Terminal Earnestness. I have to level with you, it's just not that hard to earn a reputation for funny in a magazine that regularly features the Ghastly Condition of Migrant Laborers and Why Nuclear War Is Inevitable.

Once a month Erwin Knoll, the editor, or Linda Rocawich, who has some title there, call to remind me that my column was due yesterday. I always groan and carry on as though some insufferable burden has just been added to my load: in fact, I generally read through the last month's worth of my own newspaper columns, pick out the best bits, and ship them on to *The Progressive*. I often plagiarize from myself. I like to think of this as ecological journalism: I recycle.

Texas is going broke in style. We make jokes all the way to the bankruptcy court and keep making them while we're standing in line to file. Since we know no one is going to feel sorry for us, we figure we might as well laugh.

Wanna know how to get an oilman down out of the tree? Cut the rope.

They're selling a new model Mercedes for Texas oilmen. It has no seat and no steering wheel, but that doesn't matter: they've lost their ass and don't know which way to turn anyway.

My favorite bumper sticker out around Midland-Odessa says, O LORD. JUST LET ME HAVE ONE MORE OIL BOOM: THIS TIME I PROMISE NOT TO PISS IT AWAY.

Oil people are really gamblers at heart, and that's why they don't defenestrate themselves in droves upon learning that they've lost all their money. When Texans go broke, they don't commit suicide; they start over. This is an oil bust, and oil has always been a crap game. You play craps, and sooner or later you crap out.

There aren't any big rich oil people in Texas who haven't gone belly-up two or three times over. The only good thing the late H. L. Hunt ever said was, "Money's just a way of keeping score." This is still the land where everything is assumed to be possible. There's no disgrace attached to losing your money in a bust like this one: it doesn't mean you did anything wrong, everybody's bust.

Another nice thing about Texas going broke is that so many hateful people are in Chapter 11. Nelson and Bunkie Hunt, those peerless funders of loopy fundamentalist anti-commie crusades, are taking the chapter. Eddie Chiles, the even loopier Fort Worth oilman who used to go on the radio with right-wing tirades that started, "I'm mad," is now sad instead. The bumper stickers that used to read, I'M MAD TOO, now say, I'M BROKE TOO, EDDIE.

Former Governor John Connally and his partner, Ben Barnes, are so broke there is a subgenre of Barnes-Connally jokes. (Ben Barnes went to Hong Kong, came back, and told Connally, "I've got good news and I've got bad news." "Give me the good news first; I need some good news." "The good news is that the Bank of Hong Kong has opened a $500 million line of credit for us." "Hallelujah, we're saved! All right, what's the bad news?" "We have to come up with $500 in cash.") And just the other day, Barnes locked his keys in his car. Who says there's no justice?

Then there is the wonder of the Suddenly Socialist. Oscar Wyatt, Jr., a medium-big oilman who is much devoted to proving that robber barons still live, recently observed, "Ronald Reagan is going to free-market us to death!" Tell Milton Friedman not to visit any time soon.

Of course, in any tough situation, the Texas Legislature can be counted on to make things worse. Frosty Troy, editor of the *Oklahoma Observer,* has offered to collaborate on a manual for other oil-patch states, *How to Go Broke.*

Step One: Get the governor out from underneath his desk. (The governor of Oklahoma came out from under his and promptly left for Europe. As soon as he came back, he departed on a tour of Asia.)

Step Two: Put foot firmly in governor's back and say, "Lead, you dumb sumbitch, it's what we pay you for." After this you're in real trouble because the guv is obliged to call in the Legislature.

Step Three: Hang the Legislature.

The Oklahoma Legislature decided to resolve the state's fiscal crisis by dismembering public education. Unfortunately, the O.U. football team was left intact.

In Texas, the House is taking the more traditional tack of picking on the blind, the disabled, the mentally retarded, and other citizens who haven't had the foresight to hire a pod of lobbyists. The Senate, led by Lieutenant Governor Bill Hobby, has actually proposed to raise taxes as well as cut services. This prompted Representative Sam Johnson of Plano to observe that Hobby reminded him of the communist guards in North Vietnamese prisoner-of-war camps.

That's the way our political debate usually goes around here.

The Progressive, November 1986

POLITICAL ASYLUM

Many delights accrued from the recent plebiscite here, not least of which is that we have elected our normal quota of dead people, Lyndon LaRouche followers, freelance fruitloops, and folks whose names sound like someone famous. Some of you may have been under the impression from recent magazine articles that the Great State is become a feminist paradise—home of women mayors, female state officials, wopersons of the highest caliber in public office. But democracy is not a perfect instrument.

The thanks of a grateful nation will flow toward Texas when y'all see what we have sent Washington this time. We had a major political duke-out over an empty house seat in Amarillo, up in the Panhandle. The victor in the Democratic primary was State Senator Bill Sarpalius, who got a leg up one night in January when a disgruntled patriot slugged him so hard it broke his jaw and the jaw had to be wired shut for most of the campaign. For most politicians, that would constitute an electoral handicap, but since Sarpalius is not bent over double with intellect, it proved a boon. He's a tall, nice-looking, apple-cheeked fellow, and if you don't have to listen to him, he looks good.

One of the Republicans in the primary, State Representative Chip Staniswalis, found hard going after the district attorney announced Staniswalis was under investigation for taking kickbacks from a legislative employee. That put a hitch in his getalong.

Staniswalis's problems reminded us all of the rich legal history of that Amarillo seat. Staniswalis's predecessor was State Representative Ben Bynum, who moved on to a county judgeship and then got convicted of failing to keep track of public monies properly. (He kept cashing the checks intended for a new county courthouse at liquor stores.) He's on probation while he appeals the case. His predecessor was State Representative Walter Knapp, who had no luck at all. Knapp wound up in Stripe City for a major offense involving postage and shortly after they let him out, Knapp killed first his former wife and then himself. His predecessor was State Representative Hudson Moyers, who also went to the hoosegow for buying a pickup truck with postage stamps from his legislative expense account.

Amarillo did not produce the weirdest member of the Texas Legislature, however. It's a tough call, but we think the title goes to State Representative Mike Martin from Longview, who at first appeared to be just a garden-variety right-winger from East Texas. But Martin came up with a unique plan to ensure his reelection. In 1981, Martin paid his cousin Charlie to shoot him in the arm with a shotgun, and then claimed it had been done by a satanic and communistic cult out to get him on account of his pro-family and pro-American stands in the Legislature. He said the cult was called the Guardian Angels of the Underworld. After his cousin Charlie confessed, Representative Martin was called before a grand jury, but went into hiding instead. The Texas Rangers hunted him high and hunted him low. At last they tracked him to earth at his momma's house, where he was found hiding in the stereo cabinet. He always did want to be the speaker.

Martin wound up paying a $2,000 fine because he lied to a grand jury investigating the case; and besides, in this state it is illegal to pay someone to shoot you—so don't ever come down here and try it. Martin then sued his cousin for having shot him.

Even Martin was not the strangest case in our recent electoral history. The matter of the Wrong Don Yarbrough made a notable chapter. We elected him to the state supreme court in 1976 by mistake on account of his name looks like that of a better-known Texas Democrat, the Other Don Yarborough. First thing the Wrong Don did after his victory was announce that he owed his triumph to the Lord, on account of God told him to run in the first place. It's possible that God, too, thought he was the Other Don Yarborough. Turned out the Wrong Don was being sued for a variety of malfeasances in his highly eccentric law practice and had allegedly been plotting the death of a Victoria, Texas, banker. The Wrong Don graced the bench of the high court for six months, but resigned before the legislature could impeach him. He was convicted on a perjury charge in 1978 and took it on the lam.

As a fugitive, Justice Yarbrough felt called to a mid-life career change and enrolled under another name at the very same medical school in Grenada that later became famous during our invasion of that country. The Wrong Don was finally nabbed in 1983. After paying his debt to society, he showed further enterprise. In 1986, the former justice pleaded guilty to bribing a banker and trying to launder $500,000 worth of drug money. The feds had also taped him plotting the "extermination" of his enemies. So he's back in stir, but the Wrong Don is still the most interesting guy we ever had on the Supreme Court.

Those who find the current selection of presidential candidates so unappetizing, who profess them to be pygmies all, clearly lack the tempering experience of Texas politics. Spotting the lesser of two evils in the Great State takes a strong mind and a stronger stomach.

I see nothing wrong with the people running for president. None of them drools.

AS THOUSANDS CHEER

Some days you open the paper and it's kind of like finding Fidel Castro in the refrigerator, smoking a cigar. Hard to know what to think. For instance, when the lead story is that fourteen Dallas Cowboy Cheerleaders have resigned because they believe the team's new owner is trying to make them into sex objects. Says I to myself, "No doo-doo?" (That's the George Bush influence.)

While the rest of the world has been following China's crushing of the pro-democracy movement, here in Texas we have been absorbed in the complex issues presented by the rebellion of the Dallas Cowboy Cheerleaders. The uprising, you might call it.

Here's the deal: The Dallas Cowboys, America's Team, got bought a few months back by a rich guy from Arkansas named Jerry Jones. Seemed like pretty much the end of the world at the time—the Dallas Cowboys owned by some Arkie. Alas, how far we have fallen.

Then the new owner fired Tom Landry, the only coach the Cowboys have ever had. And then he fired Tex Schramm, the only manager the team has ever had. And now he's messing with the franchise.

The girls (we all call them girls) want to retain their clean-cut, wholesome image. You may not have been aware until now that they had a clean-cut, wholesome image, but that's only because you have not studied the matter deeply. As the *Fort Worth Star-Telegram* noted in its caption under a particularly fine picture of two Cheerleaders jiggling up a storm, "Dallas Cowboy Cheerleaders Frequently Visit Nursing Homes."

But the barbarian from Arkansas wanted the girls to wear revealing costumes—halter tops and spandex bicycle pants, as opposed to the Puritanical outfits they wear now. He further said the girls could socialize with football players. Yes, I'm telling you! And he was going to scrap the rule that says the Cheerleaders can't perform where alcoholic beverages are served. There was even a rumor that he wanted the girls to make a beer commercial.

Debbie Bond, director of the Cheerleaders for ten years, resigned, saying, "I couldn't ask these girls to do something which was against my beliefs. And I would not want my daughter wearing the uniform under the present regime. It's image, reputation, standards, morals, character, principles. They all go hand in hand."

Alona Wood, a four-year veteran of the squad, said, "We wanted to be different from the other cheerleading squads. That's why we were so popular. That's why nobody could touch us. Sure it's purity—high moral standards."

Tina Miller, a three-year veteran, said, "When you tell somebody you don't associate with the Cowboy players, they love that—they put you on a pedestal."

Toni Atwater, a rookie, said, "I feel like we are a sacred, sacred organization. You can imagine—or, actually, you probably can't—the public outpouring of support and sympathy for the Cheerleaders."

In Dallas, we like girls who will stand up against tanks for traditional virtues like that. Jones backed down and tried to claim it was all just a misunderstanding, but he also kept referring to "our

girls" who he claims are "the pick of the litter." He should probably
shut up. No one is fooled. He has named a new director of cheerleading,
and he's still going to change the uniforms.

One of the more brain-spraining aspects of Texan culture is
Baptist sex. As we all know, Baptists (who stand here metaphorically
for the entire Southern fundamentalist world view) are agin sin,
which they define as drinkin', dancin', and carryin' on. Carryin' on
is the worst.

That Baptists see nothing wrong with the Dallas Cowboy
Cheerleaders, who are indisputably open-air coochie girls, is one of
those anomalies we all live with here. Because football requires the
suspension of rational thought, just as theater requires the suspension of disbelief, we see nothing odd in such phenomena as the
Kilgore Rangerettes, the Apache Belles, and other noted practition-
ers of the close-order drill and baton-twirling arts.

Objectively, there's no denying that what those girls do is dress
up in costumes that would do credit to a striptease artiste and then
prance about in front of thousands of people, shaking their bums and
jiggling their tits. This display is considered not just decent but
proper, as Jim Schutze put it, "as long as the presentation is locked
inside a bulletproof sugar-coating of overdone, over-made-up, over
hair-sprayed, ultra-exaggerated nicey-nicey wholesomeness."

Well, is that any more irrational than most other American
attitudes toward sex? It is not a subject that has ever motivated
people to do a lot of real clear thinking.

The Progressive, July 1988

TEXAS-STYLE ETHICS

Jeez, just because Jim Wright is in trouble, now they're saying everybody in Texas politics is a crook. David Broder wrote a column saying Jim Wright is just a product of his environment, and everybody knows Lyndon Johnson was outrageous, and now they've taken to quoting the old saw about how an honest man in the Texas Legislature is one who stays bought. Our name is mud.

Actually, the criterion for being considered an honest politician in Texas is as follows: If you can't take their money, drink their whiskey, screw their women, and vote against 'em anyway, you don't belong in Texas politics.

The late Woody Bean of El Paso, one of our more memorable pols, used to tell about the time he had a client who had stuck up a grocery store. The perpetrator was inept and the law was hot on his heels right after the heist, so he ditched the loot in a brown paper bag (double-bagged for safety) by an oil well out in the country. He was then apprehended. Bean interviewed him at the local hoosegow and asked, "Son, what'd you do with the money?" The perp gave detailed directions to the boodle, and Bean promptly went and found it and helped himself to a generous fee. As he drove away he said to himself, "Woodrow Wilson Bean, you are skatin' on the thin edge of ethics."

Some of Bean's friends recall him adding, "Woodrow Wilson Bean, ethics is for young lawyers."

I wouldn't say our public servants here in the Great State are without ethics. Governor Bill Clements, when asked why he had repeatedly lied about the Southern Methodist University football scandal, replied reasonably enough, "Well, there was never a Bible in the room."

State Senator Bill ("the Bull of the Brazos") Moore once defended himself against the charge that he would personally profit from a bill he was backing by saying, "I'd just make a little bit of money, I wouldn't make a whole lot."

One official with a colorful past felt so honored upon finding himself elected to statewide office that he called his staff together and said, "Boys, stealin's out."

House Speaker Gib Lewis recently found himself under attack because the Parks and Wildlife Department has been stocking his ranches with deer, elk, turkey, and bass without charging him for it. Lewis felt the complaints were unfair. "I have been helping Parks and Wildlife for seventeen years," he explained. "If they owe anyone a favor, they owe me a favor."

Lewis is not a crook; he just has the ethical sensitivity of a walnut. When he was first elected, he forgot to put some stuff on his financial-disclosure statement—a little oil well, a little airplane, a little bidness he happens to be in with some lobbyist friends. He explained that he ran out of room on the paper.

Lewis did make a mistake one time: He went to Ruidoso to watch the horseracing and let some horseracing lobbyists pay for the trip. Caught hell. So the next time he took a trip, to play golf at Pebble Beach, California, he let the taxpayers pay for it. Caught hell for that, too. So the next time he took a trip, he carefully pointed out to the press that it was *not* paid for by lobbyists and it was *not* paid for by the taxpayers: He was going as guest of the government of

South Africa. Hunting is Gib Lewis's passion, and his office is covered with the stuffed and mounted heads of the assorted endangered species he has knocked off over the years. His four-year-old granddaughter was recently in the office and stood solemnly looking at an Indian war bonnet that also graces the room. "When did you shoot the Indian, Grandpa?" she inquired.

Sid Richardson, the late Fort Worth oilman, once said to John Connally, "I'm gonna put you in the way to make a little money, John." And that's the way it has always been done in Texas. The rising politician is cut in on deals. The deals are legitimate, the profits are legitimate. It's just that the pol is never asked to put up money—his collateral is the value of his cut. When and whether there is a quid pro quo for this bidness opportunity is between the donor, the donee, and God.

I know a number of pols I count as honest who never did anything in return for such favors. Is it any ranker than getting a large campaign contribution from someone with a special interest in legislation? For virtue, try Minnesota.

The Progressive, September 1988

STATE OF
THE STATES

Good news from the Southwest! The New Mexico Legislature is about to make the biscochito the State Cookie—as soon as they figure out how to spell it. The Senate version of the State Cookie law has it as "bizcochito." A conference committee will be named.

Meanwhile, the Texas Lege is responding stoutly to news of the massacre of children in Stockton, California, by a crazed man using an assault rifle. In lesser provinces, solons are outlawing the purchase of automatic and semi-automatic weapons; in Texas, we are going to make it a capital crime to murder children on school grounds.

I could tell on opening day it was going to be a great legislative session here in the Lone Star State when Speaker Gib Lewis thanked his

colleagues for reelecting him by saying, "I am filled with humidity."
All of which tends to prove a long-held theory of mine: The really
interesting stuff in our public life is not in Washington—it's in Austin
and Albany, Boise and Baton Rouge.

Speaking of Baton Rouge, when David Duke, the newest member of the Louisiana Legislature, was the chief cheese and sheet-
washer for the Knights of the Ku Klux Klan, he took the Dale
Carnegie course in how to win friends and influence people. Honest.
At the time, the case of the Klansman who took the Carnegie course
(where they teach you to say heartily, "Gosh, isn't this a good
party?" and "My, aren't we having a lot of fun?") seemed to be just
another reason not to write fiction. Now, with any luck, the Klansman who took the Carnegie course is off on a blazing political career.

If Louisiana eventually elects Duke governor, don't expect any
sympathy from Texas. They sent us one of their barmy governors
once before—Earl Long, who was Huey's crazy brother. Earl finally
got so bad his own family shipped him off to a nuthouse in Galveston.
We kept him for six weeks and then let him go; he looked like a
perfectly normal governor to us.

Take the one we've got now, the Lonesome Guv. Our state
legislators were timorously hoping for a raise this year: It's been
fourteen years since their last one and they make $7,200 a year,
which comes to $341 a month take-home. Governor Bill Clements
came out against the pay raise and genially observed, "Some people
think they're overpaid now." Governor Clements makes $91,600 a
year; when it was pointed out to him that this leaves a significant gap
between his salary and the legislators', he quipped, "And I hope that
gap gets wider."

In an effort to narrow the gap one way if not another, Representative Keith Oakley promptly introduced a bill to cut the governor's
salary by $84,000 a year. Said Oakley, "He's sitting there saying, 'I
think legislators are overpaid,' and he's drawing $92,000 a year and
wearing a plaid jacket and going to Taos, New Mexico, all the time
and slapping us in the face like that."

It *is* embarrassing to have a governor who wears a plaid jacket
all the time.

Meanwhile, one of our more noted homeboys, Little John
Tower, has come to grief in Washington City and has now taken up
permanent residence in the Hall of Martyrs to the Media. I'll say this
for John Tower—he worked for his reputation, he earned it, and he
deserves it.

Most journalists didn't go after stories about Tower's wenching on grounds that it's not really relevant. As a general rule, it isn't. Personally, I tend to like men who like whiskey and women, and I'm not entirely sure I trust those who don't. But there's a difference between a man who propositions a colleague, an equal, even someone he meets in a singles bar who's in a position to say, "Back off, Jack," and a man who hits on women who are economically or psychologically vulnerable, who for one reason or another are not able to say no easily.

A boss who hits on his employees, an executive who hits on his secretary, a professor who hits on his students, a doctor or psychiatrist who hits on his patients—that's not lusty pursuit in a game of love played by both sexes: That's abuse of authority, that's preying on the weak, and it is morally repellent.

The Progressive, April 1989

LUBBOCK: SEAT OF REBELLION

All right, all right, so I love Lubbock. I never claimed to have exquisite taste. I'll be there with the diehards to the end, trying to explain, "No, this is a griddle with some Monopoly houses on it: *this* is Lubbock." Still, the life of all us Lubbock-lovers would be a lot easier if the Chamber of Commerce hadn't adopted the slogan "Keep Lubbock Beautiful." *Keep?*

Here's my favorite Lubbock political story: Sometime after Franklin Roosevelt died and before Swatch watches, Lubbock elected a state senator who proceeded to Austin, where he holed up in the Driskill Ho-tell with another senator-elect; they's drinkin' whiskey and "interviewin' secretaries." Comes a knock-knock-knock on the door and there's the lobbyist for the chiropractors; he offers 'em each $200 to vote for the chiropractor bill. Guy from Lubbock takes the money. Damn ol' bill comes up first week of the session. Guy from Lubbock votes against it. Hacks off the chiropractor lobbyist something serious.

"You take my money and you vote against me!" he says.

Guy from Lubbock says, "Yeah, but the doctors offered me $400 to vote against you."

Now the lobbyist is some pissed. He cusses the senator up one side and down the other. Senator finally gets to feeling resentful. He explains, "Yeah, but you knew I was weak when I took the $200."

My favorite place in Texas is Lubbock, mostly because Lubbock, like Popeye the Sailor, is what it is. Lubbock's a place that'll keep you honest. It's hard to be pretentious or affected if you're from Lubbock. Damned hard.

One thing I like about Lubbock is that people there know what sin is. There's more confusion on that issue than many people realize, with all this bushwa about being nonjudgmental. The advantage of being able to identify sin is that you can go out and do it, and enjoy it. Lubbock gives people a lot to rebel against: You don't have to waste time trying to figure out what the rules are; you can go right ahead and break 'em and see what happens.

People are always asking how come Lubbock produces so many musicians and artists. 'Cause there's dog-all else to do in the place. In Lubbock you got to make music, laugh, or go crazy. Lots of famous musicians are from Lubbock or have done time in Lubbock—Buddy Holly, Bob Wills, Waylon Jennings, Mac Davis, Joe Ely—but I like the ones who never made it. Robin Dorsey from Matador, for example, went to Tech and had a girlfriend named Patty from Muleshoe and wrote a song about her, "Her Teeth Was Stained, But Her Heart Was Pure." Dorsey's college buddies were responsible for what scholars believe is the only country-western song ever written with the correct use of the subjunctive in the title: "I Wish I Were in Dixie Tonight, But She's Out of Town."

Lubbock has a newspaper, the *Lubbock*

Avalanche-Journal, that is without redeeming social value, which is good by me because I love to pick on bad newspapers. They call Lubbock "The Hub City of the Plains"—actually, only the Chamber of Commerce ever called it that—and as Jimmie Dale Gilmore once observed, "Plain is the opposite of fancy." One of my most prized possessions is a packet of postcards entitled "Ten Scenic Views of Lubbock, Texas." It naturally includes a view of the Cotton Club, which is closed now and never was much to look at, even if it was the finest honky-tonk in all of West Texas.

Also in the ten scenic views are Prairie Dog Town, a tornado, and a lot of flat land with a lot of sky over it. I like flat land. Land you can fall off the side of makes me nervous. In Lubbock the world is about 88.3 percent sky, which I believe is the correct proportion: It takes a while to get used to, but after you do, Lubbock feels like freedom and everywhere else feels like jail.

Texas Monthly, May 1989

TOO WUSSY FOR TEXAS

Biggest fight we've had all summer here in the Great State is over what motto to put on our license plates. The Highway Commission voted early this summer to put TEXAS—THE FRIENDSHIP STATE on our plates. This was unanimously condemned as Too Wussy for Texas, and it took Bubba a couple of months to get it turned around.

Historians will recall that we had the same flap a few years ago when some unusually demented Highway Commissioners decided TEXAS—THE WILDFLOWER STATE would look good on our plates. This caused the ever-vigilant guardians of Texas *machismo* to declare that we might as well call it THE GAY RIGHTS STATE.

Now, THE FRIENDSHIP STATE is not

nearly as wussy a motto as THE WILDFLOWER STATE—and it does
have cultural roots. Our state motto is FRIENDSHIP, and our state
safety slogan is DRIVE FRIENDLY, which is ungrammatical but perfectly clear.

And it wouldn't be false advertising—Texans actually are
friendlier than normal people—at least outside the big cities, which
you can prove any day by driving into a Texas town and saying
"Hidy."

But we do have a shitkicker image to maintain, so the papers
have been rife with suggestions like YANKEE GO HOME, and FUCK
ALASKA, and TEXAS: KISS MY ASS.

If we were to go for honesty instead of public relations, we'd
wind up with something like TOO MUCH IS NOT ENOUGH or TEXAS—
LAND OF WRETCHED EXCESS. Or, perhaps, HOME OF THE FDIC.

If honesty were a national license plate policy, we'd see:

- RHODE ISLAND—LAND OF OBSCURITY
- OKLAHOMA—THE RECRUITING VIOLATIONS STATE
- MAINE—HOME OF GEORGE BUSH
- MINNESOTA—TOO DAMN COLD
- WISCONSIN—EAT CHEESE OR DIE
- CALIFORNIA—FREEWAY CONGESTION WITH OCCASIONAL
  GUNFIRE
- NEW JERSEY—ARMPIT OF THE NATION
- NORTH DAKOTA—INCREDIBLY BORING
- NEBRASKA—MORE INTERESTING THAN NORTH DAKOTA
- NEW YORK—WE'RE NOT ARROGANT, WE'RE JUST BETTER
  THAN YOU

It was a slow summer for scandal here until Bo Pilgrim, an East
Texas chicken magnate, walked onto the floor of the State Senate and
started handing out $10,000 checks with no payee filled in. He said
he wanted to encourage the senators, then meeting in special session
on the workers' compensation issue, to do right by bidness.

Turns out it's perfectly legal to walk onto the Senate floor and
start handing out checks for $10,000 made out to no one in particu-
lar. Just another campaign contribution, folks. Bo Pilgrim is a familiar sight on Texas television, where he dresses up in a pilgrim suit
and pitches ads for his fowl. He adds a certain *je ne sais quoi* to our
communal life. His chicken factory is a major source of pollution in

East Texas so, of course, the governor put him on the state Water Quality Board.

The death of Houston congressman Mickey Leland made so many hearts ache that poor Mick like to got buried under a mountain of hagiography. But you can't make a saint of a guy who laughed as much as Mickey.

My favorite Leland stories go back to the early 1970s, when he came to the Texas Legislature, one of the first blacks ever elected right out of a black district without having to get white folks' permission to run at-large. He showed up wearing an Afro and dashikis, and the Bubbas thought he was some kind of freak-radical Black Panther, and it meant the end of the world was at hand.

His first session Leland carried a generic-drug bill to help poor, sick, old people. He couldn't believe anyone would vote against poor, sick, old folks, but the drug companies and the doctors teamed up to beat his bill. After the vote, he stalked up to the medical-association lobbyists at the back of the House and in a low voice that shook with fury he hissed, "You are evil motherfuckers." They almost wet their pants on the spot. He got the bill passed in the next session.

During the 1975 speaker's race, members of the Black Caucus made a shrewd political play—they deserted the liberal-labor candidate and threw their support to Billy Wayne Clayton, a West Texas redneck, in exchange for some major committee chairmanships and heavy clout. Leland came out of the meeting with Clayton waving a tiny Confederate flag and announced, "We done sold de plantation."

I remember wondering early on if guys like Mickey were going to make a difference in the Lege. One day during his first session I saw him standing in the middle of the capitol rotunda, which is a natural amplifier, trying to get Craig Washington and Paul Ragsdale, who were peering down at him from the third-floor gallery, to come along. In a voice that stopped traffic he yelled up, "Gottdammit, are you niggers comin' down to get lunch, or what?" Yep, gonna make a difference.

And he did. He made a much bigger difference in this world than all the damned old racists who used to vote against him.

The Progressive, October 1988

CHARLIE'S ANGLES

I've been worrying about my fitness to write for *Ms.* magazine on account of I like Charlie Wilson. Good Lord, that is embarrassing. Congressman Wilson is the Hunter Thompson of the House of Representatives, a gonzo politician. He's a sexist and has made war a spectator sport. By way of redeeming social value, he's funny, a good congressman for his district, and hasn't an ounce of hypocrisy.

I can never figure out whether to laugh or to groan over Charlie. A year or so ago, I was sitting in my office minding my own business when the phone started ringing off the hook. People were gobbling with outrage over a newspaper story, "There's a congressman from Texas over on the Afghanistan border trying to kill Russians! He wants to cut off their ears!

He's wearing cowboy boots! And he's got Miss World with him!" The only thing you can say at moments like that is, "Must be Charlie Wilson."

Since his days in the Texas Legislature, Charlie has been noted for the beauties that grace his office. His standing order on secretaries is, "You can teach 'em to type, but you can't teach 'em to grow tits." A lot more people will quote that line than will notice that he's got a crackerjack staff in Washington and one of the best casework records in Congress.

He's seldom seen anywhere socially without some smashingly beautiful woman on his arm. In the sixties and seventies he was married to a lovely woman called Goose, who deserved a lot better. For the last couple of years, he's been going with a former Miss USA, whom he invariably calls "Miss World." She does have a name; it's Annelise Ilschenko. I'm told she's a perfectly nice woman, but she did look fairly funny standing in the mud in an Afghanistan refugee camp in white, high-fashion boots and a fur coat. Charlie got in trouble for taking her along on an inspection trip of an aircraft carrier not long ago. He claims he was just trying to raise the morale of the troops, but the Navy made him pay her airfare anyway.

Charlie's been living fast and hard for a long time. He finally quit drinking a few years ago because the doctors told him it was that or die. He's a good-looking man (skinny legs) who is now fifty-four and becoming quite Dorian-Gray-ish around the edges.

One of the famous Wilson drinking stories is the time in the early seventies when he imbibed heavily at a political party in Austin and, in an excess of patriotism, tried to drive his car up a flagpole. The cops hauled him down to the hoosegow and when some friends showed up to bail him out, they too were thrown in the slammer. Finally the party's host arrived with a lawyer in tow, neither of them in any condition to pass a Breathalyzer either. One of those involved still remembers Wilson, who is six-four, drawn up at full Annapolis-drilled attention, loftily instructing the arresting officer, "Sergeant, inform my friends what I'm charged with." The lawyer advised his client to shut up.

On another occasion when the juice of grape had overly affected him, Wilson borrowed a car belonging to Secret Servicemen who were guarding President Lyndon Johnson. He ditched it in an alley and it took them almost three weeks to find it. I cite these exploits in part because, in the post–Gary Hart era, it's reassuring to know

that Wilson is still with us: everyone else seems to have come down
with congenital Boy Scout-itis.

So how come he keeps getting reelected out of East Texas, an
area thick with Bible thumpers? The most common theory is that
people back in Lufkin don't know how Charlie behaves when he's
in Austin or Washington. Horsepucky. There is a far greater tolerance for eccentricity and human frailty in small Southern towns than
most folks who live in great cities have any notion of. (Of course it
helps if you were born there and the people have known you forever.)

Joe Murray, editor and publisher of the Lufkin *Daily News,*
said, "Charlie's never tried to be anything but what he is. You watch
him at that domino tournament he sponsors every year; they come
up to him and hug his neck. You can find his enemies, but they're
at the country club."

Wilson's version is, "You have to bring home the bacon, convince 'em you don't want to take no shit off them Russkies, and you
can't think of anything more obscene than gun control."

It seems to me a critical question for feminists here is, "How
come we like Charlie Wilson anyway and should we?" I asked Ann
Richards, the state treasurer and one of the wise women of Texas.
She said, "We like him because he likes us. He can't help himself.
He does." Barbara Blaine, a Washington lawyer who knows Charlie
on account of having married his old friend the writer Larry King,
says he has the personality of a charming fourteen-year-old.

I called Wilson to ask him why we like him, thinking he might
know. He said, "Feminists like me because I am an unapologetic
sexist, chauvinist redneck who takes no shit off of 'em and votes with
'em every time. I have proven that I can vote with 'em without
kissing their ass. I try not to let 'em know I vote with 'em; it's more
fun to have 'em mad at me."

In fact, Charlie's voting record on women's issues is pretty good
and, considering that he comes from East Texas, it's practically
miraculous. He has a semiliberal record on most economic and social
issues. He has always been progressive on race, he supported the
Equal Rights Amendment from the beginning, and he's pro-choice
on abortion. But he never met a weapon he didn't like or a war he
didn't think was dandy. He went off to see the Israelis fight the
Egyptians, he spent a lot of time in Nicaragua rooting for Somoza
against the Sandinistas (he has dreadful taste in dictators), and he's
been to see the Afghan rebels so many times they named a gun after
him—the Charliehorse. He's beyond his *Rambo* phase with the Af-

ghan cause—now he's into a *Lawrence of Arabia* syndrome, rides around over there on a big white horse wearing bandilleros strapped across his chest, surrounded by Afghan rebels in turbans on little brown horses. He has thoughtfully instructed the Afghan fighters in what he has told them was an old Texas war cry: "Kill the commie cocksuckers!" Charlie's rhetoric on the subject of commies is so hopelessly retro, 1950s, cold war, there's no way to deal with it. I've never suspected him of using the issue cynically: I think he believes all of it. When he was still in the Navy in 1960, he went from the Pentagon to work on John F. Kennedy's campaign every night. In many ways he's like a frozen snapshot from that era—the Kennedy liberalism, the Kennedy cold warriorism, and the Kennedy attitude toward women. The charm is his own.

He is a shrewd student of Congress, has a good feel for what will fly and what won't, how to move, how to deal. All that stuff they taught him at Annapolis about tactics and strategy pays off in the House.

One of the best stories he tells on himself is about the time his momma called Tip O'Neill. Charlie was down in Guadalajara, Mexico, studying Spanish, with a woman not his wife, in the days when he was big buddies with Somoza. Some vote came up in Washington and he had to interrupt his course to come back. "In the meantime, some godless Sandinista communist subhuman threatened my little skinny life and my mother became excited. To my mother, everybody south of Brownsville, Texas, was a Mexican; she made no distinctions between there and Tierra del Fuego. She said to me, 'You're not going back down there to Mexico.' I was forty-five years old at the time.

"When I got to Washington, Tip O'Neill called me in. He said, 'I have just spent one hour and ten minutes on the phone with your mother. I don't have an hour and ten minutes. You are not going back to Mexico.' I said, 'Look, this trip has nothing to do with the House.' He said, 'Charlie, if you want to be on the Appropriations Committee when the recess is over, you better keep your ass out of Mexico.' I ignominiously withdrew from the fight.

"The story was so good it got out on the wires and my mother got letters from other mothers all over the country who had trouble controlling their grown children. Until she died, it was her fondest scrapbook."

Ms., February 1988

A TEXAS TREASURE:
THE WIT AND WISDOM
OF ANN RICHARDS

When Ann Richards, the Texas state treasurer, finished giving the keynote address at the Democratic National Convention, media people like to fell over themselves rushing to be the first to announce, "A star is born!" Gave me a funny turn because Ann Richards has been a star for the twenty years I've known her. She once said, after she'd been up East and wowed the crowd at the National Press Club, a group she was a little afraid of, "You know how you always wonder if you're good enough to play in the Big Leagues? Like, everybody thinks you're fine here at home, but they're all friends of yours, and what do they know? They're all from Ozona. Well, I just found out—it's not any tougher in Washington than it is in Waco." So of course I knew she was going to be terrific and I told everybody she'd be terrific and it beats me why I got so nervous just before she started.

Ann Richards is smart and tough and funny and pretty, which I notice just confuses the hell out of a lot of people. Older men seem to have the most difficulty with it. Poor Eric Sevareid of CBS grumbled that her speech was okay, but didn't compare to Alben Barkley's in 1948. Turns out Alben Barkley talked for three hours in 1948, which they won't let you do anymore. Murray Kempton, the dean of liberal journalists, grumbled that the speech had "too many one-liners." But Kempton loved Jim Hightower's speech: Hightower is the Texas agriculture commissioner, who is wonderfully funny, but his whole speech was one-liners. I think what made these men and others uncomfortable was seeing a pretty woman be bitingly funny. You can tell they think it's an extremely dangerous combination. You have surely noticed how much women comedians, with the astonishing exception of Lily Tomlin, put themselves down. Phyllis Diller, Joan Rivers—funny women are expected to disarm people by playing up their own inadequacies; funny women are supposed to be like Fanny Brice or Ado Annie—funny to make up for not being pretty or not being smart.

Ann Richards is an exceptionally competent state treasurer, although I have to admit, her predecessors, Warren G. Harding and Jesse James, would have made almost anyone look good. She was also a dandy county commissioner, one of the last uncracked bastions of the good ol' boy. She can talk road graders with anyone. But it is her wit that makes her so extraordinary. If she were merely smart and sweet, like Dallas Mayor Annette Strauss, or smart and tough, like Houston Mayor Kathy Whitmire, people wouldn't rush to hear her with such delight.

Richards' humor has several dimensions. She has the timing to do jokes well. She's a fine storyteller, with a particular gift for spotting what is ludicrously characteristic about people's behavior. She's also a good mimic, delivering memorable impersonations of Texas political personalities, and sometimes does characters of her own invention. Given a setting like a benefit for a women's political group, Richards will occasionally don a rubber pig-nose, put a cigar in her mouth, and become Harry Porko, the classic Texas sexist. Harry heads Porko Electronics and has often observed, "I believe that the success of my bidness is because I have always been good to my girls.

I say to my managers, 'Be good to your girls, give 'em a little praise and a pat on the fanny, they'll work like dogs.' We've done a lot for our girls at Porko Industries. . . . We were the first to give our girls real-hair hairnets and we started the Yellow Rose Award. Give years of work without an absence and you get a little yellow plastic rose on your polyester uniform. We were the first to put daily horoscopes on the bulletin board—'cause wimmin like stuff like that—little things mean more to them than all the money in the world.

"We've got a li'l motto in all our shops that says, 'When better wimmin are made, Porko Electronics will make them.' 'Course, part of the credit goes to my ball-and-chain, Gladys. . . .'" Harry can carry on like this for hours. He enjoys repartee with women candidates who come to Porko Electronics seeking his support: "What's a nice-lookin' woman like you want to do somethin' like this—you hate your father or somethin'?" I understand Porko once appeared in the halls of the Chase Manhattan Bank when the treasurer of Texas, who had come to New York on a multimillion-dollar deal, was left waiting for a long time.

Richards is one of those people who think of, on the spot, what it takes the rest of us two weeks to come up with. You sit bolt upright in bed, well after the fact, saying, "You know what I should have said?" Ann Richards always said it.

Several years ago there was a big political do at Scholz Beer Garten in Austin and everybody who was anybody in political Texas was there, meetin' and greetin' at a furious pace. About halfway through the evening, a little group of us got the tired feet and went to lean our butts against a table by the back wall of the Garten. Like birds in a row were perched Bob Bullock, the state comptroller; me; Charlie Miles, a black man who was then head of Bullock's personnel department (and the reason Bullock had such a good record in minority hiring); and Ms. Ann Richards. Bullock, having been in Texas politics for thirty some-odd years, consequently knows every living sorry, no-account sumbitch who ever held office. A dreadful old racist judge from East Texas came up to him, "Bob, my boy, how are yew?" The two of them commenced to clap one another on the back and have big greetin'.

"Judge," said Bullock. "I want you to meet my friends. This is Molly Ivins with the *Texas Observer.*"

The judge peered up at me and said, "How yew, little lady?"

"This is Charles Miles, who heads my personnel department."

Charlie stuck out his hand and the judge got an expression on his face as though he had just stepped into a fresh cowpie. It took him a long minute before he reached out, barely touched Charlie's hand and said, "How yew, *boy*?" Then he turned with great relief to pretty, blue-eyed Ann Richards and said, "And who is this lovely lady?"

Ann beamed and said, "I am *Mrs.* Miles."

Ms., October 1988

DALLAS DOES
IT AGAIN

The Big D, that darlin' Dallas, has been in the headlines again, once more drawing national attention with its fatal tendency to flash ass. The Honorable Judge Jack Hampton touched off the fire this time by giving a light sentence to an eighteen-year-old double-murderer on grounds that his two victims were, after all, only "queers."

"These two guys that got killed wouldn't have been killed if they hadn't been cruising the streets picking up teen-age boys," Hampton explained. "I don't much care for queers cruising the streets picking up teen-age boys. I've got a teen-age son."

In the first place, Hampton got the facts all wrong. He seems not to have heard a word of the trial over which he presided. The gay victims of Richard Bednarski were not cruising the streets picking up teen-age boys; a band of teen-age boys led by Bednarski was out cruising the streets for "queers" to bash.

They had driven a good twenty miles from a suburb to Dallas's gay neighborhood to "pester the homosexuals," as one of them put it at the trial. It was among their favorite pastimes when they "got bored." Bednarski brought a gun with him, talked another boy into joining him in a plan to beat and rob the two victims, went to a park with them, and ordered them to take off their clothes. When they refused, Bednarski shot both unarmed men three times. One of them took five days to die. Afterward, Bednarski bragged about the killings.

None of these facts was in dispute at the trial.

Judge Hampton further observed, "I put prostitutes and gays at about the same level. If these boys had picked up two prostitutes and taken them to the woods and killed them, I consider that a similar case. And I'd be hard put to give somebody life for killing a prostitute."

Even in Dallas, these sentiments drew attention. I say "even in Dallas" because Dallas is just so—how to explain it? Dallas is a town that would have rooted for Goliath to beat David. It has always been run by a business-knows-best philosophy. It's also the canned-spinach capital of America.

It's a city that makes life difficult for satirists. At Christmastime in 1985, for example, a Dallas man put a life-size replica of Santa Claus in a real Sherman tank on the corner of Beverly and Lakeside, overlooking the Dallas Country Club.

People with wit like to make up aphorisms about Dallas. "Dallas is a city that honors the man who can buy a piece of art more than the artist who creates one" (A. C. Greene). "A city that can't tell the difference between change and progress" (Anon).

What Dallas hates more than anything else is bad publicity—the kind of bad publicity it got twenty-five years ago when John F. Kennedy was murdered there. Anything that touches off another round of "Dallas, City of Hate," "Dallas Is Weird," "Dallas Is Full of Right-Wing Loons" drives the town nuts.

The trouble is, most Dallasites see nothing peculiar about Bunker Hunt, so it is left to a non-Dallas sensibility to cringe when someone like Judge Hampton speaks out. Or, more precisely, there are Dallasites who also cringe, but only because they know another round of bad publicity is coming.

For a long time now, Texas liberals have been trying to figure out whether Dallas really is any worse than lots of other places or whether, as Dallasites strongly believe, it is treated unfairly. It's not that Dallas gets bum-rapped, exactly; after all, the place is more than passing strange. But it seems likely that the only reason its reputation is worse than that of, say, Lubbock, is because of the assassination. Every subsequent bit of right-wing lunacy coming from the city has the effect of a blow on a bruise.

So much of what is truly strange about Dallas never gets noticed at all. For many years, the city was proud of its zealous law'n'order prosecutor, Henry Wade, a man who could get Dallas juries to sentence people to 5,000 years in prison. But in the last seven years of his reign, Wade, who could get a death sentence any time he asked for one, never sought a death sentence in any of the fifty-six capital-murder cases in which the victim was black. Not one. Jack Hampton started out as an assistant district attorney under Henry Wade.

All of this reminds country-western fans of the old Lounge Lizards song, "I Am Going Back to Dallas to See If There Could Be Anything Worse Than Losing You."

The Progressive, February 1989

THE REAGAN ADMINISTRATION REVISITED: UNDER INDICTMENT OR UNDER AVERAGE

★ ★

"The charm of Ronald Reagan is not just that he kept telling us screwy things—it was that he believed them all. No wonder we trusted him—he never lied to us."

—*Savvy*

HOW TO SURVIVE REAGAN

Many citizens of progressive political persuasion are finding that, soul-wise, these are trying times. To be a liberal in the Reagan era—not to mention being a lefty, pinko, comsymp—strikes most of us as damned hard cheese. Duty requires the earnest liberal to spend most of his time on the *qui vive* for jackbooted fascism, in a state of profound depression over the advance of the military-industrial complex, and down in the dumps over the incurable nincompoopery of a people addicted to "The Newlywed Game."

Beloveds, fear not, neither let yourselves despair. Rejoice, I bring you good news. As a life-long Texas liberal, I have spent the whole of my existence in a political climate well to the right of that being created by Ronald Reagan and his merry zealots. Brethren and sistren, this can not only be endured, it can be laughed at. Actually, you have two other choices. You could cry or you could throw up. But crying and throwing up are bad for you, so you might as well laugh. All you need in order to laugh about Reagan is a strong stomach. A tungsten tummy.

Mike Zunk is a fellow we used to know who tried to get into the *Guinness Book of World Records* by eating a car—ground up, you understand, a small bit at a time. He just took it in as a little roughage every day. We always thought of Zunk as a Texas liberal-in-training. The rest of us toughen our stomachs by taking in the Legislature a day at a time. And now, lo, after all these years of nobody even knowing we were down here, it turns out Texas liberals are among the few folks who know how to survive Reagan. We feel just like Rudolph the Red-Nosed Reindeer.

It may be true, as Tom Lehrer believes, that satire died the day they gave Henry Kissinger the Nobel Peace Prize. But then, as Gore Vidal recently observed in another context, one must never underestimate the Scandinavian sense of humor. You have to ignore a lot of stuff in order to laugh about Reagan—dead babies and such—but years of practice with the Texas Lege is just what a body needs to get in shape for the concept of Edwin Meese as attorney general. Beer also helps.

Here are six perfectly good reasons to keep laughing during the Reagan administration:

• Things are not getting worse; things have always been this bad. Nothing is more consoling than the long perspective of history. It will perk you up no end to go back and read the works of progressives past. You will learn therein that things back then were also terrible, and what's more, they were always getting worse. This is most inspiriting.

• Things could get worse. The fact that they probably will should not be used as an excuse for tossing away this golden opportunity to rejoice in the relative delightfulness of our current situation. Is there anything to cheer us in the realization that Ed Meese is attorney general? Yes. It could have been Jesse Helms. And may yet be. Let us give thanks for Ed Meese while we yet have time.

• There is always the off chance that adversity will improve our character. Since we are all the spiritual children of the Puritans, we secretly believe suffering is good for us. I am putting this spell in the wilderness to good use myself; that awful tendency we liberals have to bleed from the heart over victims of cruelty and injustice is so off-putting. One of my New Year's resolutions is to not feel sorry for Texaco, Inc., victim of manifest injustice though it is. I hardly ever heard of anything so awfully unfair as Texaco having an $11 billion judgment put against them when it wasn't even Texaco that screwed over Pennzoil in the first place. And then they have to pay a $13 billion bond to appeal the case. Gosh, it's a good thing I have a will of iron or I'd be hard put to suppress those little twinges of sympathy.

• We're not responsible for any of this stuff. No matter how bad it gets, no matter how much they foul things up, it's not our fault. We've got a guilt-free eight years here, team, and given the amount of guilt we have to carry around with us when we have any say in how things get done, this should be our shining hour.

• A redundant reason to keep right on chortling through the Ronaldan Age is on account of lefties are more fun than righties by definition. Ever been to a YAF convention? By comparison, SDS was a Marx Brothers movie. What's the point of doing good if you can't have fun doing it? You want to wind up looking like Jeane Kirkpatrick? So smile.

• The Reagan administration is genuinely funny, honest it is. From the time we whipped Grenada in a fair fight to the day the old boy dropped off the wreath at Bitburg, this administration has been nothing but laughs. James Watt! Killer trees! Ketchup as a vegetable! Reagan cures the deficit! This is great stuff. You can't make up stuff this good.

In fact, there's another perfectly good reason to be grateful to Ronald Reagan: he's so amazing that zillions of future writers are daily being discouraged from ever trying their hands at fiction.

The Progressive, March 1986

THE FRONT LINE

Y'all can stop worrying. Ever since the president told us they were comin' in at Harlingen, everybody in Texas been gettin' ready. "The Red tide," said Ronnie, "will lap at our very borders." He meant the Texas border, of course. When the only president we've got added that the nest of terrorists and subversives in Managua is only two days' drive from Harlingen, we all knew what was next. Falfurrias, naturally, and once the commies take the Butter Capital of Texas, they'll be swarmin' up Commerce Street in downtown Dallas.

But we're prepared. You couldn't have a tougher group in your front line. Hail fahr, Texans have always been fighters. We've synchronized our Rolexes. We not gonna shoot till we see the whites of their eyes. If we have to fall back and regroup, we'll meet at the Dairy Queen in the Galleria Shopping Mall. Victory or Death! (Price of oil what it is today, we might as well die defending our country. I know Texas women who've had to turn in their Neiman-Marcus charge cards.)

Here at the battlefront, we find it's the waiting that gets to you—two whole days from Managua to Harlingen by station wagon. Now the Russians can nuke us in seventeen minutes flat by missile, but we don't have to sit around worrying about it. With the Soviets, by the time you've said, "No shit?" you're dead. But these sneaky bastards from Nicaragua—there's three million of 'em down there, there's only sixteen million Texans, and they've got us cornered between the Rio Grande and the North Pole.

The menace from Managua is without question the most fun foreign-policy event since the time we decided the Congo was a threat to our national security. There is some truly great, vintage stuff coming out, and anyone who has been refusing to listen to the administration's case on grounds that it's a pack of lies has been missing just first-rate entertainment. I, for one, especially appreciated the president's explaining to us how the Sandinistas dress up in *contra* uniforms and go around committin' atrocities, killin' their own people, so as to put the *contras* in bad smell. Do you know who them Sandinistas *are*? They're Nicaraguans, too. They've infiltrated their own country!

If y'all would listen to Ronnie more, you'd learn a good deal. We're talking Sandinistas, not just Soviet/Cuban-type commies. We're talking Bulgarians, Colonel Qaddafi, the Ayatollah of Iran, the entire drug traffic, desecration of synagogues, persecution of evangelicals, and subversion of two continents. Not to mention the invasion of Texas. All I want to know now is what Reagan's speechwriters smoke.

The Progressive, May 1986

THE GREAT INTERNATIONAL BLINK-OFF

What a great month it was for veracity, credibility, and integrity on the part of the only government we've got.

There was the swap that wasn't a swap, the deal that wasn't a deal, the disinformation campaign that wasn't a disinformation campaign, and the C-123 cargo plane we had nothing to do with.

We also had nothing to do with the people who flew the plane we had nothing to do with, nor the company that owned the plane we had nothing to do with, nor the airport off from which the plane we had nothing to do with took, nor the arms aboard the plane we had nothing to do with, nor the people who set up the operation involving the plane we had nothing to do with.

And then, having gotten us all into practice, President Reagan explained after Reykjavik that Mikhail Gorbachev screwed up chances for an arms-control agreement by offering to give up half of something they've got right now, and that we know they've got, in return for something that we don't have and that they know we don't have and that we both know we aren't about to have any time soon and that won't work when we get it. Right? Because if we gave up what we don't have and we both know we don't have and won't have any time soon and that won't work when we do get it in exchange for half of what they have right now that we know they have right now and that we can go and check to see that they give it up right now, then it wouldn't cost us a dime. See? A bad deal.

Besides, they blinked first.

It was right there on the front page of *The New York Times,* October 13, 1986. "Initial Congressional reaction tonight to the failure of President Reagan and Mikhail S. Gorbachev to reach agreement on nuclear arms control was mixed. 'The President did not blink,' said Senator Richard G. Lugar, Republican of Indiana."

Many of you have been wondering, I know, about the ophthalmological machismo that has lately dominated international relations and how it came to replace the better-known forms of *cojones* competition. For many years, my preferred form of exercise has been rapid blinking, so I am in excellent trim to explain all this.

Officials began looking for new forms of testosterone testing and virility vying about six years ago. When your main man is seventy-five, this gets a little dicey, which is obviously why they decided to enter Reagan only in blinking contests. They wanted to try him in competitive napping as well, but it's not recognized by the International Olympic Committee.

Believe me, blinking can be strenuous, so the administration introduced a simple but far-reaching innovation that changed the objective of the game. Instead of the traditional blinking goal—shutting the eyes faster and harder than the competition—the Reagan administration announced that the new object was not to blink. You don't get the same aerobic effect under the new rules, but it has a sort of yogic elegance. Just as with yoga, in order to truly excel at not blinking, you must begin by letting your mind become perfectly empty. The right sport for Ronald Reagan.

Perhaps the high point of recent events was the lying about the disinformation campaign. The press was pretty put out about it at first. The president of the Associated Press said it was "highly objectionable." *The New York Times* called it "appalling." The *Philadelphia Inquirer* said "deplorable." The editor of the *Los Angeles Times* found it "pretty disgusting."

But they were all off base, because the president denied there was any disinformation campaign and said he challenged the "veracity" of the *Washington Post.* Unfortunately, Secretary of State George Shultz explained, "Frankly, I don't have any problems with a little psychological warfare against Qaddafi." Everybody knows it's okay to lie about a guy if he's a zit.

It was a good thing that Bernard Kalb resigned over the disinformation campaign; he saved himself the pain of having to lie about the C-123. Assistant Secretary of State Elliott Abrams said of that affair, "This is an outrageous violation of international law." Of course, he wasn't talking about secret, illegal arms shipments to the *contras*; he was talking about the Nicaraguan government's temporary delay in allowing U.S. consular access to the surviving crew member of the plane we had nothing to do with.

The administration is also concerned because schoolchildren are not being taught ethics.

The Progressive, December 1986

RUNNING ON
HIS RIMS

Ah, such rich and delicious times for those who relish political uproar, for followers of fallout, connoisseurs of cover-up, wallowers of every stripe and persuasion. How sweet it is!

I have been collecting euphemisms used on television to suggest that our only president is so dumb that if you put his brains in a bee, it would fly backwards. *Confused, detached, disengaged, befuddled, lazy*, and *sedated* (that was Edwin Meese's) are a few of the genteelisms in common use—all of them downtown dull.

How about, "He's walkin' around dead and don't know enough to lie down"? Here are some others: "You can look in his eyes, but there's nobody home." "Don't have all his oars in the water." "Couldn't pour water out of a boot if the instructions was on the heel." "Fishin' with a rotten line and an empty hook." "He don't know nothin' and has that all tangled up." "Cross-threaded between the ears." "Running on his rims."

I'm just trying to be helpful here. We need some pep in discussion of the presidential dimness.

While Sam Donaldson has waxed sarcastic and George Will has been annoyed by it all. Dan Rather suffers chagrin and Peter Jennings looks worried, the only television commentator on the money has been David Letterman, who observed plaintively, "I thought you never forgot your first arms shipment to the Ayatollah." Ronald Reagan's dysfunctional memory caused Letterman to wonder what else the president might have forgotten. The words to "Happy Birthday"? Where he left the Seventh Fleet? Whether he's put out enough dry food and water for the vice president?

One thing Reagan rather clearly forgot was the involvement of Iranians in the 1983 bombing that killed 241 U.S. Marines he had sent to Lebanon. According to combined American, French, and Israeli intelligence sources, the $50,000 check that went to the "fixer" in that bombing was cashed at the Iranian embassy in Damascus.

Perhaps the most difficult question in American politics today is why anyone is still taking Ronald Reagan seriously. Nick von Hoffman was fired by CBS during Watergate for observing, "The president is the dead mouse on the floor of American politics, and the only question left is who is going to pick him up and carry him out of the room." The time has come once more to ask this painfully obvious question, whether CBS is ready for it or not.

Reagan is so much a creature of the tube that a couple of great minds came up with the same happy thought: Ida Frankel of New York and the comedian David Steinberg both observed that he belongs in a series of ads with the slick-haired fellow in the white coat who comes on and says, "I'm not a doctor. But I play one on TV," and then proceeds to give us advice about cold remedies. Reagan would be perfect saying, "I'm not a president. But I play one on TV."

I like the Reagan faithful who defend his "poor management style" (another euphemism for "a few bricks shy of a load"). Their contention is that it's a splendid style—choose the best people and let them do as they think best—and needs only a slightly more "hands-on" approach.

The best people? No amount of hands on is going to help a man who would choose Oliver North, John Poindexter, Donald Regan, William Casey, James Watt, Michael Deaver, Edwin Meese, Paul Thayer, Richard Allen, Rita Lavelle, Anne Burford, Richard Perle, Charles Wick, William French Smith—I could go on and on—to run the country. All of them are guilty of illegalities, improprieties, or simple loopiness.

The Progressive, August 1987

GRAB THE SALT

It's been said for months now that when we got to the bottom of the Iran-*contra* mess, we'd find out the president was either a fool or a liar. According to Admiral John Poindexter, he's both.

Ronald Reagan knew all along it was an arms-for-hostages deal, and he lied about it. He was too dumb to notice his own staff was supplying and running an army in Central America. He could just wear a button that says, THE BUCK STOPPED BEFORE IT GOT HERE.

Easily the most terrifying idea I have ever heard seriously proposed by a high government official was William Casey's plan to set up a private CIA to conduct covert operations. According to Oliver North, this secret agency, funded by arms sales, was to be accountable to no one in elected office.

But the most alarming statement I have heard in all this was nothing said before the congressional investigating committees. It came from a student found sunning himself on a Chicago beach by some inquiring reporter out to take the pulse of the people. "They were fighting communism so it doesn't spread," said this citizen. "We elect people to do what's right for the country. Why should we know what they do?"

Few people are more annoying than those pedants who stop a perfectly good argument dead in its tracks by saying prissily, "Now let's define our terms here." If you don't know what's under discussion by the middle of the argument, I suspect you're not going to make much of a contribution anyway. But we need to define "covert operations," if only because Lieutenant Colonel North is so confused about what they are.

During one of his remarkable defenses of the need to engage in lying and secrecy so that we can bring open government and democracy to more benighted nations than our own, North managed to put into one bag he labeled "covert operations" the roundup of the *Achille Lauro* hijackers, the bombing of Libya, the invasion of Grenada, and the sale of arms to Iran with subsequent diversion of the profits to the *contras*.

In fact, the only covert operation in the bunch is the last. All the others were military operations. You can go back and look it up. They were paid for out of the military budget, not the CIA's, and they required the commitment of U.S. military forces.

Some military operations do require secrecy, of course. Whether attempting to rescue hostages in Iran or bombing Libya, you are not wise to advertise your intentions in advance. But that does not make them covert operations. The U.S. government does not try to hide its role in them. After they are over, or even as soon as they have begun, such operations are made public. It is not the same thing as mining Nicaraguan harbors in violation of international law and then lying about it.

Before all this is over, you will hear at least several dozen times the assertion, "We all realize that some covert operations are necessary." Grab the salt and look at the record. When our covert operations work, they produce terrible things. The failures are bad enough, but the successes are real disasters.

In 1953, the CIA successfully placed the Shah of Iran back on his throne after his people had chucked him out the first time. The

CIA successfully installed a military government in Guatemala that produced twenty years of torture. The current government of Chile is a CIA product, as are the governments of Indonesia and Zaire. The Philippines dictatorship of Ferdinand Marcos came about with the knowledge and blessing of the CIA—see Ray Bonner's excellent book, *Waltzing with a Dictator*—and was, of course, supported by our government for twenty years.

Yes, we can successfully overthrow the governments of Third World countries by means of covert operations, but we always replace those governments with repressive regimes. Their collective record of murder, torture, theft, and abuse is a disgrace to this country and to everything we want it to stand for.

Moving along to the Nicaraguan end of this insanity, I spare all you progressives yet another explanation of why Oliver North's moving profession of concern for democracy in Nicaragua and for the lives of eleven-year-old girls would gag a maggot. (Why did no one think to ask him about the CIA gimme cap sported by the *contras* that says, ADMIT NOTHING—DENY EVERYTHING—MAKE COUNTER-ACCUSATIONS?)

The good news is that the Reagan administration has now put a Texas politician in charge of selling its *contra* aid package on Capitol Hill. The happy salesman is none other than that distinguished former member of Congress from Hunt, Tom Loeffler, who needed a job because he came to electoral grief in his gubernatorial bid last year. Connoisseurs of Texas politics will recall that Loeffler is the man who went to San Francisco to give a speech during his late campaign and, according to a published report, spent the entire visit holed up in his hotel room, wearing shower caps on his feet for fear of getting AIDS from the tiles in the shower.

The Progressive, September 1987

SOAP OPERA

You could probably prove, by judicious use of logarithms and congruent triangles, that real life is a lot more like soap opera than most people will admit. *As the World Turns* is now featuring a remarkable drama hinging on these questions:

Will General Noriega offer political asylum to Ed Meese? Will President Reagan recover from the amnesia that has afflicted him for seven years? Will Jimmy Swaggart return to a grateful nation bearing lipstick stigmata on his palms? Will we have to send in troops to get Meese out of the Justice Department?

Mr. Detail, our only president—"I think the Justice Department is just running along fine," he said recently—has set forth a new ethical agenda that deserves sober consideration from us all. "What I want for this country *above all else,*" he said, "is that it may always be a place where a man can get rich." Our highest purpose, our noblest goal, our finest principle, our dream of greatness.

Most of us had not counted on the president's aides, Cabinet officers, underlings, and pals to take this grand new national aim so to heart in their own individual cases.

It's such a fun administration—half of it is under average and the other half is under indictment. Reagan and I have a theory on why this has come to pass, what has driven them to it. Back in April 1980, when Mr. Detail got to discussing the causes of crime—variously attributed by other experts to poverty, emotional deprivation, mental illness, greed, Satan, and pure meanness—he observed, "History shows that when the taxes of a nation approach about 20 percent of the people's income, there begins to be a lack of respect for government. . . . When it reaches 25 percent, there comes an increase in lawlessness."

Well, you see? All the president's men are still in that dreadful, hateful, high old 38 percent bracket, which is a lot lower since the great tax reform but still not down to that barely tolerable 25 percent. Dan White used the Twinkie defense, Michael Deaver claimed Demon Rum made him do it, and the rest of the Reagan gang can claim the Tax Rationale: "Your honor, it was the income tax."

A fund-raising letter from the Republican party wafted my way recently, sent by Senator John Tower, who was "delighted to inform you that at the last membership meeting of the Republican Senatorial Inner Circle, your name was placed in nomination by Senator Phil Gramm and you were accepted for membership." Little John was also delighted to inform me that "among those who have already joined the Inner Circle are Bob Hope, Arnold Schwarzenegger, George Shultz, Mario Andretti, and Wayne Newton."

My formal invitation will be mailed in the next few days, and Tower urges me to respond instanter so I can demonstrate my "commitment to Republicanism that goes beyond mere lip service." The Shortest Senator does not mention filthy lucre, but I suspect we're talking money here, don't you? On the other hand, nominated by Phil Gramm, informed by a delighted John Tower, with Arnold Schwarzenegger and Wayne Newton as fellow members—how can I not join?

And when I do, says the letter, I'll get two fabulous, fun-filled days in Washington, highlighted by a private dinner for Inner Circle members with Mr. Detail. In addition to a day of briefings and closed-door strategy sessions on legislative policy, I'll be taking part in a small, intimate dinner—yes, small and intimate—hosted by a Republican senator, a cabinet member, or an administration official.

Now all I have to do is figure out how to get Erwin Knoll to pay my dues.

At a recent symposium on toxic waste in Colorado, it was revealed that in addition to all the noxious civilian substances we have to worry about, the U.S. government has thousands of old nerve-gas bombs lying around, and they could start leaking at any time. To find out whether the dread leak has finally sprung, the government periodically sends a bunny rabbit into the storage area. If the rabbit dies, the nerve gas is leaking, said a government spokesman.

That or the bombs are pregnant.

The Great Mentioner is now mentioning Phil Gramm as a possible running mate for George Bush. Damn shrewd move. They could use a Texan on the Republican ticket.

The Progressive, October 1987

PERSIAN DIVERSION

Hair in the butter" is what we say in East Texas to describe a sensitive situation. The Great Iranian Arms Caper is not only hair in the butter, I'd say someone's thrown a skunk in the church house as well. I don't know how the rest of you are bearing up, but I'm still stuck on the mystery of the cake and the Bible.

You recall that the first wind we got of this *megillah* was that the president's former national-security adviser had gone to Iran, looking to make friends, and had taken along some gifts—a Bible and a cake.

"Say what?" we all said. "Took a Bible?" If the White House wanted to make friends, why didn't anyone think to take a nice leatherbound Koran, maybe with gold lettering, preferably in Farsi? Why are we sending these people a Bible in English?

Ever since then, we've been learning more about this damned fool venture, but no new questions occur. "Say what?" and "Didn't anyone think?" continue to cover all the new information that comes out. Of course, it has since been denied that we ever sent a Bible, but all of the denials have deniability. The Iranians say we sent a Bible, and they were honest enough to call Ronald Reagan's explanation of all this "mere lies."

I especially like the part when something new and more horrible is revealed and they announce that Edwin Meese will investigate. The very thought of Ed Meese—with his keen legal sensibility, his sensitive ethical antennae—renders me cheerful beyond all description. I know some of you humorless old lefties think we shouldn't gloat publicly over Reagan's difficulties. Listen, my momma may have raised a mean child, but she raised no hypocrites. I love this. I can't wait to read the papers every morning. I'm entitled to this satisfaction. It has not been easy to be anti-Reagan in Texas for the last six years. Damn right, I'm gloating.

One interesting aspect of the big mess is the political sociology of lying. The Republic has sunk to such a state that our public servants not only lie but brag about it and even seem to consider it their chief function. Damage control, deniability, spin, turn. Donald Regan's description of himself as a pooper-scooper is already classic: "Some of us are like a shovel brigade that follows a parade down Main Street cleaning up."

Watching the "spin doctors" at work is fascinating: The first step is to blame the media for everything. If the "delicate negotiations" go awry, it is the press's fault.

They even persuaded the most recently released hostage to stand on the White House lawn and declaim, in a voice shaking with emotion, that the lives of the hostages still in captivity depended on restraint by the media.

Several developments later, Reagan was still carrying on about "the sharks circling."

One of my favorite moments was when the president told us his purpose in all this was to bring an end to the terrible war between Iraq and Iran. He sent arms to bring peace. This is the famous putting-out-the-fire-with-kerosene ploy. Remember the graffito from Vietnam—FIGHTING FOR PEACE IS LIKE FUCKING FOR CHASTITY? Ah, said the president with great lucidity, it's true we shipped weapons to Iran, but they were *defensive* weapons. If the man had a brain, he'd play with it.

Another great moment was when Richard Nixon appeared on television urging complete candor as the best possible option.

Also outstanding was when the Prez called Oliver North "a national hero." Same Oliver North he had fired only the week before on grounds that North is the only man in the entire world who knew that profits from the illegal sale of arms had been illegally turned over to the *contras*. As Senator Bob Dole said, not even Ripley would believe it. But the administration is clearly counting on North to go down with his lips buttoned. Ollie North, meet G. Gordon Liddy. Would you guys like a couple of candles to hold your hands over?

The Progressive, November 1986

DON'T WORRY, THEY'RE HAPPY

Ron and Nancy. Let's face it, they were the eighties. Okay, so his mind is mired somewhere in the dawn of social Darwinism and she's a brittle, shallow woman obsessed with appearances, but then, it was that kind of decade, wasn't it? No fair blaming it on them—they were what the country wanted. They never made you think, never had any doubts, never met a problem that couldn't be solved by public relations, and they didn't raise your taxes. It was Don't Worry, Be Happy City—all done on borrowed money, with glitz and mirrors, while the social fabric rotted, the infrastructure crumbled, the environment slowly became nightmarish, and the deficit grew and grew. The least we can do is thank them for the wonderful memories.

The charm of Ronald Reagan is not just that he kept telling us screwy things, it was that he believed them all. No wonder we trusted him, he never lied to us. That patented Reagan ability to believe what he wants to—damn the facts, full speed ahead—gave the entire decade its *Alice in Wonderland* quality. You just never knew what the president would take into his head next—or what odd things were already lurking in there. His stubbornness, even defiance, in the face of facts ("stupid things," he once called them in a memorable slip) was nothing short of splendid. It made no difference how often you told him something he didn't want to believe. The man *still* thought you could buy vodka with food stamps, that he never traded arms for hostages, and that the Soviet Union has sent billions of dollars of weapons to the Sandinistas. This is the man who proved that ignorance is no handicap to the presidency.

The elements of berserker comedy that so distinguished Reagan's presidency were there right from the start. During the 1980 campaign—shortly after he announced that cars don't cause pollution, trees do—scholars in the press corps took to classifying Reagan's departures from reality. We're not talking bloopers here—like the time he toasted Bolivia—in Brazil; greeted his own Secretary of Housing as "Mr. Mayor"; called President Samuel Doe of Liberia "Chairman Moe"; and announced at a 1982 GOP fund-raiser, "We are trying to get unemployment to go up, and I think we're going to succeed." We all trip on our tongues from time to time and there's no great harm done. These errors go beyond *faux pas.* Journalists Mark Green and Gail MacColl finally sorted his errors into six classes: obvious exaggerations, material omissions, contrived anecdotes, voodoo statistics, denials of unpleasant facts, and flat untruths.

One of my favorite episodes came early in the administration, in 1981, when then-Secretary of State Alexander Haig announced to an appalled world (we hadn't twigged yet) that the Soviet Union was using chemical warfare in Southeast Asia, spraying a lethal "yellow rain" on remote tribes that led to a terrible sickness and then death. The godless commies were apparently practicing on remote tribal people to see if the poison worked. Oh, the horror.

Later, scientists around the world identified the "yellow rain" as bee shit. It seems that Asian bees occasionally leave their hives, fly up to a considerable altitude, and dump en masse. The resulting clouds of bee doody frightened the tribes but never, it turned out, killed anyone. The Reagan administration never withdrew the charge and never apologized for it.

In 1986, when Reagan was told the Congressional Budget Office had statistics showing a dramatic redistribution of wealth from the poor to the rich, he twinkled endearingly and said, "Oh, I don't think that's true." That's a classic example of the simplicity, the straightforwardness of his approach to unwelcome news. It was one of his favorite phrases.

Some days, having Reagan for president was like finding Castro in the refrigerator: Remember the time he appointed thirteen people to a commission on AIDS—including a sex therapist who thought you could get the disease from toilet seats; some fruitloop who claimed gays were engaging in "blood terrorism" by deliberately donating infected blood; and a longtime friend of Reagan's who ran a controversial "AIDS testing clinic" out of her van? No one on the commission was a medical specialist with any experience in treating AIDS. It was really awfully funny, if you didn't care about AIDS.

Sometimes you could tell Reagan was confusing old movies he had seen with reality: On November 29, 1983, he told Israeli Prime Minister Yitzhak Shamir that he was part of a crew filming the liberation of the Nazi death camps. On February 15, 1984, he repeated this claim to the Nazi-hunter Simon Wiesenthal. Of course, Reagan never left the United States during World War II—he spent the war in Hollywood making training films for the Air Corps.

Other times, it was just hard to know what to think: On February 18, 1984, following a half-hour with the Lebanese foreign minister, who was trying to explain the intricate relations between the many political factions in his country, Reagan suddenly said, "You know, your nose looks just like Danny Thomas's."

By December 1987, the deficit had become so staggering that a "budget summit" was called between the White House and Congress. The deal was that Congress had to come up with half of an agreed-upon sum by making cuts in social spending, and that Reagan would come up with the other half by cutting military spending. The congressional delegation arrived at the White House and laid out its cuts. Reagan then laid out his new military budget, but it had no cuts in it—it had increases. "Mr. President," said Speaker Jim Wright gently, "you were supposed to *cut* the military budget."

"Oh, spending on the military doesn't increase the deficit," replied Reagan cheerfully. "Cap," he gestured to the end of the table, "explain it to them." Looking slightly sheepish, since he was talking to the members of Congress who know most about financing government, Caspar Weinberger rose to his feet and launched into a spiel he had obviously given often before. He said money spent on the military goes out into the economy, you see, and is spread around, and then it trickles down, you see, and then it has a multiplier effect, and because of the multiplier effect, the treasury gets back more money than it spends on the military, you see, so it doesn't increase the deficit at all. And then he sat down. Reagan turned confidently to the congressmen and said, "You see?" He had then been president for seven years.

And his timing was fabulous. Remember Thanksgiving Day 1982, when the administration chose to swell the national sense of gratitude by announcing plans to tax unemployment benefits? Ed Meese explained that they wanted to "make it less attractive to be unemployed."

And what a sense of humor. Remember his joke that went out over the air during a radio mike check in 1984? "My fellow Americans," said Reagan, "I'm pleased to tell you today that I've signed legislation that will outlaw Russia forever. We begin bombing in five minutes." Heh, heh, heh.

He was always a man of the people: During the 1984 campaign, his advisers made Reagan go into a McDonald's. He sat down and asked, "What do I order?"

They said he was lazy and confused, but he prepared in advance: A script discovered by Sam Donaldson revealed that even Reagan's most casual comments in meetings were written on three-by-five cards for him. ("Otis, what are your thoughts on this?")

He inspired all around him with awe at his work habits: According to several Reagan aides, in the wake of the Iran-*contra* scandal, there was serious talk of invoking the 25th Amendment to remove him from office because he wouldn't come to work—all he wanted to do was watch movies and television.

He was the pro-family president and he believes in family values—just ask his son Michael, who wrote a vicious book about him; his daughter Maureen, who wrote a pathetic book about him; his daughter Patty, who also wrote a nasty book about him and Nancy; or his son Ron, Jr., who has not yet finished his book. Or any of his grandchildren, whose names he can't remember.

He was the candidate of the Moral Majority and the Religious Right: Unfortunately, his entire administration was so riddled with corruption that much is still being uncovered. The man brought James Watt, Ed Meese, Ray Donovan, and Silent Sam Pierce into the cabinet. He brought Michael Deaver, Lyn Nofziger, Donald

Regan, John Poindexter, and Oliver North into the White House. In 1985, the last year for which we have the full numbers, 563 federal officials were indicted and 470 convicted, a tenfold increase over the highwater mark that was reached with Watergate. It's gotten worse every year since and may go even higher this year, if only because of the HUD scandal.

Reagan also put a splendid assortment of nuts, racists, and wackos into other high public offices. Remember the woman appointee who had written a book claiming, "American blacks insist on preserving their jungle freedoms, their women, their avoidance of personal responsibility, and their abhorrence of the work ethic"; and the woman at the Department of Education who turned out to believe that handicapped people "have invited their fate"; and the federal program to encourage chastity among teenagers that urged girls "to pretend that Jesus is your date"?

My personal favorite: On October 25, 1983, the United States of America (population 250 million), the mightiest nation on earth, invaded the island of Grenada (pop. 86,000) by air, land, and sea. And we whipped those suckers in a fair fight. We sent in almost 7,000 fighting men, armed to the teeth, along with ships, planes, guns, missiles, and tanks, to face a situation that we had (1) helped create by ignoring Maurice Bishop's pleas for help, (2) was none of our business anyway, (3) did not involve American medical students, who neither needed nor wanted our help, and (4) at worst could have been handled by a couple of Texas Rangers. The local population was mostly armed with sticks, and the 800 Cuban construction workers who were supposed to be commie soldiers either dropped their guns or never got to them at all. According to the Pentagon's own post-invasion analysis, none of the sixteen Americans killed in the invasion died by enemy fire; they all died by accident. The press, for the first time in the history of the nation, was not permitted to accompany U.S. troops into action—and only would have reported that we had bombed the local mental hospital anyway. President Reagan slept through the whole thing, as was his wont in moments of national crisis. Nevertheless, he went on television that night, after we had defeated the entire military might of Grenada, a place smaller than Cleveland, and his voice trembled with emotion as he said, "This—is our finest hour." The army later gave out 8,612 medals for heroism in the great Grenadan invasion, even though fewer than 7,000 men took part.

As for Nancy, my own feeling is that it's unfair to pick on

her—irresistible, but unfair, in that the only reason she ever entered the public eye was as Reagan's consort. Whatever vanities, follies, selfishness, or even excesses of loyalty that may distinguish her, none of them would have ever come in for public lampooning had the woman married a rich dentist. Many, including Donald Regan, saw her as the power-behind-the-throne, as the stronger, more manipulative partner, the one who supposedly made Reagan into a right winger to begin with. Oh, poop. That's just the same old sorry sexist stereotype about the scheming woman that's been used against every wife-of-a-powerful-man from Napoleon to Lincoln to Roosevelt. There's no evidence that Nancy Reagan's occasional interference in her husband's schedule, staff, or public presentation was ever anything more than protectiveness or perhaps overprotectiveness. That he was slightly dotty by the end of his second term was clear to everyone, and her fierce desire to protect him from demands beyond his fading abilities can only be considered commendable in human terms.

Aside from tempting personal idiosyncracies—such as her sweet, feminine little pearl-handled revolver, which can make such a sweet, feminine little pearl-handled bullet hole—Mrs. Reagan should be given a walk. Acquit her of malign political intent; the best evidence is that she is infinitely more interested in clothes than in any public issue. That her folly on that topic has no apparent limits is her problem, not ours.

Of more legitimate public concern, although probably of marginal impact, is her effect as a role model. Mrs. Reagan chose to be—first, last, and always—a Wife. By the testimony of her own children, it was a role she put well ahead of that of Mother. That she has no independent life is apparent: he *is* her career and she is unquestionably an enormous political asset to him. I never met an honest man yet, no matter what his politics, who wouldn't confess that he would adore to have a woman look at him the way Nancy *always* looks at Ronnie. "The Gaze" was famous among journalists and political insiders. Through every single speech of his, Mrs. Reagan looked at him with total attention, as if she were witnessing one of the wonders of the world. It was a fantastic performance when you consider how many times she had to sit through that drivel.

So here's to Nancy, the Gaze, and eight years of not much else. When not calling her "friend," the astrologer, to see if it was a good day for the Prexy to travel, she followed the advice of her image maker and sought to shed her reputation as a vain, vapid clothes-horse by valiantly combatting the drug epidemic with the most ring-ingly inane and inappropriate slogan in the history of folly: "Just Say No." All who have been saved from drugs by Nancy Reagan, please raise your hands. Thank you.

Savvy, October 1989

WE THE PEOPLE

Constitutionally speaking, it seems to me that in this, the bicentennial year of the glorious document, we fall roughly into three groups. There are those who consider the old charter perfect as written. Their reverence for the work of the founders is such that they wish to see it altered neither jot nor tittle and are original intenters all. One can observe them frequently on the *MacNeil/Lehrer* program wearing three-piece suits and horn-rim glasses; they are distinguished by an air of premature pomposity. I used to wonder where the *MacNeil/Lehrer* folks ever found these people, but I have since learned from Russell Baker that they are mass produced by the Heritage Foundation. They commune with the founders concerning original intent by the same means Oral Roberts re-

ceives instructions from the Lord. Such is their reverence for the
founders that they are not only rendered bilious to this good day by
the emancipation of slaves and the enfranchisement of women, but
are still dyspeptic over direct election of senators and apoplectic over
granting the vote to nonpropertied white males.

Does the Reagan Supreme Court decree that the death penalty
shall be limited largely to black people? Some specimen in a three-
piece suit appears instantly to announce this was the dearest wish of
the founding fathers. Do the Supremes decree that accused citizens
can be held in prison until they can prove their innocence? Some
peckerwood from a right-wing think tank immediately declares this
was the very scheme most cherished by Thomas Jefferson himself.
As our only attorney general observed not long ago, "You don't have
many suspects who are innocent of a crime. That's contradictory. If
a person is innocent of a crime, then he is not a suspect." I was
amazed by that statement: I hadn't realized Ed Meese knew what a
contradiction is.

What's really astounding about these brickheads who claim to
be in touch with the original intent of the founders is (1) none of them
seem to have read what the founders wrote, from Thomas Jefferson's
essays to Jamie Madison's notes, and (2) you know damn well if they
had been alive at the time of the American Revolution, they all
would have been Tories.

Then, in the second group, there are the citizens of this great
nation who have yet to hear about the Constitution. A great many
of them live in Texas. You know how fond we are as a nation of those
polls that show we're hopeless dunces—"72 percent of all Americans, when asked to locate Japan on a map, put it to the right of
Chile"—that kind of thing. "Sixty-eight percent believe Chou En-Lai
is a shrimp/noodle dish," and so forth. Then we all cluck abut how
dumb we are. Well, whenever they run one of those tests on the Bill
of Rights, some depressingly high percentage of Americans immediately identifies the list as the work of Karl Marx. "What communist
swill!" reply 41.7 percent, or whatever the number is this year.

Many citizens in this category serve in the Texas Legislature.
Take my word for it. This is why, when the Robert Borks of the
world, with the complacence of perfect ignorance, announce that
questions concerning our fundamental liberties can be safely entrusted to the state legislatures, I can be found on my knees with my
liver quivering. Enough said; you know the problem.

Then there are the rest of us.

I submit to you that only half the reason the Constitution is a great and living document is because our foundin' daddies were about the smartest sumbitches ever walked and also because they wrote right in there how to keep changing the old charter as need arises. The other half of the credit for the beauty of the Constitution goes to 200 years worth of American misfits, troublemakers, hell-raisers, eccentrics, mavericks, anti-Establishmentarians, and outsiders who are ever ready and happy to do battle.

In my opinion, there's not a thing wrong with the ideals and mechanisms outlined and the liberties set forth in the Constitution of the United States. The only problem was, the founders left a lot of people out of the Constitution. They left out poor people and black people and female people. It is possible to read the history of this country as one long struggle to extend the liberties established in our Constitution to everyone in America. And it still goes on today.

Texas Observer, September 11, 1987

THE DISCREET SMARM OF THE BUSHWAZEE: CAMPAIGN NOTES AND THE FIRST YEAR

★ ★

"There are certain minimal standards for citizenship—real Texans do not use the word *summer* as a verb. Real Texans do not wear blue slacks with little green whales all over them. And real Texans never refer to trouble as "deep doo-doo."

—MOLLY IVINS,
Gannett Center Journal

THE WORD'S
THE THING

Told you so. I *told* you George Bush was going to turn out to be more fun than a church-singin'-with-supper-on-the-grounds. How can you not love his thing thing? They asked him why he thought he was trailing Michael Dukakis, and the Veeper said it's the problem he has with "the vision thing."

He's also having a little difficulty with the minority thing. A few weeks ago, Bush was commiserating with a black ghetto kid who said he hated homework. "Ah," said Bush, *"comme ci, comme ça."* Yo, mo'-fo'. Reporters traveling with Bush have taken to keeping track of his French. "He's back on *'C'est la vie.'* Three times today."

Next, Bush was interviewed by Ted Koppel, whom he kept calling "Dan." Koppel was finally reduced to pleading, "Please, Mr. Vice President, don't call me Dan. It's so Freudian. Call me Peter, call me Tom, anything but Dan."

I think this is not a Dan thing but a word thing with Bush. While trying to express how close he is to President Reagan, Bush said, "For seven-and-a-half years I've worked alongside him, and I'm proud to be his partner. We've had triumphs, we've made mistakes, we've had sex." He didn't mean that: "Setbacks. We've had setbacks," he quickly amended. There's just slippage from time to time in the links between his mouth and his mind.

The continuing debate over whether Bush is a Texan surfaced again during the state Democratic convention, when some fun-lovers rented Bush's "home"—his address of convenience, a suite at the Houstonian Hotel—and held a Bologna Bash and Boogie here. The bookcases in Bush's "house" feature Reader's Digest Condensed Editions.

Texas Agriculture Commissioner Jim Hightower, reflecting on Bush's "stay-the-course" strategy, said, "If ignorance ever goes to $40 a barrel, I want the drillin' rights on that man's head."

The Progressive, August 1988

TEXAS GEORGE

George Bush's distinguished career as a raving twit suffered serious setback when he went *mano a mano* against Dan Rather and came out looking more like Chuck Bronson than Tweetie Bird, his usual alter ego. Everyone said Bush savaged Rather. Cover of *Time*. The whole schmear. Bless my soul.

As a senior chronicler of Bush's life and times as Wienie One, I found it hard to comprehend this episode until I saw a postfight interview with Rather. He had not intended to be rude, said the anchorman, he'd just been trying to do his job. "I have the greatest respect for the office of the vice presidency," said Rather. Is that right? It explains a lot.

"It was like combat," burbled the Veeper a day later, ". . . that guy makes Lesley Stahl look like a pussy." I knew my man was back in form.

Out in Iowa, Bush was confronted by a young woman who accused him of favoring abortion. Bush hotly denied it; absolutely not, said he, I am totally opposed to abortion. After the meeting he went up to this woman, who was holding a Jack Kemp flier in her hand, took it away from her, tore it into pieces, and said, "*Fini!*" French in Iowa. *Quel fromage!*

When he lost a straw poll in Iowa, the Veeper blamed it on his supporters being off "at their daughters' coming-out parties or teeing up at the golf course for that crucial last round." The comment did not burnish my man's image as a son of the soil.

Then *The Wall Street Journal* asked him what went through his mind when his plane was shot down in World War II. "Well," replied Bush, "you go back to your fundamental values. I thought about Mother and Dad and the strength I got from them. And God and faith, and the separation of church and state." And who among you shall be so churlish as to doubt that our man Bush was contemplating the separation of church and state as his plane hurtled toward the sea?

After Iowa it was on to New Hampshire, where invitations went out: "Come for burgers and bloodies with the Bushes." Across the length and breadth of the Granite State he trooped, swearing that he was the truest, bluest Yankee who ever lived. It was fascinating to see him metamorphose into a Texan a week later wearing cowboy hat and neckerchief as he rode horseback in the Houston Live-Stock Show parade: "Ah am one of y'all."

Bush's finest day back in the 1984 campaign started in Minnesota when he had to get up at 6 A.M. and milk a cow in order to demonstrate his concern for the plight of the American farmer. Protocol calls for the politician-demonstrating-concern-for-plight-of-farmer to wear a plaid shirt, and Bush showed up in the correct red plaid. But he had it on under a pinstripe, State Department suit. Either Bush had forgotten how to milk, or that cow was a Democrat. He couldn't get a drop out of her. Bush also forgot that cows are retromingent, a word one seldom gets to use. Cows are the only mammals that pee backwards. That's why one should never walk behind them, even though they don't kick.

It went like that all day. Every time someone handed him a baby, the little nipper would commence to scream as though it had been stuck with a pin. Bush got to Green Bay, Wisconsin, and told the crowd there how much he loves the Minnesota Vikings.

This was a few days after Bush's debate with Geraldine Ferraro, in the course of which Bush had claimed that Walter Mondale said our Marines in Lebanon had died in shame. Mondale had said no such thing; he said Americans had died in vain in Lebanon. Bush held a painfully absurd press conference trying to prove with a dictionary that "in shame" and "in vain" mean the same thing. Mondale was royally hacked about this and said, "George Bush doesn't have the manhood to apologize." This comment was relayed to Bush, by now in California, and he was asked to respond. Said the Veep, "Well, on the manhood thing, I'll put mine up against his any time." Reporters stood there, pencil frozen in wonder. "Did he say that? Did you hear him say that?"

Late that night, as Bush climbed the ramp of his plane for the trip to his next campaign stop, the press turned out to see if he would answer one last question. No, he indicated, no more questions. He waved once and called, "So long." About half the press corps replied spontaneously, "*How* long, George?"

The *Washington Post* was once driven to describe Bush as "the Cliff Barnes of American politics—blustering, opportunistic, craven, and hopelessly ineffective all at once." To some of us, such sins pale in comparison to the fact that the man voluntarily renounced his Texas citizenship in 1984. He tried to take a $123,000 tax deduction by claiming that his real residence is in Kennebunkport, Maine.

There is a curious duality in people's reactions to Bush. Some listen to him and dismiss him instantly as a "preppy dweeb." Others hear him on a good day and come away saying, "This guy has a lot of knowledge and a lot of experience. He is not a lightweight." Twenty years ago, after Congressman George Bush voted for the 1968 Civil Rights Housing Act, there was hell to pay back in his right-wing Houston district. He stood up at a series of public meetings in front of God and everybody, took screaming, abuse, threats, and still refused to apologize for that vote. As it happens, it was also the last time I ever saw him do anything I admired. George Bush is one of those people whom neither time nor circumstance has treated kindly. God knows, he started with enough advantages of birth, talent, and education, but somehow as he has gotten older, he seems to become less and less.

It is true that the vice presidency is a job that makes anyone who occupies it look small: even Lyndon Johnson was pathetic as vice president. But Bush's smallness is in the man, not the job. He has an incurable tendency to toady. In 1974, a Yankee Republican who was an old Washington hand and a friend of former Senator Prescott Bush, George's father, said, "I can't think of a man I've ever known for whom I have greater respect than Pres' Bush. I knew him during all his years in the Senate [1952–1963] and I never once doubted his judgment or his integrity. Hell, he talked back to Joe McCarthy as a freshman senator and that was a damn tough thing to do. I've always been kind of sorry his son turned out to be such a jerk. George has been kissing Nixon's ass ever since he came up here."

Nixon named Bush chairman of the Republican party in the midst of the Watergate scandal. It was not a happy moment in GOP history. Even so, Bush did more than just ignore the stench of that administration in its last months—the corruption, the arrogance, the lawbreaking, the signs of mental unbalance. Through it all George Bush burbled inanely and chirruped cheerfully. Micawber as a sycophant.

For seven years now he has been a fawning cheerleader for Ronald Reagan. He said last year, "Even if it costs me my political career, I'm not going to distance myself from the president." If he distanced himself from the president, he'd have no political career.

Since the interview with Rather, Bush's stock response to all questions about the Iran-*contra* scandal is, "If you would look at page 502 of the Congressional report, you will see that the report clears me completely." He says this with great impatience, as though the question were simpleminded. Page 502 of the Congressional report on the Iran-*contra* scandal from the dissenting minority report was written by the eight Reagan loyalists on the committee. It was so bad, three Republicans refused to sign it, and Senator Warren Rudman (R.–N.H.) called it "pathetic."

Ms., May 1988

MAGNOLIAS
AND MOONSHINE

Watching the candidates metamorphose into Southerners was sort of like watching *The Fly.* Bob Dole claimed to be a Southerner-in-law. Paul Simon noted he is from southern Illinois. Albert Gore, Jr., fondly reminisced about shoveling pig manure, and Pat Robertson ate grits in public. George Bush, who only the week before had been in New Hampshire claiming to be the full-blooded Yankee—Drink Syrup or Die—turned up in Houston wearing boots, cowboy hat, and neckerchief. Behind them came a great pack of journalists, baying and yipping. "What about the South? Explain the South."

As it was in March, so shall it be during the general election campaign. You'll hear lots of commentary between now and November about how the "pivotal voters," whom the pollsters and consultants have decided are white Southern males, will vote. But what the pundits and commentators understand about the South could fit on the tip of a ballpoint pen, as I found out last March during the frantic buildup to Super Tuesday voting.

Local scribes tried to help. We gave interviews, turned over our reliable sources and colorful characters. "Someone from the KKK? Sure. I'll call 'em up and tell 'em to get out their sheets." You could tell what the candidates thought of the South; they opened their mouths and mush gushed forth. Ours was the "no message" primary. To a man they bravely endorsed a strong national defense, courageously defended traditional family values, and daringly opposed higher taxes.

Upon arriving in Dixie, they commenced to use the word *leadership* more and *compassion* less. There was a dire shortage of humor in the exercise. None of them campaigned in the South; they campaigned in eighty-five major media markets. But they did remember that you have to talk slowly and simply to Southerners, that you must not upset us by bringing up any idea that postdates 1954. So Jesse Jackson won, which is logical since it makes no sense. Keep in mind that Southerners are so conservative they voted for Franklin Roosevelt, so isolationist they voted for Richard Nixon, so populist they voted for Barry Goldwater, so aristocratic they voted for George Wallace, and that they see nothing peculiar in any of this.

It's possible to put this more kindly—it's even possible to be proud of it—but the bottom line is that Southerners are crazy. "Incurably romantic" is the polite version. "Nuts" is the way Florence King, a distinguished daughter of Virginia, puts it.

King claims she first noticed this while at the University of Mississippi when she was party to a drunken kidnapping that ended up in a rowboat in the middle of a lake at 2:00 A.M. with a hysterical Southern belle hissing, "Kill him, Wade, kill him!" While King wondered what she was doing there and how a sane person could get into something so bizarre, the answer came to her: "I am not sane, I'm a Southerner." This "click" of recognition is much like the famous "clicks" that come to women on their way to realizing they are feminists. To accept that simple, elementary common sense is never going to rule your life, or even play much of a role, is to acknowledge your Southernness.

Let us detour here to address the generalization problem. Of course it's silly and shallow to make sweeping statements about enormous numbers of people who differ more from some folks in their own hometowns than they ever will from the majority of people in other regions. Still, but, yet, however, the French *are* observably different from the British, even though generalizations are inherently superficial, and Bretons differ from Gascons. There is a fashionable intellectual perception that America is becoming more and more alike from one end to the other, that it's all covered with interstate highways and Howard Johnsons. Horsepucky. The most amazing thing about this country is its diversity, and the persistence of its regional and cultural differences.

If you go someplace where people come from all over America—say the Grand Canyon or Disneyland—you will find you can consistently pick out two kinds of Americans from all the others: Midwesterners and Southerners. Middle Westerners tend to be exceptionally sensible people. Almost everything they say makes you want to nod and mutter. "Yep, that's right."

If, for example, you hear someone say, "Ethel, I told you if you wore your high heels on the hike, you'd get sore feet," you know right away that he is from the Midwest and Ethel is from the South. Because Midwestern women do not wear high heels on hikes; they are too sensible. But to Southern women, appearance is more important than pain. Florence King even argues that *faux pas* matter more than sins to Southerners. We often lie in the interest of kindness, seemliness, or social ease. Perhaps it would help Yankees to think of this as something of an Oriental approach to life, in which the concept of "face" has great importance. Personally, I don't think there's a single damn Oriental thing about it, but it beats having Yankees think we're stupid.

Which is, of course, the major cultural impression Yankees have of Southerners, an impression more deeply embedded than that of magnolias, moonshine, and mint juleps, even stronger than the image of red-faced, nigger-hating bigots. The extent to which a Southern accent is associated with low IQ in American popular culture is hard to exaggerate. Look at all those World War II movies: three guys wind up in the Army together from basic training to heroic death. The hero is always a handsome, brave, blonde kid from the Midwest. His pals are a smart, wisecracking New Yorker—some kind of dark-haired ethnic—and a Southern slope-headed ridge-runner too dumb to tell c'mon from sic 'em.

.   .   .

A few months ago in Mobile, Alabama, I stopped a lady in the street and said, "Ma'am, can you tell me how to get to the bus station from here?" She said, "Why yes, honey, I can. You see that yellow house up at the corner? That's the old Jessup house there. Jefferson Jessup, he was in the grocery trade. They had a daughter who married a boy from Montgomery. He had a brother who had a goiter, but everyone liked him anyway. . . ." And with that she was off on the history of the entire Jessup clan, a compelling saga which I thoroughly enjoyed.

Southerners habitually think in terms of clan relationships. This is a friend's mother calling to make dinner reservations at a local restaurant: "This's Miz Henry callin'. My son's in town and he's got his darlin' wife here too, with both little boys. Then Big Buck's brother Bartley is here and we've got a newspaper lady here, too. So that's eight people comin' at 8 o'clock, we're sorry to be so late, can y'all handle that?"

I suspect that African griots, the respected elders whose function it was to carry the tribal history in their heads, sounded very much like elderly Southern women. That emphasis on family, which can be maddening and is often pretentious hooey, makes the South one of the last places in America where money is not suzerain. It's not looked down on, you understand; it's just not everything.

One of the nicest things about Southerners is their large tolerance for eccentricity. By legend, Southern families tend to have loony relatives stashed in the attic: in my experience, they are not kept in attics at all—they wander around loose, suffering from harmless delusions, such as their own direct descent from Mary Queen of Scots. Another of Florence King's dicta is: "Southern mental life is a Cecil B. De Mille screenplay sired by a Sir Walter Scott novel." This affinity for purple romanticism accounts for the fact that Southerners will overdramatize anything. Reserve and understatement are not Southern virtues. One coed to another: "And then I realized my bag did not match my shoes and I thought I would *die!*"

Since the entire region wallowed in misery after the Civil War, we quite understandably have developed an acute nostalgia—things *were* better for nineteenth-century Southerners before the War of Northern Aggression. Ever since, white Southerners have romanticized, exaggerated, and prettified the antebellum South. This phenomenon runs in waves: there was a bad spell of it shortly after the turn of the century, causing untold numbers of historical societies and chapters of the Daughters of the Confederacy to blossom. The publication of *Gone with the Wind* set off another round. The film of *GWTW* used to be required viewing in the public schools. Margaret Mitchell had a number of imitators—you can find one for every taste—including Frances Parkinson Keyes, Frank Yerby, and Erskine Caldwell.

What difference can dated fiction possibly make in the real world, in the politics of 1988? Is Jo of *Little Women* not still an important role model for little girls? Well, so is Scarlett O'Hara. Cheerleaders, beauty queens, belles, flirts—that whole set of roles for women still holds cultural sway in the South. In her definitive work, *Southern Ladies and Gentlemen,* Florence King observes, "The cult of southern womanhood . . . requires [a female] to be frigid, passionate, sweet, bitchy, animated, and scatterbrained all at the same time. . . . A horrifying number of us succeed, which accounts for that popular southern female pastime, having a breakdown."

Racism in the South today is still complex. There is a generational difference developing. Young whites are demonstrably more tolerant than their elders, while young blacks are either more impatient than theirs or they're buppies. A young black man in New York recently dismissed the civil rights movement by saying that all it had done was "get rid of colored drinking fountains—big deal." It was a bigger deal than he will ever know. Those struggles weren't about drinking fountains; they were about dignity. Blacks and white liberals who grew up in the South before the civil rights movement tend to be persistently optimistic. To have lived here before is to know how much and how fast things can change. All of us have our own memories of it—a troop of colored Cub Scouts (we always said "colored" then) sitting dejectedly on the curb in front of a Dallas movie theater, where they had just been denied permission to see *King of Kings,* a film about the life of Christ. Still, while legal and political changes in the South have been dramatic, economic change for Southern blacks is painfully slow.

After the law, the major source of racial change in the South is football. In Pat Conroy's very Southern novel *The Prince of Tides,* he describes the first time a white boy ever handed off a football to a black boy in a small South Carolina town. In a moving passage, he credits "the Southerners' awesome love of sport" with breaking down resistance to integration and winning out over the "bruised history" that has brought this lone black kid into the backfield.

Texans too have an awesome love of sport; our problem is we're tacky. When the University of Texas at Austin finally started a black player in 1970, he was promptly tackled by a black player from the opposing team. Though it may be apocryphal, it is widely reported here that a famous UT booster rose in the stands and screamed, "Goddammit, ref, get that nigger off our colored boy."

The kind of integration Conroy describes in the high school team has united some communities. In other areas, integration just means that all-white teams now play against all-black teams and the result is often a public outpouring of racism.

Sometimes racial progress is noticeable in unexpected areas. Working-class Southerners have always been assumed to be the obdurate racists in the region. I have heard country club Southerners—the kind who always say "Nigra" rather than "nigger"—mourn over how bad "trashy people" like Bull Connor made the South look to the rest of the country. (Eugene "Bull" Connor, children, was the commissioner of police in Birmingham, Alabama, at the time Dr. King was thrown into jail in that city. He sicced police dogs on black marchers and turned fire hoses on children. He was the archetypal red-faced, mean, dumb, racist Southern lawman. Birmingham now has a black mayor.)

One might assume that middle-class whites would be more amenable to integration than the butter-and-egg man, because working-class whites are in competition for the same jobs and have the most to fear from blacks economically. As it turns out, working-class whites and blacks may be closer to real integration than middle-class white Southerners, who use their money to avoid blacks in schools, housing, restaurants, and so forth. You see more integration in the bowling alleys—where the guys from Don's Cement or Dickey's Beer Distributor wear the same team shirts and give each other high fives after a strike—than in the posh clubs.

The most thoroughly integrated institution in America is almost certainly the U.S. Army, which doesn't get much credit. In March, *Newsweek* ran a special report on its cover—"Black & White: How Integrated Is America?"—and never even mentioned the military.

The Southern passion for military service first astonished the rest of the country in 1898, when Southerners signed up in droves to avenge the *Maine.* It was the country's first war since Appomattox, and for thirty-three years Yankees had questioned Southern loyalty. The intense patriotism of Southerners persists to this good day (six out of eight of the men involved in the Iran-hostage rescue mission were Southerners). Conventional wisdom holds that the officer corps is still predominantly Southern, and the ranks are full of working-class and rural Southern kids, black and white. "Has your boy done his service yet?" is a common question in the South (including among Chicanos).

Southern machismo is part of the military's appeal: one theory about why so many Southerners enlist in the military is that they just want to get the hell out of the house and away from all those sweetly domineering women. So how come all these macho Southern white males voted for George Bush? Because it makes no sense, of course.

A reporter for the *Washington Post,* describing a rally of Kentucky coal miners for Jackson, said, "It looked like Crackers for Jackson. These people would stand up and say, 'Ah am fer Jesse,' and I couldn't believe they weren't talking about Jesse Helms." A little Yankee bigotry showing there. It crops up in the oddest places. *Texas Monthly* ran a profile of George Bush and the second paragraph says, "Bush is not a wimp. . . . The drama of his life . . . consists of his repeatedly deciding to reject the safe, standard course and to do something unusual and dangerous. He risked his life and became a Navy pilot right out of high school. He moved to Texas after college instead of taking a job in New York." *He moved to Texas?* How unusual and dangerous! In 1948, when the Comanches were still raiding Midland!

Pat Clark, a black woman who heads Klanwatch, the organization that keeps track of KKK activities, was raised in New Jersey but now lives in Montgomery. She notes not differences in kind between Southern and Northern racism but differences in public reaction. "When there was trouble in Forsyth County, the very next weekend 20,000 people from all over the country showed up to march there. At right about the same time, there was the trouble in Howard Beach in New York City. That too got lots of media attention, but 20,000 people from all over the country didn't show up to march in protest of Howard Beach."

Perhaps the South deserves the persistence of the Southerner-as-bigot stereotype, but that should not itself be the basis for fresh bigotries. P. J. O'Rourke is a right-winger of the cool school: he's young, he's hip, he writes for *Rolling Stone.* During an interview on Canadian Broadcasting, O'Rourke said of Pat Robertson's followers, "I hate fundamentalists. I think they're dangerous. I'm afraid of them. They're terrible for the Republican party. I wish they'd crawl back under their rocks." If that's not religious bigotry, then how does it differ from anti-Catholicism or anti-Semitism?

According to the Gallup Poll, there are more than 50 million Evangelical Christians in America, and they sure do come in a lot of different flavors. Yankee journalists who assumed Pat Robertson was going to show tremendous strength in the Southern primary have now learned that—and so has Brother Robertson. The South killed his candidacy.

The first response of your basic secular humanist to this respectable bigotry against born-again Christians is always to point out that fundamentalists themselves are notoriously intolerant. And some of them sure as sin are. But the kettle being black is no excuse for this kind of ugliness. Dr. Os Guinness, a student of religious conflict, says:

> In the face of modernity, liberal believers believe less strongly and conservative believers believe more strongly. The result is this fruitless and bitter contention. American opinion makers must take their own share of the responsibility for this, because American intellectuals have made their own contribution to a situation that tends more and more to polarized extremes. America is both the most modern and the most religious modern nation in the world. Many intellectuals suffer from culture shock in their own country.

Fundamentalists aren't evil; they're worried. They're afraid of modernity, worried about the family, repelled by abortion, and yearn for traditional values. All of us sinners like to see a hypocrite brought down, and sweet was the fall of Jim and Tammy Faye. And Jimmy Swaggart had done his share of hatcheting other preachers. What goes around comes around, Brother Swaggart. But you know who his followers are? They're straight out of *Let Us Now Praise Famous Men*. All their lives they've suffered from poverty, isolation, no opportunity, poor diet, poor education, and the scorn of others. There was a time when progressives did not sneer at folks like that.

The Southern primary should be read separately from Super Tuesday, the larger political event that included twenty states, Massachusetts among them, and American Samoa. The eleven states of the old Confederacy divided neatly into two regions: Broke and Not

Broke. The oil states—Texas and Louisiana—are brokes. Jesse Jackson won both. His victory in Texas has gone completely unsung because the state has a two-tier system. The television networks used the raw vote totals, which were Dukakis 32.7 percent and Jackson 24.6 percent. But the Texas party uses a weighted system based on a region's party strength, so Jackson finished the first round with 42 delegates to Dukakis's 43. In the second round, the caucuses on primary night, Jackson beat Dukakis: even though the party is still figuring the results from Senate district conventions, the campaign offices agree that Jackson has more delegates than Dukakis. ABC's exit poll showed Jackson got 14 percent of the white Texas vote and 20 percent of the Hispanic, on which the Dukakis campaign had concentrated. That more white Texans voted for Jackson than in other Southern states is likely due to Jim Hightower, the popular state agriculture commissioner, who was the only white official elected statewide anywhere in the South to endorse Jackson.

It was one of those rare, genuinely moving moments in politics—Jackson and Hightower stood together on Texas Independence Day at the front of the Senate chamber with a portrait of Jefferson Davis behind them and a full-length Stonewall Jackson in Confederate uniform off to one side. Hightower's backers had begged him not to do it—conventional wisdom is that he'll lose a lot of Jewish contributors. But he said that day, "As hard as I have tried to remain neutral, I could not escape the inner voice of integrity saying that Jesse Jackson was forcefully, proudly, and successfully carrying the populist program I espouse. If he was standing for my principles, why was I not standing for him?

"If it's dangerous to talk to yourself, it's probably even dicier to listen, but I did, of course. I've had plenty of advice saying I'm a fool, but as I've often said, there's nothing in the middle of the road but yellow stripes and dead armadillos. So here I am where I always should have been."

The Confederacy can alternately be read as a coherent cultural entity except for its two bookends, Texas and Florida, which are dissimilar both from the other Southern states and from one another. Jackson took seven states: Texas, Louisiana, Mississippi, Alabama, Georgia, Virginia, and South Carolina. Gore won three: Tennessee, Arkansas, and North Carolina, while Dukakis got Florida.

Meanwhile, Bush was sweeping everywhere on the Republican side. Democratic turnout from state to state in the South ranges between two and three times that of Republican turnout. However, the polls, for whatever use they are this far out, show it will be hard for a Democrat to beat Bush in the South come November. That's the South that's Not Broke and thinks Reagan stands tall against the commies.

Quite a few political reporters bet on politics. Among those who do it and make money, none of them put money on what the South will do.

Mother Jones, June 1988

THE DISCREET SMARM
OF THE BUSHWAZEE

There used to be a fellow in the Texas Senate named Carlos Ashley, who retired after some unpleasantness about a retainer from the insurance industry. Ashley wrote cowboy poetry— he was known as the state's "poet lariat"—and I still remember the conclusion of one of his more thoughtful works: "When the final scale is balanced in the field of loss and gain/Not one inauguration's worth a good, slow, two-inch rain." Having been in Washington, D.C., for the Bush Inauguration, I find deeper meaning in this rhyme today.

First rat out of the trap we got a fully inflatable, kinder, gentler George Bush. The Noonan version is, as it turns out, quite a bit clearer than unscripted Bush, as we all found out later in the week at the new president's first press conference.

"We've got to have a little time," Bush told reporters, in answering a question about relations with the Soviet Union. "We're not about to let this Soviet thing put—put us in the mood of, of foot—mode of foot-draggers. We're going to be out front." That certainly cleared things up.

On Inaugural Day, Bush had rather remarkably made only one stupid move—despite the unfortunate Bush-Noonan lapse into cliché at the end of an otherwise fine speech (the "new breeze" turning the page of the chapter in the unfolding story: I was afraid for a minute there the winds of change would start blowing the sands of time).

The blunder was a promise to wipe out the "scourge of drugs" during his administration. Almost as certain as death and taxes is the prospect that there will continue to be a serious drug problem in this country in 1992.

Among Washington Insiders, there was little sense of a "new chapter." The whole *megillah* was treated by them for what it was: say, much like a long-expected promotion within a large corporation. One of the surprises about the whole affair for me was how little the Republicans seemed to mourn the departure of Ronald Reagan. But perhaps that's because what stayed the same is more noticeable than what changed.

The Washington press corps, for example, remains thoroughly Reaganized, reporting on the First Family with the zeal of courtiers in the time of Louis XIV; the dramatic, earthshaking change from Reagan red to Bush blue is discussed among them with all the seriousness due cabinet appointments. The press corps seemed so ecstatic to have a president who stays awake, in fact, that they've all declared him the greatest ruler since Augustus. He appears sincere in his desire to be the education president, to eradicate homelessness, and all the rest, but this means, of course, that he will be one of the victims of the expectations he is raising.

The fact is, the nation's underlying economic problems are so critical that you might wonder whether Bush can fulfill *any* of his many promises.

His promised emphasis, for example, on ethics in government took a brutal hit as Bush tried to get one up on the Gipper by bravely dragging a scandal right *into* the cabinet rather than leaving top aides time to develop major problems in office over time, as Reagan kindly did. I quite agree with Bush's impulse: why *wait*? John Tower, after all, revealed he was a man of "some discipline." Many of us wanted to know *how much* and *which kind*?

Two days before the $25 million inauguration, a crowd of several hundred homeless people stood across the street chanting, "Shame! Shame!" as a thousand rich Republicans in limousine after limousine swept up the front entrance of the newly restored Union Station for a $1,500-a-plate dinner.

The Republicans stepped forth, resplendent in $1,200 red, white, and blue spangled shoes, and gowns by Galanos and Yves Saint-Laurent. The homeless favored a layered look, topped by street-chic wool caps and accessorized by gloves or mittens with the fingers worn out.

Official Republicans were properly sorry about the state of the homeless. George Bush the Younger said, "I know this is something my father feels strongly about." Unofficial Republicans, such as a handsome, white-haired man from San Francisco, were more blunt: "I just think it's become a cliché, it's been done, it's not new, you know?"

One thing the Reagan years have accomplished is to take away the sting and shock of seeing homeless people in a land of plenty. The juxtaposition of extreme poverty and extreme wealth no longer seems obscene because it's so familiar. It's been done, you know?

There were so many additional bizarre moments during Inaugural Week, it will take some future anthropologist to work them all out. Precisely 225 Bush relatives descended on Washington for the inauguration, of varying degrees of consanguinity and affinity; this occasionally led to surreal moments in which you suddenly noticed that every other person in a room with you looked eerily like George Bush.

You were constantly rubbing shoulders with the unbelievably powerful; at one shindig I was introduced without warning to William Webster—formerly FBI, now CIA—and all I could think of to say was, "Hi, you have a file on me."

And then there was a "From George to George (Washington to Bush)" children's program, which seemed to be a lovely idea in conception but produced a few puzzling results.

There was, for example, a five-story chair sitting on the Washington Mall that turns out to have been a giant replica—made by U.S. Buddhist children—of the chair George Washington used when he was president. You may well ask what *was* the point of a five-story chair made by Buddhist children. The only thought that occurred to me as I marveled over the sight was that it would take one hell of a large butt to fill it.

Homeless people were on the mall as well, of course; they're everywhere, sleeping in the parks and esplanades. The latest studies show that 25 percent of them have full-time jobs, but they make only minimum wage and cannot afford a place to live.

On Inaugural Day, Senator Bob Dole, who voted a few months ago against increasing the minimum wage, addressed members of Team 100—the *richest* Republicans—who had given more than $100,000 to the party. With his endearing frankness, Dole explained the sly maneuvering leading up to a 50 percent wage increase for the distinguished members of Congress. To stop the increase, opponents had to get both houses of Congress to vote no.

"We in the Senate will all righteously vote no, which will have no effect, and then will watch anxiously to make sure that our colleagues in the House don't vote at all, and that will ensure passage of the raise. Of course, my wife has a new job, so it's no big deal to me." Really, you'll have to trust me, it was just so cute the way he said it.

That was the strategy, but it didn't work. Don't cry yet. Dole and his colleagues last got a salary increase in 1987 and, at $89,500, they make an average of $43 an hour.

The minimum wage is $3.35 an hour and was last raised more than eight years ago. A woman trying to support two children by working full time for minimum wage is almost $2,000 below the poverty level.

So, how long will it take for kinder, gentler to kick in?

Mother Jones, April 1989

DUMB BANKERS, MAVERICKS TOO

Cries of alarm are ringing through Washington city—"The Texans are coming! The Texans are upon us!" Journalistic brethren from the Northeast have called to inquire, "What does it all mean? Is there a Texas way of governing? Is there a Texas point of view?" You understand we are talking about a range of political Texans that runs from Henry B. Gonzalez, the ancient Chicano radical, who at seventy-one slugged hell out of some sumbitch who called him a commie, to that trio of displaced preppies Jim Baker, Bob Mosbacher, and Georgie Bush. If you insist on a comprehensive comment, a one-size-fits-all: What it means, folks, is a serious setback for vegetarianism. Where you find Texans, there shall ye also find meat-eaters. The only cultural advantage to being Texan is that we never have to apologize for being carnivorous.

I gather the nation's capital has yet to recover from the last time it was overrun by a horde of Visigoths from the Great State, led by the Horrible Head Hun, Lyndon Johnson. Fear not, Eastern effeters, none of these new guys is going to pull up his shirt and show you the scar from his gallbladder operation. But I guarantee we've sent you two citizens who will remind everyone where the word *maverick* comes from. (The first Texas Maverick was a rancher who refused to brand his cattle, so that if you found an unmarked cow in your herd, you knew it was a Maverick.) The two new congressional committee chairs from Texas—Gonzalez and Jack Brooks—are as far from Bob Forehead as it's possible to get.

Wait till you see Brooks, the new head of the Judiciary Committee, in action. Come to think of it, you already have. He was the only guy on the Iran-*contra* committees last summer with any guts, remember? The one who kept trying to wade into *contra* drug smuggling and all that other stuff the good little boys had promised to stay away from. The thing about Brooks is that he just doesn't care, except about the Ninth Congressional District, where they think he's God. In the Ninth it is widely believed that Brooks personally ordered Hurricane Gilbert to steer clear of Beaumont/Port Arthur—with powers greater than the prayers of Pat Robertson! Brooks does not give a flying fart about what is seemly, proper, politic, not done, or about whose reputation gets hurt, making it look good, or public relations.

As for Henry B, he's been going his own road for so long no one could make him shape up. It's been chic to snicker a bit at Henry B in recent years—he's overweight, he has an accent and bad hair, he talks too much and believes too passionately in things that are not neo. But I notice Washington seldom snickers long at those with power. Some rainy afternoon, you should get someone who was there to tell you about the time in 1957 when Henry B. Gonzalez filibustered against the segregation bills in the Texas Legislature for thirty-six hours and two minutes. The charm of having Henry B as chair of the Banking Committee during the S&L catastrophe and what promises to be a spirited round of re-regulation is that Henry B understands two important things: Bankers all have hearts like caraway seeds, and bankers as a group are dumb. I am pleased to report that the phrase "dumb as a Dallas banker" has now made its way into the Texan language.

Charlie Wilson, the East Texas Representative and hero of Afghanistan (recently lionized on *60 Minutes,* which was a refreshing change, since the last time *60 Minutes* paid any attention to Charlie it was on account of that unpleasant business about the cocaine), came up with a scheme to save Speaker Jim Wright from the nasty schemers who hauled him before the House Ethics Committee. Wilson suggests that no one should be allowed to serve on the House Ethics Committee who has not himself been investigated. He claims this would cut down on the hypocrisy and the sanctimony, and would produce a committee of people who understand how much lawyers cost and who could recognize chicken shit when they see it. Wilson was himself on the Ethics Committee until it had to investigate him: He claims he got the seat by observing to Mo Udall, as he studied the list of the members, "Damn, there's not a sonofabitch on here who likes pussy or whiskey. They're not representative of the Democratic Caucus." Udall agreed and put Wilson on.

The State Legislature convenes in January, but we are trying not to think about it. Finest new member of the State Senate is Bill Haley, a funeral home director from Center. Last year some friends took Haley to eat at a swanky Austin restaurant. Faced with an absurdly pretentious wine steward, Haley, who is suspected of being more than mildly literate, became a complete naïf. The steward finally came around with a tray of after-dinner drinks. "How much is that kind, a glass?" inquired Haley.

"Zat, monsieur, is six dollars ze glass," replied the steward.

"Oh my," said Haley in wonder. "And that kind, how much is that a glass?"

"Zat, monsieur, is ze very best we have in ze house. Zat is twenty-five dollars a glass."

"Twenty-five dollars a glass!" squealed Haley. "Why, you wouldn't want to pee for a month, would you?"

Cultural notes from around the Great State: A citizen fed up with "lawyers running the country" has filed a $1 billion class action lawsuit against the entire legal profession. Daniel Madison of Austin is suing the American Bar Association, the Texas Supreme Court, the University of Texas Law School, and the Law School Council for violation of antitrust laws, claiming they conspire to keep power out of the hands of nonlawyers. "If you're rich, you can have all the justice you want, but if you're a working-class citizen, you may get little or none. That's the system in America and I intend to prove it," said Madison.

Proving once more that the legal profession is a disgrace, Texas lawyers passed up a chance to elect Oliver Heard president of the Bar Association. Heard was caught in a nude modeling studio during a police raid in the middle of his campaign for the state bar office. Heard claimed he just went into the place to use the bathroom, but came to electoral grief anyway.

The Nation, January 23, 1989

THE CZAR
IS HOOKED

Praise the Lord and pass the RICO statute, here comes a substitute for the cold war, just in time. Boy, was I worried! The entire foreign-policy establishment, from State to CIA to DIA to NSC, had gone into depression, funk, the toilet. They were moulting and dying up at the Council on Foreign Relations.

Reminded me of the time I took clinical psychology in college so that I wouldn't have to take real science. They gave me a rat in a Skinner box, and I was supposed to teach it that it had to press a bar in order to get a food pellet. It was a bright little rat and learned that in no time. Then I was supposed to teach it that it had to press the bar twice to get a food pellet. But my rat overlearned, which, as I recall, is something that can be plotted on a bell curve.

My rat would press the bar once, and when it didn't get a food pellet, instead of trying again, it developed a neurotic ritual: it would turn around three times to the left, tossing its head pitiably, and then fall over backward. I swear to God. It never did learn to press twice, just became more and more neurotic. I ruined a perfectly good rat and felt guilty about it for years.

Any fool can see that our foreign-policy folks have overlearned the cold war. Now that they're required to do something else, they've developed the most astonishing neurotic rituals. I was afraid that any minute we'd see Henry Kissinger turning three times to the left and falling over backwards. But here in the nick comes the War on Drugs, God bless us everyone.

Already Czar William Bennett is sniffing out the quislings in the War on Drugs: In addition to the usual suspects—intellectuals and the American Civil Liberties Union—we find such novel doves as William F. Buckley, Jr., Milton Friedman, and former Secretary of State George Shultz, all backing the "scandalous" notion of legalizing drugs.

Ha! Just the kind of people who thought commies should be legal back in the old days—Un-American, effeminate, and probably drop Latin phrases into their conversation. In an especially happy twist, the Czar suggests these parlor druggies may be motivated by racism.

Alas, the Czar himself is a drug addict. He's got a three-pack-a-day tobacco jones he just can't lick. Happily, his drug has been legalized. But he knows full well this is not the solution for people addicted to *dangerous* drugs. (According to the Surgeon General, 2,000 people in the United States died of cocaine use last year. In the same year, cigarettes killed 390,000.)

Lewis Lapham, who is clearly a drug dupe, recently wrote in *Harper's* magazine, "Bennett's voice is the voice of an intolerant scold, narrow and shrill and mean-spirited, the voice of a man afraid of liberty and mistrustful of freedom. He believes that it is the government's duty to impose on people a puritanical code of behavior best exemplified by the discipline in place at an unheated boarding school. He never misses the chance to demand more police, more jails, more judges, more arrests, more punishments, more people serving millennia of 'serious time.' "

Well! I know disloyalty when I see it and I'm reporting Lapham to the House Un-American Activities Committee.

The War on Drugs is the perfect substitute for the cold war. We can continue to pursue policies that don't work on the cheerful assumption that if we just do more of what doesn't work, it will solve the problem. This is in the splendid tradition of the Vietnam War and other glorious episodes in the nation's past.

I especially like the level of argument propounded by the Czar, who claims those who favor legalization want to sell PCP and meth in the Jiffy Mart. I sort of thought, myself, that we were talking about an improved system of methadone clinics, or something like the British system where addicts have to register with the government and go to a doctor. But the Czar says that's not what we're talking about, and he knows best.

In the meantime, the Drug Enforcement Agency has been corrupted, poor city cops are out there pissing on a towering inferno, the scumbags of the universe are becoming obscenely wealthy, and once again we have an enemy against whom we can spend more and more and more money, deploy more and more weapons—and never, ever win. It's heaven.

In 1931, President Hoover assigned a task force to study Prohibition. It was called the Wickersham Commission, and in the immemorial manner of government blue-ribbon panels, this little beauty studied the problem, compiled lots of evidence, and arrived at the politically correct conclusion. F.P.A., a columnist for the *New York World*, then wrote this synopsis of the report so no one would have to bother to read it:

> *Prohibition is an awful flop.*
> *We like it.*
> *It can't stop what it's meant*
>   *to stop.*
> *We like it.*
> *It's left a trail of graft*
>   *and slime.*
> *It's filled our land with vice*
>   *and crime.*
> *It don't prohibit worth a dime.*
> *Nevertheless, we're for it.*

And anybody who isn't is a rotten intellectual.

The Progressive, February 1990

KINDER AND
GENTLER ALREADY

President Bush wants the spooks in the CIA freed up to assassinate foreign leaders at will, but he has vetoed the bill that would have provided abortions for poor women who are the victims of rape or incest. How nice: a kinder, gentler nation already.

I'm worried about My Man George because in Washington, the city where everyone says what everyone else says, everyone is saying the guy is a wimp. Or, as George puts it, they're calling him "the *W* word"—and it doesn't stand for *wussy.* Trouble is, when a lot of people start calling Bush a wimp, he tends to go into some kind of a snit to prove his standing in what he once memorably referred to as "the manhood thing."

When he was a mere veep, Bush was limited to verbal displays of testosterone, like the time he said he'd "kicked a little ass" after debating Geraldine Ferraro (who had actually hammered him pretty good). But his current job gives him a lot more scope for "the manhood thing." Since the coup against Colonel Manuel Noriega, which was supposed to be "Bush's Grenada," has come to naught, one winces to think what he might do next if he gets really upset about "the W word." If I may make a modest suggestion, how about we invade Grenada again? They seem to like it, and we're pretty sure to win.

Our only Prexy refused to sign the bill making it highly illegal to burn the American flag; he let it become law without his name on it on grounds that we really should amend the Constitution on this burning issue. Bush's last birthday cake was in the form of the American flag, and *he ate it*—stars, stripes, and all. Think about where that flag wound up—I call that desecration.

Here in Texas, we got off to a glorious start in the gubernatorial race when Republican candidate Jack Rains issued a ten-point Program on Education, which he said we need because kids today aren't learning a thing in school. His points were numbered 1, 2, 3, 4, 6, 7, 8, 9, 10.

But the story that has been haunting me lately concerns efforts by the Harvard Business School to teach ethics to its students. Seems John McArthur, dean of the school since 1980, has been pleading with the students not to "go through life focused only on Number One"—to little apparent avail, so far.

Albert Gordon, a Harvard fund-raiser and chairman emeritus of Kidder Peabody, said, "I hope they don't take the ethics issue too far because human nature and the free-market system will doom it to failure. They run the risk that some students could decide to go to other schools in the future."

So far, though, the dread addition of ethics to the curriculum does not seem to have stemmed the tide of aspiring future earners of $70,000-a-year-to-start. According to a wire-service story, the school attracted 6,200 applicants this year, and 5,400 had to be rejected. Some of them were so distraught they threatened to sue the university.

As part of McArthur's effort to weed out people interested only in lucre, the admissions process now includes thirteen questions and nine essays, rather than a standardized test, and takes hours to complete. To make the cut, students must answer a few questions about ethics.

For example, they are asked to explain, in the application, how they managed an ethical dilemma they have experienced. But according to Laura Gordon Fisher, the school's admissions director, many students say they have never encountered an ethical dilemma.

"It's amazing how many people admit they've never experienced a moral dilemma," said Fisher. "Some applicants want to know if they should fabricate one."

Reminds me of the old question, if a dog could talk, what would it say? If these kids were to make up an ethical dilemma, what do you suppose it would be?

The Progressive, December 1989

POST-INVASION PACIFICATION

The unfortunate *faux pas* concerning Manuel Noriega's cocaine stash is entirely understandable. As the U.S. Army explained, it was "in the excitement of the moment" that American soldiers searching Noriega's refrigerator mistook a bunch of white powder for his "personal supply" of the dreaded drug. Upon analysis, the powder turned out to be tamale flour, *masa harina,* which is also used for thickening chili and making tortillas and gorditas.

Clearer evidence of the need for women in combat I have never come across; in fact, the entire incident cries out for the institution of the drafting of Texas women.

This is the most embarrassing cross-cultural snafu since the time President Gerald Ford came to Texas and tried to eat a tamale without taking the shuck off. (Actually, Ford suffered an equally embarrassing lapse on that same campaign trip when an insufficient acquaintance with Texan culture caused him to enunciate "Remember the Alamo" as a question. This, children, is why Jimmy Carter carried Texas in 1976.)

Turns out this whole invasion bidness is fraught with potential embarrassment. The American press covered itself with something other than glory by breathlessly breaking records to report the color of Noriega's underwear (red) and the nature of his pornography collection (which may yet turn out to be the family album) before they got around to mentioning that we seem to have killed several hundred civilians in the course of the glorious invasion.

My favorite episode, invasion-wise, remains the vicious rock 'n' roll assault on the papal nunciature in Panama City while Old Zitface holed up there. (You recall that Our Boys broke out their boom boxes and blasted the living hell out of those dictator shelterers. No wonder they turned him over in jig time. Great stuff, eh?)

But the *piece de resistance* of the whole schmear is our post-invasion pacification program. Having upset every living person between the Rio Grande and Tierra del Fuego with one more display of our respect for the sovereignty of other nations, our only president then proposed to settle everyone down by dispatching the ineffable Dan Quayle on a peace mission. To tell them all they looked like happy campers to him. Unfortunately, as one country after another elected not to receive Danny Q., his mission had to be scaled back. They finally let him out to say hidy to the maitre d' at a Taco Bell.

Now we get to have even more fun trying to try the general. Comes the question, can we find twelve Americans who have not yet made up their minds about Noriega? My friends, fear not. The invincible ignorance of the American people, so often deplored by short-sighted pundits, is what will make it possible to find scores of citizens who have never the hell *heard* of Manuel Noriega. This is a great country, 250 million strong, and we can all sleep soundly at night knowing there are among us more than twelve who have no opinion. About anything. Many well-informed journalists profess to be among them.

It's been a bad time generally for our reputation among the neighbors to the south. Our allies in El Salvador murdered six priests, their housekeeper, and her daughter. Such a public-relations gaffe! Everyone knows it doesn't matter how many thousands of peasants our allies in El Salvador slaughter, but offing the clergy upsets people every time.

Also, nuns. Killing nuns is very bad PR; so annoying of our allies to keep committing this bêtise. I know what you're going to say: "Oh, you liberals, all you ever do is complain. You never propose any solutions."

All right, here's a helpful suggestion. Many Americans are now joining twelve-step groups in order to overcome assorted bad habits. Perhaps the CIA could start a chapter of Nun Killers Anonymous for the *contras*.

The Progressive, March 1990

MIMIC MEN

Writing for *Mother Jones* has been a bit of puzzlement for me. It's such a Left Coast publication. (Here in the Great State, we think of the East as the Right Coast.) *MJ* is so trendy and hip, it's hard to imagine what it might learn from a state where *queer, commie,* and *nigger* are still in common usage in political dialogue.

Clearly, we in Texas are not yet ready to move on to describing the handicapped as "differently abled." On the other hand, there's a lot to be said for residual common sense. Sometimes I think Texas exists as a reality check for those who might wander too far toward the precious.

Unfortunately, the folks who most need a reality check seldom read *Mother Jones.* Those who seem to me to have strayed furthest into some make-believe ideological world are the neoconservatives. They have actually managed to convince themselves the world is run by (or at least greatly influenced by) folk of the liberal persuasion. I suppose if you spend your life in academe, you might conclude this is actually so: that indeed it requires great courage and a singularly independent mind to go against "the prevailing liberal orthodoxy." Whenever I see this line of argument, I say to myself, "Ah, there's a sumbitch who has never spent time in a state legislature."

Confusing the academy with the world is a dumb and dangerous thing to do. In the real world, money talks, bullshit walks. In a state legislature, clout meets clout, money meets money, interest fights interest, and only the strong prevail. Which is why ordinary folks keep losing.

Should this strike you as an unduly Darwinian view of what is, after all, a liberal, Western democracy, I can only commend you to Reality School. Go and study how the laws are made and then tell me if I lie.

The forty-first president of the United States is not having a happy effect upon your nation's capital. Calling George Bush shallow is like calling a dwarf short. He's a conventional creature, perfectly amiable—in fact, he has lovely manners when he's not upset (his mom deserves a hand)—but every principle he holds is based on a recent opinion poll. Even though he vacillates constantly, he is not a hopeless twit, a total Twinkie, or a damn fool. That's a misimpression based on the fact that, as *Newsweek* magazine once put it, "At least once a day he achieves a level of transcendent dorkiness." Bush merely has twit tendencies. Unfortunately, the entire Federal City now needs to be dipped for the same ticks.

Observe Congress—silly, vacillating, with no earthly idea what to do unless it has an opinion poll in front of it. Here's the Democratic party—silly, vacillating, no earthly idea what to do unless it has an opinion poll in front of it. And citizens, observe the press—silly, vacillating, no earthly idea what to do except take another opinion poll. It's almost the only form of enterprise reporting left in Washington.

The man who ran on the slogan "Ready on Day One" has been in office for a year, and the only issue for which he has shown real passion is a capital-gains tax cut to benefit all the rich pond scum who piled up boodle during the Reagan years. And even his commitment to a capital-gains reduction was the result of pique. According to several published reports, Bush didn't become obsessive about the capital-gains cut until House Majority Leader Dick Gephardt gigged Bush by saying, "The president has named a lot of his friends to be ambassadors; I guess this proposal is to take care of those who didn't get named." Gephardt also said, "The limousines are circling the White House." Well! George Bush was miffed! Yes, he was. And his people put out word that the Prez considered Gephardt's remarks unsporting and "overly personal." Sheesh. "Weeks later Bush remains so offended he can barely bring himself to say hello to Gephardt," *Newsweek* reported.

That episode would be sufficiently silly on its own, but half the Democrats in town took up the chorus—after voting for the capital-gains cut because the timber and real-estate industries displayed such touching enthusiasm for it. Said Representative Les AuCoin of Oregon, "The thing I think our party has missed is that the American people do not buy in, in any fundamental way, to a class-warfare political argument." We have a president who vetoed Congress's first effort to raise the minimum wage in thirteen years but supports a tax cut for the richest people in the nation, and House Democrats are offended that anyone should introduce the notion of class-warfare politics into the discussion? You could have knocked me over with Dan Quayle's brain. Breathes there a Democrat with soul so dead he cannot recognize that as an issue from heaven? A normal Democrat would kill for an issue like that. But not the House Democrats. Like Les AuCoin, they recoiled in horror from the thought of "class-warfare politics." What the hell do they think the Republicans are practicing—mah-jongg?

This is such a timid and fearful bunch of pols that they're blind to the obvious. They're so afraid someone will accuse them of being "soft on defense" that they've missed the fact that now is the time to be squishy on defense. The military cuts proposed by Bush would have been put into effect even if nothing had changed in Eastern Europe—he cut nothing more than the most wretched of the Reagan excess: Remember David Stockman's explanation of how the Pentagon budget came to be swollen beyond all intention by a fatal error in the base figure? The proposed cuts barely rectify that error. The process of converting jobs from defense to civilian purposes has been studied for years, and Democrats should be saying, "Here's how we do it." And then, of course, the more inviting prospect, "And here's what we do with the boodle we save."

The low point of Bush's performance so far came the day the Berlin Wall came down. The fall of the wall was a genuinely thrilling event. Okay, we all know George Bush suffers from this sort of verbal dyslexia and that on his bad days he can barely make himself intelligible. We cannot hope that he will find the immortal combination of words to crystallize and articulate for us all the emotions and hopes that attend such a stirring, historical event. Churchill the guy is not. But his highest rhetorical flourish on that day was "I think it's a good development." It was enough to remind one of the always timely question, "Is God punishing us?"

Part of Bush's problem is that he is not a well-educated man—he just went to good schools. On paper, his real-world education is encouraging—he built a business, held a variety of important government posts (you figure he has to have learned something)—until you look at it closely. In the oil patch, Bush's old partner is credited with building Zapata Oil. And the government jobs were all appointments to positions where he couldn't do much harm, except for his one-year stint at the CIA, where he did real harm. A few reporters have put a lot of investigative time into case studies on Bush's tenure at the CIA: How well did he know General Noriega? Did he help cover up the Letelier assassination? And then there was his finest hour—wiretapping Micronesia for reasons critical to our national security. But the real damage done during Bush's tenure as the spook spokesman was in policy. That was the era of the "B Team," the crowd of neoconservative defense experts headed by Richard Perle, who were called in by Bush and allowed to override the CIA's own top Sovietologists and military analysts. The immense defense buildup of the Reagan years was based on the B Team's erroneous analysis of the Soviet threat. Its intention was to force the Soviets to "spend themselves into the grave." Both CIA and DIA analysts now agree that the Soviets didn't bite; they never tried to match our Reagan-era buildup because their economy was already collapsing—while we spent our country into social disintegration all by ourselves.

That's one more reason why the emergence of an invertebrate press corps is so troubling. There have been several unsparing diagnoses of the press lately, such as Noam Chomsky's analysis of our institutional ailments in *Manufacturing Consent,* and Mark Hertsgaard's look at our collective cowardice in *On Bended Knee.* None of the deplorable trends noted by these critics in either print or broadcast journalism is new—they're just getting worse.

The most disturbing development among the Washington press

corps is a collective amnesia about the purpose of a newspaper—which is to gather news. The mortal sins of the press have always been our sins of omission, not our sins of commission, no matter what you may have heard about bias, hubris, or anything else. It is the stories we don't get, the ones we miss, pass over, fail to recognize, don't pick up on, that will send us to hell. The list of what we missed during the Reagan years includes everything that mattered—we missed Iran-*contra,* HUD, S&Ls, and the entire game plan until David Stockman told us what it was. And then we sat around criticizing Stockman for a tattle-tale.

When you consider that Max Frankel, now the editor of *The New York Times,* was the paper's Washington Bureau chief when it got beaten to a pulp on the Watergate story, you have some idea of what the problem is there. The *Times* sends out reporters to write down the words of powerful people, who frequently lie. The *Times* then prints the words and has its columnists double-dome them. It serves as a megaphone for official lies and then lets some zippy thinker like Flora Lewis or Abe Rosenthal gum it over for us. No one is out getting the news.

Journalistic bum-kissing has reached new depths. Nancy Reagan, according to her book *My Turn,* never could have made it through those dark and terrible days after the Iran-*contra* scandal broke—when her dopey husband had just been exposed as a liar, again—had it not been for the love, encouragement, and constant support she received from her "pals"—George Will, Katharine Graham, Mike Wallace, and Meg Greenfield, editor of the *Washington Post* editorial page. Isn't that *nice?* As I. F. Stone pointed out, the only way for a journalist to remain independent is "to sit in your tub and not want anything. As soon as you want something, they've got you!" That includes wanting the approval of the powerful and even the approval of your peers. Perhaps especially of your peers.

At the national convention of the Society of Professional Journalists in October 1989, the featured speaker at the main banquet was Al Neuharth, a press baron of whom the best that can be said is that he is not as bad as Rupert Murdoch. When asked why Neuharth, the man who invented *USA Today* so newspapers could be just as bad as TV, had been asked to speak to professional journalists, an official of the organization explained that Neuharth's company has contributed a lot of money to the group. And these are the people who are supposed to explain why we need campaign finance reform.

It may seem that the moment is ripe for despair, but we can be thankful for the spur of ambition. Many, many senators would like to be president, and so they have considerable interest in carving out an alternative to George Bush's record. This can lead to fairly funny results: one listens to Lloyd Bentsen, the old Tory Democrat, suddenly blossoming into populist rhetoric on the capital-gains tax issue, and one is left wondering, Okay, who put the Tabasco sauce in his grits?

George Bush's Washington is not threatening, as Washington was under Nixon. Nor is it dangerously ludicrous, as it was under Reagan. Instead, it's like half-cooked candy before it reaches the "soft ball" stage—you can get it together, but it's just mush; it has no form, no shape, no coherence. Since Bush is not venal, mean, nor nearly as daffy as Reagan, the American people, notoriously tolerant when it comes to their presidents, may be ready to cut the guy slack. "Well, he doesn't look great so far, but let's give him a chance" is the common line. "Wait until we see him face a real crisis," they say in D.C. But as Chekhov once observed, "Any idiot can face a crisis; it is this day-to-day living that wears you out." We have just graduated from an eight-year course in the inadvisability of doing nothing while social problems fester. We're about to discover that inaction in the face of unraveling disaster is just as bad when it's the result of indecision as it is when it's the result of ideology.

Mother Jones, February 1990

POST-ELECTION
GLOATING

Many pleasures ensued from the recent plebiscite, not least among them the flattening of the Houston city councilman who proposed, during a debate on changing the name of the Houston airport to honor the late Representative Mickey Leland, that we just call it "Nigger International." Guy looked like a road kill after election day.

As a devout believer in post-election gloating, I particularly enjoyed the spectacle of Republican politicians undergoing conversion experiences on the abortion issue—especially those who converted after long talks with their wives, with whom they apparently have long talks every twenty-five years or so. I haven't seen so many people getting right with God since my last tent revival.

Down here in the Great State we're all balled up on the issue of workers' compensation, which is one of those sexless issues that creates horrendous political gridlock by pitting lawyers against bidness against insurance against workers. Comp insurance rates have gone up 170 percent here in two years because Texas has such an abysmal industrial accident rate, but you can't convince a Texas bidnessman of that.

"What do you mean a high accident rate? What do they base that on? All those fraudulent claims that are filed by all those adjective-deleted workers and their adjectival-interjection lawyers?" demanded one irate bidnessman.

Actually, the high accident rate is based on the more than 800 mangled bodies that get carted off Texas worksites every year. As the man in the Monty Python sketch said, that is an ex-parrot. It is not a fraudulent claim.

Bush's linguistic inadequacy has never been more painfully apparent than it was on the day the Berlin Wall came down. People rejoiced the world over, and one so yearned for someone who would crystallize and articulate those feelings. But Bush can barely make himself intelligible some days.

The policy is much like the rhetoric: vapid, inadequate, and confused in response to one astounding development after another. We must certainly concur that the policies of the cold war should not be tossed aside lightly; they should be thrown aside with great force. But the United States seems destined to be the last country in the neighborhood to get dipped for cold war ticks.

Secretary of State James Baker said, both of German unification and of aid to Eastern Europe, "There are many things, it seems to me, that have to take place in between. One of those is fair and free and even multiparty elections. Another is movement to a free economic system, free markets, free enterprise."

Whoa! It's one thing for America to root for, encourage, and reward the blossoming of democracy. That's what our country stands for, those are our most fundamental principles. But nowhere in the Declaration of Independence or the Constitution of the United States is there anything about a free economic system, free markets, or free enterprise. Some of our closest allies have socialist or mixed economies, and some have higher standards of living than we do. (We now rank fifth behind Switzerland, Germany, Denmark, and Sweden, with Japan closing fast.)

We have no right to force capitalism on other countries or to require it of them. In fact, the contradictions of advanced capitalism (a fine Marxist phrase) have been glaringly apparent around here lately; the savings-and-loan industry offers some instructive points.

The country really needs a democratization of the control of capital. Decisions over the lending of money and the price charged for borrowing it are too vital to be left in the hands of bankers or any special interest. It is, after all, our money—our bank deposits and savings. The strategies of lending the money—whether for corporate takeovers or for home ownership and college education—should be a matter of public policy.

The platform of the Populist Alliance observes that the performance of our economy must not be judged merely on the Dow-Jones Index but on the opportunity available to the many and the benefits offered to all families and communities: "The beauty of the free-enterprise system is not in the corporate banditry and quick-profit machinations of the powerful few, but in the industriousness of the many family businesses, inventors, minority firms, dirt farmers, cooperatives, entrepreneurs, worker-owned companies, and other independent enterprises."

We need a national economic policy that spreads investment more widely and more wisely than we do now—and that takes account of the environmental impact of economic activity. We'll be doing no great favor to the people of Eastern Europe if we insist on exporting the state corporatism that increasingly dominates our own economy and that Republicans keep confusing with freedom.

The Progressive, January 1990

THE GOLF . . . ER,
GULF . . . CRISIS

The only fun I've found so far in the Gulf Crisis is the faintly comic sight of George Bush galloping around the golf course like a fool in the rain to prove what a cool, unworried fellow he is. Unless you count the gladsome tidings that the Western leader who went to meet Saddam Hussein face-to-face is Kurt Waldheim.

Otherwise, it's been bizarrely grim, having to listen to Henry Kissinger night after night carefully enunciating "strategic interests" and "surgical bombing." Lord, can't we at least agree that there is no such thing as "surgical bombing"? You don't do it on an operating table with a laser, for Christ's sake.

Who are these idiots advocating an attack on Iraq? In the name of God, why? We've stopped Saddam Hussein, we've got him surrounded and cut off, so now we let him negotiate the best deal he can: He's not holding any cards, what have we got to lose?

There are two kinds of bottom line in this deal; one is that war costs hell's own money. Sooner rather than later, it will be much, much cheaper for us to conserve energy than to kill tens of thousands of people.

The second is what we put on the tombstones when they start shipping the bodies home: HE DIED TO KEEP OIL AT $17-A-BARREL? MAKING THE WORLD SAFE FOR FEUDAL ISLAMIC FIEFDOMS doesn't have much of a ring to it. Everyone who has ever lost someone he or she loved in a war has an obligation to talk back to these chest-thumping jackasses who are so anxious to get other people's sons killed.

Now that I've gotten that off my chest, let us proceed to the case of the man-hunting prison board member, Jerry Hodge, just another reason I'm proud to be a Texan. Hodge is the fellow who took a couple of his pals along on a prison-board practice manhunt with dogs and then, afterwards, gave them jackets tastefully inscribed, THE ULTIMATE HUNT.

The object of the practice manhunts is to train the dogs to track down real escaped prisoners should the need arise. Of course, the state did have to settle $14,000 on two "dog boys" in 1983 after some enthusiastic hounds made hamburger out of 'em. But now the dog boys wear protective clothing and there's only been one seriously bitten in the last three years.

Poor Jerry Hodge felt hurt and disappointed when the press commenced to make a stink about his sporting ways. He had the hardest time getting the press to understand that there is nothing wrong with manhunting for fun. In a truly open-hearted gesture, he offered to let the press hunt *him* down with dogs so we could see for ourselves what good, clean fun it is.

Quite naturally, the Texas press took up the offer with gusto. Except we want to bring our own dogs. McNeely of the *Statesman* has a cock-a-poo named Tinkerbelle, a fine little tracker. Ramsay of the *Herald* offers the services of Bear, who can climb tall fences. Kilday of the *News* will bring Sparky the Wonder Dog, a Schnauzer. Cutbirth of the *Telegram* has a promising pup named Josh. And here in South Austin, I know two particularly amiable pit bulls named Ripper and Slasher. They'll enjoy the Hodge-hunt.

Otherwise, life in the Great State is rocking through the dog days with its usual panache. Our politicians have undertaken a festive round of lying in television ads. No one mentions the *T* word, although the latest estimate on the size of the state's deficit ($3 to $5 billion) caused Speaker Gib Lewis to observe during a budget hearing, "I move we recess to go outside and throw up."

I've started a new collection—explanations offered by oil-company spokesmen for the astronomical rise in gas prices ten minutes after Saddam Hussein invaded Kuwait. I particularly like the wounded-dignity-inflicted-by-ignorant-peasants approach, as in, "Anyone who accuses us of price gouging simply does not understand the complex and involved mechanisms of oil pricing." Buy low, sell high; takes Einstein to understand it.

The New York Times actually offered us a thoughtful thumbsucker on "The Psychology of Oil Pricing." Where's Freud when we need him? My favorite was when the television crews dug up some gas-pump jockey down at Joe Bob's Exxon and asked him how come he was raising his prices. "Uh," he said. "This is a real competitive bidness."

The Progressive, October 1990

SEASON OF DREAR

The ornaments are packed, the tree is down, and here come the bills, Ry-Krisp and cottage cheese, war, recession, and the Texas Legislature. On the whole, the outlook for 1991 is not glorious.

But we must find cheer where we can in this season of drear, so look on the bright side—at least Dan Quayle is still veep.

While buckling up for a kinder, gentler war, let me offer some *mots* for meditation from the Reverend W. N. Otwell of Fort Worth, a fundamentalist divine of some note here in the Great State. W.N. frequently chats with the Big Amigo, so he knows whereof he speaks. Just now, W.N. is real upset about us sending women to fight in Saudi Arabia.

"We believe," he says, "that God's word

and God's people are being mocked, and the leaders of this country are laughing in the face of Almighty God when they pervert His purpose for the woman and the mother by allowing them to suit up in a man's military uniform and serve in a combat situation." (Note the possibility that Pastor Otwell might not object to women in skirts serving on the front lines.)

W.N. says the Bible tells us women are to obey their husbands, not their military commanders. And further, "Although we have respect for the office of the President, the Congress, and our military leaders, they cannot and will not get away with mocking God. *God is not mocked!* To take a mother from her children so she can defend able-bodied men is unbiblical, immoral, and outright wimpish! Where are the men of America? Where is our leadership? Don't think for one minute that God is pleased with this sick mess!"

So there.

On more frivolous fronts, the country is heading into a banana (it is considered seditious to use the word *recession*), the banking industry appears to be prepared to imitate the S&L debacle, and the administration's response is to deregulate the banks.

I love those articles on the bidness pages and in the bidness magazines explaining to us economic illiterates that though the banking mess looks like the S&L mess, smells like the S&L mess, and quacks like the S&L mess, it is not going to be like the S&L mess. And the reason deregulation, which caused the S&L mess, will save the banks is because what we need is bigger banks. So we can be competitive with the Japanese, you see.

Friends, this is horsepucky. In Texas, which does lead the nation in some things, we were picking through the briquettes of the S&L bonfire before anyone in Washington even noticed the smoke. We know the consequences of having fewer and bigger banks, and then again bigger and fewer banks. My Aunt Eula's bank in Fort Worth has been swallowed so many times by bigger banks, she calls it "Edible National." North Carolina National Bank bought most of our banks. We say, NCNB stands for No Credit to Nobody.

If you think the oil industry is tons of fun the way it is now, wait until you see a banking industry with seven majors. Seems to me that it's a simple concept—the concentration of wealth is a Bad Idea. Since capital tends to concentrate, it is one of the functions of government to oppose this tendency. That's why we used to have antimonopoly laws and the like.

When you see government encouraging the concentration of wealth, check your wallet.

The Progressive, February 1991

WIMMIN, AND
ANCILLARY MATTERS

★ ★

"If you want to take the pulse of the people in
this country, listen to country-western music. I
first knew the Moral Majority was past its
prime and Pat Robertson would go nowhere
when I heard 'I Wrote a Hot Check to Jesus'
on country radio, followed by 'Would Jesus
Wear a Rolex on His Television Show?' "

—MOLLY IVINS,
Ms.

TEXAS WOMEN: TRUE GRIT AND ALL THE REST

Writing a humor column for *Ms.* magazine always sounded like the punch-line of a joke to me. That estimable publication tends toward the sober. There's something awfully daunting about having a box that says "Humor" on what you write, a set-up for people to say, "*This* is supposed to be *funny*?" Still, being female is often a comical proposition in this world, and being a Texas feminist is a particularly oxymoronic vocation.

Writing for and about women in various publications over the years has given me the opportunity to write more personal pieces than political reporting allows, and I am grateful.

They used to say that Texas was hell on women and horses—I don't know why they stopped. Surely not because much of the citizenry has had its consciousness raised, as they say in the jargon of the women's movement, on the issue of sexism. Just a few months ago one of our state representatives felt moved to compare women and horses—it was the similarity he wanted to emphasize. Of course some Texas legislator can be found to say any fool thing, but this guy's comments met with general agreement from his colleagues. One can always dismiss the entire Legislature as a particularly deplorable set of Texans, but as Sen. Carl Parker observes, if you took all the fools out of the Lege, it wouldn't be a representative body anymore.

I should confess that I've always been more of an observer than a participant in Texas Womanhood: the spirit was willing but I was declared ineligible on grounds of size early. You can't be six feet tall and cute, both. I think I was first named captain of the basketball team when I was four and that's what I've been ever since. I spent my girlhood as a Clydesdale among thoroughbreds. I clopped along amongst them cheerfully, admiring their grace, but the strange training rituals they went through left me secretly relieved that no one would ever expect me to step on a racetrack. I think it is quite possible to grow up in Texas as an utter failure in flirting, gentility, cheerleading, sexpottery, and manipulation and still be without any permanent scars. Except one. We'd all rather be blonde.

Please understand I'm not whining when I point out that Texas sexism is of an especially rank and noxious variety—this is more a Texas brag. It is my belief that it is virulence of Texas sexism that accounts for the strength of Texas women. It's what we have to overcome that makes us formidable survivors, say I with some complacency.

As has been noted elsewhere, there are several strains of Texan culture: They are all rotten for women. There is the Southern belle nonsense of our Confederate heritage, that little-woman-on-a-pedestal, flirtatious, "you're so cute when you're mad," Scarlett O'Hara myth that leads, quite naturally, to the equally pernicious legend of the Iron Magnolia. Then there's the machismo of our Latin heritage, which affects not only our Chicana sisters, but has been integrated into Texas culture quite as thoroughly as barbecue, rodeo, and Tex-Mex food.

Next up is the pervasive good-ol'-boyism of the *Redneckus texensis,* that remarkable tribe that has made the pickup truck with the gun rack across the back window and the beer cans flying out the window a synonym for Texans worldwide. Country music is a good place to investigate and find reflected the attitudes of kickers toward women (never ask what a kicker kicks). It's your basic, familiar virgin/whore dichotomy—either your "Good-Hearted Woman" or "Your Cheatin' Heart," with the emphasis on the honky-tonk angels. Nor is the jock idolatry that permeates the state helpful to our gender: Football is not a game here, it's a matter of blood and death. Woman's role in the state's national game is limited, significantly, to cheerleading. In this regard, I can say with great confidence that Texas changeth not—the hopelessly intense, heartbreaking longing with which most Texas girls still want to be cheerleader can be observed at every high school, every September.*

Last but not least in the litany of cultures that help make the lives of Texas women so challenging is the legacy of the frontier—not the frontier that Texas women lived on, but the one John Wayne lived on. Anyone who knows the real history of the frontier knows it is a saga of the strength of women. They worked as hard as men, they fought as hard as men, they suffered as much as men. But in the cowboy movies that most contemporary Texans grew up on, the big, strong man always protects "the little lady" or "the gals" from whatever peril threatens. Such nonsense. Mary Ann Goodnight was often left alone at the JA Ranch near the Palo Duro Canyon. One day in 1877, a cowboy rode into her camp with three chickens in a sack as a present for her. He naturally expected her to cook and eat the fowl, but Goodnight kept them as pets. She wrote in her diary, "No one can ever know how much company they were." Life for farm and ranch wives didn't improve much over the next 100 years. Ruth White raised nine children on a farm near High, Texas, in the 1920s and thirties. She used to say, "Everything on this farm is either hungry or heavy."

All of these strains lead to a form of sexism so deeply ingrained in the culture that it's often difficult to distinguish the disgusting from the outrageous or the offensive from the amusing. One not infrequently sees cars or trucks sporting the bumper sticker HAVE FUN—BEAT THE HELL OUT OF SOMEONE YOU LOVE. Another is: IF YOU LOVE SOMETHING, SET IT FREE. IF IT DOESN'T COME BACK, TRACK IT DOWN AND KILL IT. I once heard a legislator order a lobbyist, "Get me two sweathogs for tonight." At a benefit "roast" for the battered women's shelter in El Paso early in 1985, a couple of the male politicians told rape jokes to amuse the crowd. Most

---

*In February 1991, a woman in Channelview, Texas, was indicted for plotting the murder of the mother of her own daughter's chief rival for the cheerleading squad. The trial is pending.

Texas sexism is not intended to be offensive—it's entirely uncon-
scious. A colleague of mine was touring the new death chamber in
Huntsville last year with a group of other reporters. Their guide
called to warn those inside they were coming through, saying, "I'm
coming over with eight reporters and one woman." Stuff like that
happens to you four or five times a day for long enough, it will wear
you down some.

Other forms of the phenomenon are, of course, less delightsome.
Women everywhere are victims of violence with depressing regular-
ity. Texas is a more violent place than most of the rest of America,
for reasons having to do with guns, machismo, frontier traditions,
and the heterogeneous population. While the law theoretically applies to male and female alike, by unspoken convention, a man who
offs his wife or girlfriend is seldom charged with murder one: we
wind up filed under the misnomer manslaughter.

That's the bad news for Texas women—the good news is that
all this adversity has certainly made us a bodacious bunch of over-
comers. And rather pleasant as a group, I always think, since having
a sense of humor about men is not a luxury here; it's a necessity. The
feminists often carry on about the importance of role models and
how little girls need positive role models. When I was a kid, my
choice of Texas role models went from Ma Ferguson to the Kilgore
Rangerettes. Of course I wanted to be a Rangerette: Ever seen a
picture of Ma? Not that we haven't got real women heroes, of course,
just that we were never taught anything about them. You used to
have to take Texas history two or three times in order to get a high
school diploma in this state: The Yellow Rose of Texas and Belle
Starr were the only women in our history books. Kaye Northcott
notes that all the big cities in the state have men's last names—
Houston, Austin, Dallas. All women got was some small towns
called after their front names: Alice, Electra, Marfa. This is probably
because, as Eleanor Brackenridge of San Antonio (1837–1924) so
elegantly put it, "Foolish modesty lags behind while brazen impu-
dence goes forth and eats the pudding." Brackenridge did her part
to correct the lag by founding the Texas Woman Suffrage Association in 1913.

It is astonishing how recently Texas women have achieved equal
legal rights. I guess you could say we made steady progress even
before we could vote—the state did raise the age of consent for a
woman from 7 to 10 in 1890—but it went a little smoother after we

got some say in it. Until June 26, 1918, all Texans could vote except "idiots, imbeciles, aliens, the insane and women." The battle over woman's suffrage in Texas was long and fierce. Contempt and ridicule were the favored weapons against women. Women earned the right to vote through years of struggle; the precious victory was not something handed to us by generous men. From that struggle emerged a generation of Texas women whose political skills and leadership abilities have affected Texas politics for decades. Even so, Texas women were not permitted to serve on juries until 1954. As late as 1969, married women did not have full property rights. And until 1972, under Article 1220 of the Texas Penal Code, a man could murder his wife and her lover if he found them "in a compromising position" and get away with it as "justifiable homicide." Women, you understand, did not have equal shooting rights. Although Texas was one of the first states to ratify the Equal Rights Amendment, which has been part of the Texas Constitution since 1972, we continue to work for fairer laws concerning problems such as divorce, rape, child custody, and access to credit.

Texas women are just as divided by race, class, age, and educational level as are other varieties of human beings. There's a pat description of "what every Texas woman wants" that varies a bit from city to city, but the formula that Dallas females have been labeled with goes something like this: "Be a Pi Phi at Texas or SMU, marry a man who'll buy you a house in Highland Park, hold the wedding at Highland Park Methodist (flowers by Kendall Bailey), join the Junior League, send the kids to St. Mark's and Hockaday in the winter and Camps Longhorn and Waldemar in the summer, plus cotillion lessons at the Dallas Country Club, have an unlimited charge account at Neiman's as a birthright but buy almost all your clothes at Highland Park Village from Harold's or the Polo Shop, get your hair done at Paul Neinast's or Lou's and drive a Jeep Wagoneer for carpooling and a Mercedes for fun." There is a kicker equivalent of this scenario that starts, "Every Texas girl's dream is a double-wide in a Lubbock trailer park. . . ." But I personally believe it is unwise ever to be funny at the expense of kicker women. I once met a kicker lady who was wearing a blouse of such a vivid pink you could close your eyes and still see the color; this confection was perked up with some big rhinestone buttons and a lot of ruffles across an impressive bosom. "My," said I, "where did you get that blouse?" She gave me a level look and drawled. "Honey, it come from mah coutouri-ay, Jay Cee Penn-ay." And if that ain't class, you *can* kiss my grits.

To my partisan eye, it seems that Texas women are more animated and friendly than those from, say, Nebraska. I suspect this comes from early training: Girls in Texas high schools are expected to walk through the halls smiling and saying "Hi" to everyone they meet. Being enthusiastic is bred into us, as is a certain amount of obligatory social hypocrisy stemming from the Southern tradition of manners, which does rather tend to emphasize pleasantness more than honesty in social situations. Many Texas women have an odd greeting call—when they haven't seen a good friend for a long time, the first glimpse will provoke the cry, "Oooooooo—honey, how good to see yew again!" It sounds sort of like the "Soooooey, pig" call.

Mostly Texas women are tough in some very fundamental ways. Not unfeminine, nor necessarily unladylike, just tough. It may be possible for a little girl to grow to womanhood in this state entirely sheltered from the rampant sexism all around her—but it's damned difficult. The result is that Texas women tend to know how to cope. We can cope with put-downs and come-ons, with preachers and hustlers, with drunks and cowboys. And when it's all over, if we stick together and work, we'll come out better than the sister who's buried in a grave near Marble Falls under a stone that says, "Rudolph Richter, 1822–1915, and Wife."

Texas Celebrates, 1986

HONKY TONKING

I can remember being embarrassed about liking country-western music, but I can't remember when I quit. It was a long time before they put Willie Nelson on the cover of *Newsweek*. Since there's a country song about everything important in life, there's one about this too—"I Was Country, When Country Wasn't Cool."

Being hopelessly uncool is the least of the sins of country music. Back when I went to college, listening to Dave Brubeck and Edith Piaf was a fundamental prerequisite for sophistication, on a par with losing your virginity. Knowing a lot of Ernest Tubb songs didn't do squat for the reputation of the aspiring cosmopolite.

Country music was also politically incorrect. The folkies were on the right side of issues:

Bob Dylan and Joan Baez sang at civil rights rallies; it seemed more than likely that Bull Connor listened to country.

The Beatles, Janis Joplin, the Jefferson Airplane, the Doors—everybody anybody listened to in the 1960s was against the Vietnam War. From the country side, Merle Haggard contributed "I'm Proud to Be an Okie from Muskogee." (Hippies quickly turned "Okie" into a longhair anthem and Kinky Friedman contributed a version entitled "I Am Just an Asshole from El Paso.")

And to be a feminist country music fan is an exercise in cultural masochism. There you are trying to uphold the personhood of the female sex, while listening to "She Got the Gold Mine, I Got the Shaft" or "Don't the Girls All Get Prettier at Closing Time." Women in country music are either saints or sluts, but they're mostly sluts. She's either a "good-hearted woman" or a "honky-tonk angel." There are more hard-hearted women in country music ("I Gave Her a Ring, She Gave Me the Finger"), despicable bimbos ("Ruuuby, Don't Take Your Love to Town"), and heartless gold diggers ("Satin Sheets to Lie On, Satin Pillow to Cry On") than the scholars can count. Even the great women country singers aren't much help. The immortal Patsy Cline was mostly lovesick for some worthless heel ("I Fall to Pieces") and Tammy Wynette's greatest contribution was to advise us "Stand by Your Man." (Tammy has stood by several of them.)

Not until the great Loretta Lynn, who is also musically lovelorn with great frequency but shows more spunk about it, did we hear some country songs that can be considered feminist. "Don't Come Home A-Drinkin' with Lovin' on Your Mind" is one of Loretta's better ass-kickin' anthems. The high-spirited spoof "Put Another Log on the Fire" is a classic parody of sexism: "Now, don't I let you wash the car on Sunday?/Don't I warn you when you're gettin' fat?/Ain't I gonna take you fishin' with me someday?/Well, a man can't love a woman more than that." Evidence of the impact of the Women's Movement on country music can be found in the hit song "If I Said You Had a Beautiful Body, Would You Hold It Against Me?"

But this is fairly limited evidence of redeeming social value in the genre. So what do we see in it? For one thing, how can you not love a tradition that produces such songs as "You Done Stompt on my Heart, an' Squished That Sucker Flat"? (Featuring the refrain "Sweetheart, you just sorta/stompt on my aorta.") Or "Everything

You Touch Turns to Dirt." Many cultures have popular song forms that reflect the people's concerns. In Latin cultures the *corridos,* written by immortal poets such as Garcia Lorca, give voice to the yearnings of the voiceless. In our culture, "Take This Job and Shove It" serves much the same function.

If you want to take the pulse of the people in this country, listen to country-western music. I first knew a mighty religious wave was gathering when I heard ditties like "Drop-kick Me, Jesus, Through the Goalposts of Life." I also knew the Moral Majority was past its prime and Pat Robertson would go nowhere when I heard "I Wrote a Hot Check to Jesus" on country radio, followed by "Would Jesus Wear a Rolex on His Television Show?"

Contrary to popular opinion, it is not easy to write country songs: many try and fail. One guy who never made it is Robin Dorsey from Matador, Texas. He went to Tech and had a girlfriend from Muleshoe about whom he wrote the love song "Her Teeth Was Stained but Her Heart Was Pure." She took offense and quit him over it, which caused him to write the tragedy-love song "I Don't Know Whether to Commit Suicide Tonight or Go Bowlin'."

Country music is easily parodied and much despised by intellectuals, but like soap operas, it is much more like real life than your elitists will admit. What do most people truly care about? International arms control? Monetary policy? Deconstructive criticism? Hell, no. What they care about most is love ("We Used to Kiss Each Other on the Lips, but Now It's All Over"). Betrayal ("Your Cheatin' Heart"). Revenge ("I'm Gonna Hire a Wino to Decorate Our Home"; "Who's Sorry Now?"). Death ("Wreck on the Highway"). Booze ("Four on the Floor and a Fifth under the Seat"; "She's Actin' Single, I'm Drinkin' Doubles"). Money ("If You've Got the Money, Honey, I've Got the Time"). Loneliness ("Hello, Walls"). Tragedy-love songs ("She Used My Tears To Wash Her Socks"; "My Bride's Wedding Dress Was Wash-and-Wear").

Now here we're talking major themes. In a song called "You Never Even Called Me by My Name," which author Steve Goodman labeled "the perfect country-western song," momma, trucks, trains, and prison are also suggested as mandatory country-western themes.

In this country we waste an enormous amount of time and energy disapproving of one another in three categories where only personal taste matters: hair, sports, and music. We need not review the family trauma, high dudgeon, tsk-tsking, and lawsuits caused over the years by hair and how people wear it. Consider the equally futile expenditure of energy in condemning other people's sports. And in music, good Lord, the zeal put into denouncing rock, sneering at opera, finding classical a bore, jazz passé, bluegrass fit only for snuff-dippers—why, it's stupefying. It's incomprehensible.

I am open to the argument that Ludwig van Beethoven has contributed more great music to the world than has Earl Scruggs. But there is a tiresome neoconservative argument these days that holds relativism responsible for all the evil in the modern world. These folks denounce the abandonment of absolute standards in everything—morality, taste, the postal service. As though the fact that people enjoy reading *The Three Musketeers* were a menace to Dante. I have felt the sting of their snotty scorn, the lash of their haughty sneers, and what I have to say is "You Are Just Another Sticky Wheel on the Grocery Cart of Life."

Ms., September 1988

THE ROMANCE
OF FOOTBALL

Do real feminists like football? Any fool can see it's the ultimate sexist game. Not only do women never get to play, but their only role in the entire proceeding is to stand on the sidelines and root for those who do, not a life-metaphor even Phyl Schlafly would embrace.

I suspect many of us are born liking it; it's a condition consequent to our birthplace. Marlyn Schwartz, who may appear to be a Dallas career woman but who is actually "a Mobile guhl" and always will be, observes, "I can't imagine not liking football because I'm from the South and Texas and I didn't know there was another topic. It was amazing to me when I grew up and finally visited the East and found out people can get through entire dinners without talking about it. But I was also amazed to learn the South had lost the Civil War—we always called it the War of Northern Aggression—which has since led me to suspect there was a lot they left out of my education."

For cultural reasons too complex to go into here, Nebraska women are also congenital football fans, though they are seldom confused about who won the War of Northern Aggression.

Many of us take up football as a lingua franca. If, for example, you live in Dallas, it is possible to strike up a conversation with anyone at all—CEOs, shoeshine boys, your garbageman, or the barkeep—by inquiring, "How about those 'Pokes?" It is useful in the ensuing chat to know whether the Dallas Cowboys have lately won, lost, or are on strike, but not absolutely necessary.

In the reverse-sexism school of feminism, "all those cute asses" is the most commonly cited reason for watching the game. While this may have merit as an aesthetic argument, it is woefully short on principle.

For many women, football is just a social occasion. They enjoy the pageantry if they go in person, and enjoy socializing with their friends even more. They don't give two hoots about the game. Political activist Liz Carpenter, who is sixty-seven, says she liked the game because her late husband Les did. "It is not one of the things I have kept up in widowhood," she said. Carolyn Barta, columnist for the *Dallas Morning News,* said, "For women of my generation, those of us who grew up competitive but were discouraged from competing— we were not encouraged to fight for or compete for anything, especially with men—football was a way of letting out those competitive instincts." You can release a lot of pent-up aggression at a football game.

In Pat Conroy's very Southern novel *The Prince of Tides,* there is much of the lore and romance of the game, but even his protagonist-coach admits, "the only good thing about football . . . the only thing good at all, is that it can be a lot of fun to play." And, as previously noted, that rules us out. On the other hand, that we'll never get to play shouldn't rule us out as fans: I'm never going to figureskate either, but I like to watch other people do it.

A more typical coach in Conroy's novel tells his high school team:

Tonight I'm gonna learn and the town's gonna learn who my hitters are. . . . Real hitters. Now a real hitter is a headhunter who puts his head in the chest of his opponents and ain't happy if his opponent is still breathing after the play. A real hitter doesn't know what fear is except when he sees it in the eyes of a ball carrier he's about to split in half. A real hitter loves pain, loves the screaming and the sweating and the brawling and the hatred of life down in the trenches. He likes to be at the spot where the blood flows and the teeth get kicked out. That's what this sport's all about, men. It's war, pure and simple. Now tonight, you go out there and kick butt all over that field. If something moves, hit it. . . .

"Now do I have me some hitters?" he screamed, veins throbbing . . .

"Yes, sir," we screamed back.

"Do I have some fucking hitters?"

"Yes, sir."

"Do I have me some goddamn headhunters?"

"Yes, sir."

"Am I going to see blood?"

"Yes, sir."

"Am I going to see their guts hanging off your helmets?"

"Yes, sir."

"Am I going to hear their bones breaking all over the field?"

"Yes, sir," we happy hitters cried aloud.

"Let us pray," he said.

As it happens, chess is also a game of war, pure and simple, but it lacks the *je ne sais quoi* so neatly described above.

Football has become real Christian in recent years, a source of distress to many fans. Guys like Joe Namath, Don Meredith, Billy Kilmer—when you saw them on their knees you knew it was because they'd been hit. Nowadays it's hard to tell. Other fans are turned off by the greed and commercialism of the pros and, increasingly, of college ball. High school football remains the last bastion of high-intensity, pure-emotion football. At the recent Texas state championship playoff game between Plano and Houston-Stratford (it's usually between Plano and somebody), a thoughtful fan told me he was rooting for Plano, which is like rooting for Goliath against David. "Because," he explained, "you never forget losing the Big Game, not for your whole life, but even the thrill of being the underdog who wins the Big Game is not as great as the mortification of losing if you are the favorite."

Football is strategically less interesting than baseball but is emotionally more gripping because it is violent. All that hitting and pounding and standing up with a crowd and screaming—it's called catharsis. When the game is well played, it looks easy, it has a rhythm, it's like good sex or great dancing, it's really exciting. Besides, it's cheaper than the movies and a lot more interesting than golf.

Ms., March 1988

IN FITNESS
AND IN WEALTH

Ah, spa. A combination of luxury hotel and summer camp. A week or two of healthy food, exercise classes, and massage. All for a little less than a year at Harvard. Of course, what you get depends on where you spa.

My friend Pankratz and I hied ourselves off to The Greenhouse last year, a fancy place near Dallas associated with Neiman-Marcus. My dears! Breakfast in bed, folks waiting on you hand and foot; drop a towel and before you could pick it up, someone else already had. You got into the hot tub to soothe your weary body after forty-five fun minutes of dancing to show tunes, and some flunky would rush over with a glass of ice water lest you get too hot in the hot tub. After you went into the steam room, they had your shower running to cool you off right away. You would be *appalled* (spa people frequently speak in italics) at how easy it is to get used to that kind of thing.

Spas are big on self-esteem. No matter how much of an uncoordinated blimp you may be, the staffers find something encouraging to say about you in every area of endeavor. Pankratz came back from Walking Clinic and announced proudly, "The instructor says I have perfect stride."

"Perfect stride?"

"*Perfect* stride."

I went off to makeup class and the instructor studied my face for a long time. Just as I was bracing myself for the announcement, "First no-hoper I ever saw," she triumphantly came up with the redeeming feature, "My dear," said she, "you have a *fabulous* space between your eyes."

With a strong sense of one-upmanship, I informed Pankratz that *I* have a fabulous space between my eyes. She promptly topped it: "My masseuse says I have *great* elasticity." I can't compete with great elasticity.

It first occurred to us that The Greenhouse was not our kind of spa when we noticed many of our fellow inmates wearing major diamonds. We have no minor diamonds. Many Greenhousers substitute shopping for aerobics, and the results are awesome. I know because they all dress for dinner. Dirty sweats do not pass muster at Greenhouse dinners. So the first night there, an animated lady given to rattling her diamonds chirruped, "Let's go around the table and say who we're going to vote for in the presidential election." You think they all said Bush, don't you? Nah. All of 'em said, "*George,* of course!"

Came my turn, and I had to confess, "Actually, I'm a Democrat." Not so much horror as genuine consternation followed this announcement. The diamond rattler finally leaned over and inquired, with an expression delicately poised between shock and disgust, "Dear, do you . . . *work*?"

Despite the splendid efforts of The Greenhouse, Pankratz and I once more achieved utter flabdom by the summer, so we decided a tougher place was needed and headed for Baja California to Rancho La Puerta, famed for its vegetarian cuisine, mountain hikes, and New Age thoughtfulness.

In the New Age, none of the vegetables are their regular color— it's all red lettuce, yellow bell peppers, golden beets. It's hard to keep up when you regularly eat chicken-fried steak, but I tried. I tried meditation, visualization, affirmation, tofu, oat bran, herbal tea, t'ai chi, and yoga. I like yoga—at last, exercise without sweat.

They kept telling us we had to get in touch with our bodies. Mine isn't all that communicative but I heard from it on Tuesday morning when I genially proposed, "Body, how'd you like to go to the nine o'clock class in vigorous toning with resistance?"

Clear as a bell my body said, "Listen, bitch, do it and you die."

Great, I'm finally in touch with my body and it turns out to have the personality of a Mafioso. They tell you to listen to your body, so I went to the hot tub instead.

But I'm in favor of the New Age. For one thing, it has historical grounding in the Old Age. Norman Vincent Peale would recognize it at once. So would Emile Coué, who during the 1920s got people to repeat, "Day by day in every way, I am getting better and better."

As Bud Trillin wrote, such matters are best discussed without the words *wacko* or *nutso*: if someone says she believes in the paranormal power of crystals or the curative power of a man who treats hay fever by making sure your toes are properly aligned, the correct response is, "It's a free country."

One day I was at my best class, New Age Relaxation (I was real good at nap in kindergarten, too), and the instructor said in a soothing New Age voice, "Think of something about yourself that you really like. Take it into yourself. Hold it close to your center. Our most important task is to love ourselves, unconditionally. Each of us must do this for peace to be in the world."

I'm thinking, "Oh, shit," because I always have a hard time finding my center and on top of that I can't think of anything about myself I like and world peace depends on this and what can I use . . . then it came to me and I took it right to my center. I have a *fabulous* space between my eyes.

Ms., November 1989

HAIR DUPE

I don't know about y'all, but what I hate most about moving is finding a new hair colorist. Last time I moved was from Dallas, where I had spent three years in the hands of a hair-coloring artiste. The man had made me a redhead, a condition to which I had never aspired and for which I have no natural talent, but you cannot argue with an artiste. You also have to pay artistes a lot. "It's the way I *see* you," he explained.

I moved to South Austin, home of the Bubbas and the Bubbettes, where our municipal motto is "South Austin, Texas, a Great Place to Buy Auto Parts." Figured I'd find some nice lady in a beauty parlor and I could tell her what color I thought my hair should be. Off I went to Groner Pitts's sister's La Delle's Beauty Shoppe, spelled with two P's and an E, on south

First Street, and a hair colorist named Esther Ann. Me and Esther Ann are settin' there lookin' at my roots in the mirror. I say, "Esther Ann, I want to dye my hair natural. Let's color the whole thing silver-gray and then I can let it grow out and I won't have to worry about it anymore."

Esther Ann said, "Honey, I cain't."

I said, "Esther Ann, how come?"

She said, "Dear, you're sprang."

I said, "Do what?"

She said, "You're sprang. You can't have a winter color like silver next to your face, it won't go." Esther Ann is into color charts based on the seasons, just like the makeup ladies at Bergdorf Goodman in New York City. Creeping chic has come to South Austin.

Next Esther Ann and I had to decide what color blonde I was going to be. The range of choices is staggering. How do women make up their minds about all these colors, I asked Esther Ann. She informs me that some women get their hair dyed to match their dogs. If you had an Irish setter or a golden retriever, or even an apricot poodle, that might be okay, but my dog is black with a white spot on her chest. Might be sharp if I ran with a punk set. Wonder what it would look like if someone matched her bluetick hound?

Since blonde is also a popular color for cabinets, you could conceivably dye your hair to match your cupboards and truly blend into the woodwork.

I have a friend who recently stopped dyeing her hair just to find out what color it is. It had been thirty years since she'd seen its natural shade and she was curious. Turned out to be a nice browny-blonde and she likes it so well she kept it. It looks real natural too.

Some shades you never see anymore: a good bleached blonde is hard to find nowadays. Marilyn Monroe, Jean Harlow—where are those blondes of yesteryear? You have to find a five-and-dime in a small town, the kind where the waitresses still sport colored handkerchiefs folded like flowers on their chests, to find that shade of blonde. I like the punk mockery of letting the dark roots show, like Madonna. But Esther Ann informs me sternly that Madonna looks tacky. I'm living in the middle of the White Trash Hall of Fame, but I'm not allowed to look like Madonna. The fashion magazines often ask, "What does your 'look' say about you?" Madonna's says: "Slut!," which is a clear fashion statement, just what the magazines advise.

I'm now a strawberry blonde because Esther Ann didn't want me to make too dramatic a departure from my former condition of redheadedness. I used to cry and wish I were dead for several weeks when somebody changed my hair color. But we live in an era when California bodybuilders dye their hair two-tone, like old convertibles: dark on the sides and blonde on the top. It's hard to look strange anymore.

Ms., September 1988

UNCONVENTIONAL WISDOM

The great quadrennial national circus is upon us: three rings, cast of thousands, red, white, and blue balloons by the ton, red, white, and blue bullshit by the hour, confusion, exhaustion, alcohol, and the fate of the nation.

Part of the fascination of political conventions is their bizarre combinations of humanity. Politics does make strange bedfellows: in 1972 in Miami, Nixon's Secretary of Transportation John Volpe did the frug with Anna Chennault, the Tiger Lady, while a Chinese girl sang "Never on Sunday" in Yiddish. It could only have been a political convention.

One of the main reasons conventions always look like an anthill that's just been stepped on is that several thousand bright people have to develop a new pecking order in less than a week. It takes achievement, reputation, moxie, and ambition to get to be a convention delegate. But though you may be Ms. Everything back in Lard Lake, Indiana, when you get to the Bigs, you have to start over. Meeting and greeting, wheeling and dealing, who do you know and what do you want?

There are those who affect to find conventions boring because they no longer nominate the candidates. I say with Mr. Johnson that a man tired of political conventions is tired of life, for there is at political conventions all that life can afford. Except for peace and quiet. People-watching at its finest. Stars are born at conventions. William Jennings Bryan electrified the Democrats in 1896 with his "You shall not crucify mankind upon a cross of gold" speech. And he had no microphone. Hubert Humphrey in 1948 and Mario Cuomo in 1984 talked their way into national prominence. Last bows are taken at conventions, defeated favorites cheered madly, old champions from yesteryear lionized once more. Sentimentality, low drama, and the occasional display of mob ugliness are staples at conventions. History does in fact get made at the absurd, damned things. In 1932, Franklin Roosevelt flew through a storm to Chicago and became the first presidential candidate to actually accept the nomination in person. FDR made another unforgettable gesture back in '24 when fresh from his bout with polio, he tottered to the podium to nominate Al Smith. That was the worst zoo in the history of conventions. It took the Democratic party 103 ballots to gut itself, shaft Al Smith, and nominate the not-unforgettable John W. Davis. One thousand ninety-eight delegates sweltered in the heat at Madison Square Garden. After the 103rd ballot, a Florida citizen sent a telegram suggesting the party change its symbol from one donkey to 1,098 jackasses.

Sometimes political conventions reflect larger political realities in intensified form. It first became clear to the public that the right wing had captured the Republican party when Nelson Rockefeller stood before the convention in 1964 and was booed so long he couldn't speak. Likewise, it was clear Vietnam had torn the nation apart when it tore the Democratic party to shreds in Chicago in 1968.

Many connoisseurs believe conventions took a turn for the worse in 1952, when television forced decorum upon the assembled politicos. But not that much decorum, if you recall what Mayor Daley screamed at Senator Abe Ribicoff in 1968. (Daley later claimed he was merely yelling "You fink, you fink.") Eisenhower was the first packaged candidate, the first to hire a Madison Avenue ad agency to sell him like a deodorant.

This year we are suffering from the acute excitement shortage caused by the nominees. The Democrats have chosen a policy wonk and the Republicans a fatuous twit. Everyone enjoys inventing lines about how dull they are: Mike Dukakis's idea of a hot night is rearranging his sock drawer; after he won the New York primary, he went out and painted the town beige. The Republicans have put up a man whose most memorable contribution to political rhetoric is "deep doo-doo." Bush thinks "gosh darn" are fighting words.

The purveyors of conventional wisdom are compounding the problem by making rational suggestions about the veepancy. Lloyd Bentsen for the Democrats. George Deukmejian for the Republicans. Or Sam Nunn and Jim Thompson. Or Dale Bumpers and Dick Thornburgh. *Please.* These are tickets of such excruciating blandness, we finally would hold an election and have nobody come. Let's hear a little imagination in the veepancy sweeps. How about Senator Barbara Mikulski because she's peppy and would make Dukakis look tall? Why not Phil Gramm because the Republicans need a Texan on their ticket? Jimmy Carter because he made peace in the Middle East, got hostages out of Iran, and battled a killer rabbit. Bush and Bruce Springsteen. Duke and Cher.

At the Democratic convention, you want to watch what Jesse Jackson does, and what is done to and for him. Whether Dukakis can finesse the Jackson question is critical to the Democrats' chances. According to the polls, if the Democrats seem to be giving Jackson too much (vice president is too much and a cabinet post may be too), or appear to be letting him dictate the party's platform, then they'll lose the South. On the other hand, if they appear to neglect or condescend to Jackson, they'll lose the whole black vote, not because blacks will vote for Bush—they just won't vote. Jackson has a strong record of party loyalty—he worked his butt off for Mondale in 1984 even though many party elders had treated him like a leper. But he has been working so hard for so long, he may not be in full control of his emotions by convention time. It hurts to let a dream go, and emotion and exhaustion play a far larger role in shaping our national destiny than is generally acknowledged. As Bobby Kennedy said of how Lyndon Johnson became his brother's running mate, "None of this ever would have happened if we'd just gotten some sleep."

The Dukakis-Harvard crowd is not likely to deal well with

Jackson—it tends to be a tight, rigid group, short on humor, poor at handling emotion, and of the opinion that a Southern accent indicates a low IQ. A couple of Southern white boys will be doing the negotiating—watch for Bert Lance of Georgia and Jim Hightower of Texas. Jackson must be granted first the intangibles—respect and dignity. He can then play for policy commitments (the high road) or appointments (the power road).

Another thing to watch for at the Democratic shindig is what they do to make Dukakis cuddly. The man has got no Elvis. He needs a charisma transplant. By convention time, they should have found someone who can write jokes for him: if they haven't, it can't be done. He will doubtlessly be forced to do *Zorba* dances for the cameras, and his wife will be brought into play. Kitty Dukakis has some Elvis.

On the Republican side, Bush has to dance a similar tightrope with regard to the right wing, which neither likes nor trusts him and tends to be paranoid in any case. Bush has been assiduously sucking up to this group all year—he got Jerry Falwell's endorsement, declared Oliver North a hero, and has sworn to oppose abortion. But he must move to cement their affection without alienating the bedroom liberals in the party—those who, like the Reagans, are divorced, seldom attend church, and are tolerant of gays. According to Don Regan's book, Nancy Reagan said, "I don't give a damn about the right-to-lifers" and many upper-class Republicans privately feel the same way. The right wing is not about to defect to Dukakis any more than blacks will vote for Bush, but the GOP needs more than their votes: it needs their energy and their enthusiasm, it needs them to lick stamps, post signs, staff phone banks, and ring doorbells. Ronald Reagan's attractive personality has papered over the differences in the Republican party. George Bush's personality is probably not adhesive enough to retain the "Reagan Democrats," the blue-collar, working-class Americans who liked Reagan's flag-waving and kick-ass foreign policy, but who have been shafted by his economic policies.

The differences in the Republican party are not just ideological, they are class differences: this is seen most clearly among Republican women. At the 1984 convention in Dallas, about half the Republican women looked like Nancy Reagan—Adolfo dresses, Chanel suits, hair by Mr. Julius—what Tom Wolfe calls "Social X-rays." The rest of the Republican women were given to polyester pantsuits, weight problems, and the name Wanda. The two camps loathed one another.

Another potential development at the Republican convention is that we'll all come to like George Bush, who is as easy to like as he is hard to respect. Once people get used to his fatuous bonhomie, it's actually rather endearing. He is given to saying silly things—his theory of caribou procreation will long be treasured—but banality is not a sin. It may not help Bush win the election, but most of us could end up being rather fond of him, as people are of Gerald Ford.

One more helpful hint: pay no attention to what the conventions do to the polls. Dukakis should surge after the Democratic Convention—it's the effect of exposure. But the Republicans have the last shot and they have long to prepare. The Democrats will attack and the Republicans will have their responses ready. Then the campaign will start. The polls start to mean something around mid-September. Beware the citizen who becomes passionate about this election—anyone who is capable of convincing herself that either of these candidates bears the stamp of greatness is given to self-delusion. We have here the choice between a Ford and a Chevy. You might get a break on the price with a Ford, maybe a little better service with the Chevy. . . . Talk it over with people who know cars, or in this case, politics. Consult the editorial equivalent of *Consumer Reports.* Make your choice based on the real policy differences between these guys and how their policies will affect your life. You should pay no attention to the razzmatazz, demagoguery, hoopla, and all that jazz. But it's un-American not to enjoy it.

Ms., August 1988

ELEPHANT WALK

Keeping up with sisters of the Republican persuasion will keep a body cheerful all the day long. Upon hearing that Phyllis Schlafly, the most serious case of Episcopal thighs in America, was giving a party with the theme "Laissez les bons temps rouler," I rushed to the scene. There was Schlafly, carefully posed on a marble staircase at the New Orleans Museum of Art, greeting her guests in front of a full-length portrait of Marie Antoinette.

Was it possible I'd been underestimating her all these years—perhaps she has a sense of humor after all. "Let them eat salmon pâté," she would announce. But no. We asked her why she thinks George Bush suffers from a gender gap. She said, "George Bush is married to one wife and he has a gorgeous family. I don't know what more any woman could want." It is hard to imagine.

And did the good times roll? With party girls like Jeane Kirkpatrick there as guests of honor to get wild, need you ask? "Boogie till you puke, Jeane," I cried encouragingly. Texas Governor Bill Clements, asked about the gender gap, replied, "I think George Bush is very good-looking. That Dukakis just can't attract men." With Republicans, it's just rip and read, right off the ticker.

Next day the mad social whirl continued with a National Rifle Association luncheon featuring Senator Phil Gramm and Arnold Schwarzenegger. (Sometimes I think I make this stuff up.) Emcee Charlton Heston noted that the pesky press had been pushing poor Schwarzenegger as to what he, a member-in-law of the Kennedy clan, was doing at an NRA bash. "Arnold, you haven't been in this country long enough to know that if John Kennedy had been alive, he'd have been here too—he was a member!" There is that to be considered.

The selection of J. Danforth Quayle for the veep nomination drove the Republicans to new heights of ratiocination. The ineffable Clements said, "Texas is probably the greatest quail-hunting area in the United States, so we can relate to Mr. Quayle. You find them in the bush. That's where Mr. Quayle is: he's in the bush with Bush." Senator John McCain of Arizona was one of many who predicted Quayle would close the gender gap for Bush because he's so good-looking. Actually, Quayle looks exactly like Princess Di, while Mrs. Quayle looks exactly like Prince Charles. What more could any woman want?

The touching faith of Republicans that women are susceptible to handsome candidates is contradicted by history. In 1960, women voted for Nixon over Kennedy by 54 to 46 percent, thus proving conclusively we don't vote romance, no matter what our other failures of judgment may be. At the Conservative Victory Gala in New Orleans, Bunkie Hunt, Jerry Falwell, Elliott Abrams, Howie Phillips, Don Hodel, and Adolfo Calero were all *ecstatic* about Quayle. The political rule is, if your hardliners are happy, you've made a mistake.

Don Hodel, the interior secretary who makes you wish they'd bring back Jim Watt, is a darling of the right wing. He told the following joke at a luncheon for the Louisiana delegation: "Some things change and some things do not. Who'd have thought someday

I'd be richer than John Connally, more religious than Jim and Tammy Faye, and more of a ladies' man than Rock Hudson?" The audience laughed quite merrily. He added, "I guess I should have told that one at the *other* convention." Where they enjoy jokes about dead AIDS victims so much more.

Listening to Republicans bloviate for hours on end has a curious effect on the brain. When they announce, "And the door prize is breakfast with Ollie North!" you scarcely wince. The usual split between the two flavors of Republican women was once more in evidence. Half the women look like Nancy Reagan; the other half tend to wear polyester pantsuits. The groups loathe one another. The reason Nancy Reagan so memorably snapped, "I don't give a damn about those right-to-lifers," is because they are not of her class. They are pushy and badly dressed and their passionate zeal is dreadfully gauche.

But there is a third strain of Republican women these days. This is the party that threw away its own best female talent because it was feminist—Jill Ruckelshaus, Mary Louise Smith, anyone who wouldn't cater to the new right's social agenda. But while the party's platform and its tone are still firmly in the grip of reactionaries, social reality is all around these people. Their convention was chaired by Liddy Dole, who is, one feels mortally certain, not opposed to the dissemination of birth-control information. Senator Nancy Kassebaum makes sense on many topics without using the rhetoric of the right. Mrs. J. Danforth Quayle is herself a lawyer and, on the face, far brighter than her husband. The only problem with this sort of bright, well-educated, suburban-mom-driving-a-wood-stationwagon school of Republican woman is her smugness. Were this quality something fleetingly felt or observed, one could mark it down to subjective impression, but it comes out in Republican politics as well. Political self-righteousness is not the exclusive property of any one party: what is funny is how indignant Republicans get when they realize that Democrats consider *themselves* morally superior.

One depressing aspect of the Republican convention was the "perfectly lovely family" syndrome—the endless emphasis on the "Father Knows Best" family. Back to the fifties. The Reagans have been using this gig for years now despite abundant evidence their own family is a trifle abnormal. But the world is full of people who do not spring from happy families: it makes their lives that much harder when others wander about pretending to have perfect home lives. The notion that this is the norm is even more dispiriting.

One might well observe that the Democrats are equally guilty of this practice, but in fact Kitty Dukakis is noticeably her own person. Listening to Republicans gossip about her, one senses still that nasty condemnation of any woman who dares to step out of line. The Republicans privately spread salacious gossip about her: Senator Steve Symms of Idaho publicly claimed he had heard that Kitty Dukakis once burned an American flag. And there was an interesting passage-at-arms involving George Bush's sister, Nancy Bush Ellis, a suburban matron from Connecticut. Speaking of Ann Richards' keynote address to the Democratic convention, which included the memorable "silver foot in his mouth" dig at George Bush, Ellis said she thought it was "bitchy, catty, and demeaning to women." *Bitchy* and *catty* are, of course, words used only to demean women. Had Ellis chosen to call the speech mean, nasty, and vindictive—or anything else from the long list of splendid invective our language offers—it would have been less telling. One is reminded of Barbara Bush's having called Geraldine Ferraro something that "rhymes with rich." Apparently genteelisms are a family habit.

Ms., August 1988

GOOD OL' DEBS

When I heard about the Debutantes for Christ, each and every one of whom has accepted Jesus as her personal savior, I knew it was time to start explaining about Texas debutantes. Helen Handley, who was presented by the Order of the Alamo at the Fiesta de San Jacinto in San Antonio in 1933—her title was Pahwarati of Madras, Duchess of the Deep Sea Divers, in the Court of India—has maintained for years that the way we do debutantes in Texas is passing strange. In Helen's family alone, there have been one Queen of Debutantes, one Duchess Butterfly in the Court of the Insects, one Duchess of the Falling Star in the Court of the Universe, and one Princess Horse Chestnut in the Court of the Trees.

Debutantes here do not have coming-out parties at which they wear white gowns and make curtsies to society at private balls. Hell, we have *much* more fun than that. You have to see it to believe it, but Texas debutantes often spend more than $20,000 on elaborate gowns, some with trains that are works of art. In Laredo, there are two sets of debutantes presented annually on George Washington's birthday: the Society of Martha Washington presents mostly Anglo girls: the Princess Pocahontas Council presents mostly Mexican-American girls who dress in Indian costumes, hand-sewn and decorated with beads and feathers.

Some grouch always points out that Laredo is in the poorest part of the United States and there are hungry people within yards of this annual shindig. The official response is that the pageant fosters patriotism and helps keep alive the customs and legends of a vanishing race—besides, it provides employment for local seamstresses.

The most elaborate and prestigious of all the Texas debutante shows is Fiesta in San Antonio, where the gowns are mind-bogglingly costly and ornate. The presentation is made at the Municipal Auditorium, and the girls enter one by one, each dragging an immense train. Instead of a simple curtsy, Texas debs sink slowly to the floor (this requires really good quadriceps) and touch their foreheads to the floor in front of their "dukes." They then look up at the "duke" (you don't want to dwell too much on the symbolism of this posture), and with his permission they slowly rise from the floor (which takes great quadriceps). They are then seated on risers until the entire stage is covered with these immense trains, glittering in the lights.

Texas debs get to do more than make one bow in their hometowns—they can go on the circuit and be presented as visiting royalty at courts in other cities. Another good gig is the Rose Festival in Tyler, where debs can ride in the annual Rose Parade. All this has far more in common with the traditions of Mardi Gras and carnival than it does with the demure deb parties in Greenwich, Connecticut, and Boston, Massachusetts. In Hispanic culture, a girl's *quinceañera,* her fifteenth birthday, is traditionally celebrated as her coming-of-age, and this tradition too has worked its way into South Texas debutante traditions.

In the big cities, Houston and Dallas, the top society debs are presented in standard white but they still do the full kowtow, forehead to floor. In both cities, girls who don't quite make the first social cut are presented at secondary balls with less status. It's a business—for a fee, women will arrange a debut for girls who haven't the social clout to swing it on their own. These girls are sometimes trotted around to shopping malls and supermarket openings just like beauty queens. The black and brown communities in these cities each have a debutante presentation, each extremely elegant and *comme il faut.*

The debuts vary with the personality of the towns. In Amarillo, a perfectly sensible place, a girl can make her debut as a Symphony Belle for $100 and is then obliged to usher at the symphony for the next year. She only has to pay for a $20,000 dress if she wants to join the Fiesta in San Antonio.

The $20,000 limit on dresses is occasionally exceeded. Two years ago, when the daughter of a prominent Houston family was presented, her family turned the pattern for the gown over to the family architect, who improved upon it.

I suppose I should condemn all this on grounds that it is an elaborate display of wealth and snobbery, and a painfully absurd misuse of money when there is suffering all around us. But Texas debutantes are like Las Vegas or a thousand-pound cheese or a submarine sandwich as long as a football field. Doesn't matter whether you like it or not—you have to admit it's really something. Even if you can't define what.

Helen Engelking Mather Handley, who did not "take" as a debutante—she is tall, strong-minded, and flat-chested, any one of which is the kiss of death in San Antonio—says the best part of making a debut is the food and the second best is riding in the parade. "There I was, bowing to the left, bowing to the right, smiling to the left, smiling to the right, when I noticed a great milling in the street ahead of me. As I went by, they cheered like mad—it was the girls from the red-light district. Of course they cheered—we were in the same line of work."

Ms., July 1988

THE WOMEN
WHO RUN TEXAS

Texas, where men are men and women are mayors! The Great State, where the men rope cows and the women run the place! It's a helluva development. Five out of the ten largest cities in Texas currently have women mayors. Over the past few years, seven of the ten have elected women as mayors—Houston, Dallas, San Antonio, El Paso, Corpus Christi, Austin, Garland—and that's not even counting all the smaller fry, over a hundred women mayors in all. In Bubba's home state the folks getting elected are named Kathy, Suzie, Betty, Lila, Annette, and Lynn.

If this had happened in some "civilized," progressive state that is always on the cutting edge of social change—say, Oregon or Massachusetts—it would be considered interesting and encouraging. But no one has ever accused Texas of being in the vanguard of social progress. This is the most *macho* state in the U.S. of A. By lore, legend, and fact, Texas is "hell" on women and horses. Until 1918, the state maintained a legal class consisting of "idiots, aliens, the insane and women," and it's been slow going ever since.

Texas women are socialized to want to be cheerleaders and then beauty queens. Any passable-looking female in the state can become at least third runner-up for Miss Miracle Mulch or Miss Congeniality at the Onion Festival. Texas women's role models are the Kilgore Rangerettes, the Apache Belles, and the Dallas Cowboy Cheerleaders. Football is Texas's state religion and women's traditional role there has been to cheer for the guys. Texas women were never allowed to play.

But now, all of a sudden, Texas women are running whole cities, with multibillion-dollar budgets. Straight from "Hey, honey" and "Yew cute li'l thang," to "Madam Mayor" and "Yes, Mayor, right away."

Just what *is* going on? The outsiders tend to be more skeptical than the insiders about what this all means. Some observers have suggested that women can now get elected as mayors of major cities because male politicians have realized that it's an impossible job, the meat grinder of American politics; not the beginning, but the end of many a promising career in public life. Maybe. The job of big-city mayor does have a killer reputation.

On the other hand, nobody is giving the job away. All these women have had to fight like dogs to get elected, and they still face a host of male challengers ready to spend millions to beat them at the end of every term. The same special interests that have always dominated civic politics—real-estate developers, road contractors, municipal employees—are still here; it's still a high-stakes game and the chips on the table are still money and power. Now the question is whether women politicians will insist on playing for different stakes—like our children's lives.

It's possible that the rash of women mayors in Texas is neither coincidence nor breakthrough, but one more small step for womankind on a long journey. Women across the country have been increasingly active in local politics. Most of them started in areas "traditional" for women: the schools—from the PTA to the school board is not that long a leap. Parks and recreation—from the garden club (never underestimate the garden clubs) and Girl Scout leadership to city parks and recreation is just a short hop. The arts—lots of nice ladies start out in the Junior League volunteering as docents at the art museum as part of a traditional social pattern and soon get hooked on the challenge of the tougher jobs—how to raise money for a new wing at the museum or for a symphony hall, how to put together a political coalition that will back a children's art program. Pretty soon these ladies from the Junior League know an awful lot about how to raise money, organize, build coalitions, get publicity. Friends, they're in politics.

From various city boards and commissions, the next step is the city council. And after a few terms on the city council, why not run for mayor? Dick Murray of Houston, a top political pollster, says women candidates, at least on the municipal level, actually have a slight edge over male candidates: Women are thought less likely to succumb to corruption than men. On the other hand, the drawback for women pols is still money: It's harder for a woman candidate to raise money than it is for a man. Fund-raising networks that support only women candidates, such as EMILY's List, do not begin to redress that imbalance. And there is a "glass ceiling" for women in politics, just as there is in almost every other field: Women can rise only so high, but no higher without exceptional ability.

But the women mayors of Texas have a different take on what this all means. They *do* see it as a breakthrough. Their collective conclusion is, "It's over, and we won." Mayor Kathy Whitmire of Houston says, "There will never be another time when a woman's ability to serve in the public sector will be questioned simply because she is a woman." Mayor Annette Strauss of Dallas says, "Gender and even race are now issues only to a few—qualifications are what people focus on." Mayor Suzie Azar of El Paso says flatly, "There's nothing we can't do."

Tip O'Neill's famous political maxim is, "All politics is local." The following stories of the five women mayors among Texas's ten largest cities, and one suburban Dallas mayor, is pure O'Neill. Their paths to power have been different, and the ways in which they use power are so strikingly distinct from one another that one is tempted to conclude that not one of them could have been elected in another's city.

The Book on Kathy Whitmire is simple: "She's tiny, but she's tough." And if you want to know how tough, consider that Whitmire, five-term mayor of the biggest, brawlingest, sprawlingest, whis-key-and-trombone town in the whole state of Texas, is barely five feet tall. There is such a thing as "sizism" in this world, as well as sexism: Smaller people have a harder time being taken seriously. And here's Houston's Kathy Whitmire, the ultimate li'l-ol-gal—young, tiny, blonde, and irreparably cute. Poor thing even has dimples.

As a result, Whitmire not only compensated, but overcompensated. She developed a glacial dignity worthy of Margaret Thatcher at her most magisterial. No one knew about Whitmire's dimples because she never smiled. In her first mayoral campaign in 1981, Whitmire was the ultimate technocrat, perfectly competent, all evidence of her sex toned down with her severe suits, hairdo, and glasses, and her no-nonsense demeanor. She had an excellent record as the city's controller and could discuss the municipal budget in mind-numbing detail. Her presentation to the world: She's no woman, she's an accountant. (Whitmire is, in fact, a CPA, which explains how she became the city's chief budget officer to begin with.) Houston, happily for Whitmire, is crawling with ambitious yuppies who all dress for success and knew her to be one of their own.

As the years have passed, and Whitmire's self-confidence in office has grown, little shoots of humor have come up here and there, and her image has softened and changed. When she got a new, more flattering hairdo, it made the front page of *The Wall Street Journal.* In addition, the first time she wore jeans in public (her third term) it was front-page news in the local papers. Kathy Whitmire was always a lot more likable than her initial public image, but to talk with her now—this pleasant, competent, straight-shooting, hard-working, really nice woman—is to be reminded of how uptight she used to be. The old defensiveness is gone. She now can show little vulnerabilities and laugh at herself and at the absurdities of public life with new ease.

This year she appointed Elizabeth Watson as the city's first woman police chief. (Whitmire had earlier appointed Lee Brown as the first black police chief in Houston; he was so successful that New York City hired him.) It was a high-profile, high-risk appointment—talk about nontraditional roles, a woman police chief is one right-in-your-face for every *macho* stereotype of authority left in this world. Nonetheless, the appointment received rave reviews and Whitmire said, laughing, "I spent two days with Elizabeth preparing her for the worst, coaching her, giving all this advice because I remember how hard it was for me when I first got elected and got hit with all that publicity. But she's taking to it like a duck to water."

Whitmire's political career is the product of the women's movement, and she never fails to give credit where it's due. Her late husband, Jim Whitmire, also a CPA with whom she had an accounting firm, was another source of encouragement. He had been interested in city politics. However, his health weakened and he died from complications of diabetes, leaving Kathy a widow by the time she was thirty. Not only does she not play on her young widowhood for public sympathy, she never discusses it at all. Jim's brother John is now a state senator, who frequently has political quarrels with his sister-in-law, the mayor. But John Whitmire also says, "Her devotion to my brother during the last year of his life was extraordinary; she nursed him to the end and I will never forget that."

Whitmire, who more than any of the other women mayors devotes endless hours to promoting women's causes, points out, "It's not just women mayors running the state's largest cities. Look who's running Houston—there's a woman head of the state's largest school district, a woman CEO at the hospital district, a woman head of the Housing Authority, a woman president of the Chamber of Commerce." And now a woman chief of police. You don't need to ask Kathy Whitmire if having women in political power makes a difference.

Mayor Annette Strauss of Dallas is, in many ways, Whitmire's opposite. A generation older, she appears soft, feminine, ladylike, a traditional wife and mother, who also is constantly smiling, and has a friendly and warm way. The stock-in-trade here is not competence, but charm. Strauss is a great listener because she knows how much it means to people to be listened to. Her hair is always perfect, her makeup is always perfect, her figure is always perfect, her nails are always perfect (in Dallas, this is *de rigueur*). She often wears those sweet flowered dresses (the expensive kind) with little ruffles around the neck. Very Neiman-Marcus. Strauss's political weapons are persuasion and compromise. She is a consensus creator, both because it is her personal style and because it is the Dallas political style. Kathy Whitmire has real power—Annette Strauss works in a system designed to have a weak mayor and a strong city manager. Whitmire earns $130,000 a year; Strauss is paid $50 per city council meeting. Basically Dallas still operates with a *noblesse oblige,* volunteer city government, which is why the city was dominated for so long by a small financial and social elite. Dallas was an operating oligarchy for most of the century and has been opened up to "outsiders" such as blacks and browns only in recent years and as the result of court rulings.

Strauss may be the most easily and most often underestimated of Texas's women mayors. Because her husband, Ted, is a wealthy banker (and brother of Bob Strauss, the famous Texas wheeler-dealer and former national chairman of the Democratic party), people tend to assume that Strauss is a classic example of the upper-class woman who has never had to struggle for anything. Only those who don't know Dallas make that assumption. Perhaps Strauss would have come up through the traditional Dallas women's power network— Junior League, art museum, symphony, opera, hospital boards and finally to city boards and commissions, and thence to the city council and finally the mayoralty. Except for one thing. The Dallas Junior League didn't admit Jews when Strauss came to Dallas. In fact, the first Jewish member of the city's Junior League was one of Strauss's daughters. Strauss says, "I have encountered more discrimination as a Jew in Dallas than I ever have as a woman."

Annette Strauss's résumé does include all those classic volunteer boards—hospital, symphony, museum. But before she was named to the boards of *the* museum, *the* opera, *the* hospital, one finds in the small print of her résumé several years of service on the Jewish hospital board, the Council of Jewish Women, the Jewish women's federation. She was breaking that barrier with almost every step she took in Dallas.

Strauss's alliances with the city's other "outsiders," the black and brown communities, go way back. There were twenty-five or thirty years of nice, sweet, ladylike, do-good service with the Dallas Black Dance Theater, the Junior Black Academy and so forth—not surprising, except that nice, white upper-class Dallas ladies didn't do that back then. Only Annette Strauss did.

Strauss exemplifies a peculiarly feminine political tactic. One reason she is an unusually effective mayor, even in a weak-mayor system, is because she doesn't insist on taking credit for her accomplishments. That's a really sneaky, underhanded, and useful trick. Probably the only safe generalization about people in politics is that they all have big egos. And they also live on publicity. So anyone who's willing to give away public credit has a huge bargaining chip.

Trouble is, in politics, to have power you have to be perceived as having power. If you keep letting other people take all the credit for what you accomplish, no one thinks you have strength. Women have, out of necessity, always been skilled at indirect manipulation, which in turn creates its own resentments. Strauss is learning to balance all these factors on a city council that features some of the most diverse and difficult personalities imaginable.

Out west in El Paso, where nothing is ever very much like anywhere else, the mayor is Suzie Azar and she is a tough broad. Well, she is. And as a rule, the farther west you go, the better folks like women like that. With Azar, what you see is what you get; she doesn't play games, she is who she is, and she's no softy. She's a good-looking woman who sometimes has to fight a weight problem. She was a divorced mother of two daughters for many years, put herself through college and then married her boss, a rich guy in the liquor business. She likes him and he likes her. His money helped her mayoral race. But it helped even more that she served four years on the city council and that she knows what she's doing.

If you wonder where it came from—that combination of competence and courage that gave Azar the will to fly—well, it came from flying. Azar holds pilot ratings for commercial, single-engine, multi-engine, instrument, and glider aircraft, and is a certified flight instructor. She is active in the Civil Air Patrol, the local air show, and women pilots' groups. Azar is hooked on flying. She tried it once, she liked it, and she just kept doing it. Funny thing about flying—it's one of those occupations that makes women realize their potential. They say, if I can do this, I can probably do almost anything. And Suzie Azar is really good at it.

Lila Cockrell is the role model for all the grandma mayors of Texas and a class act to boot. The only deceptive thing about Cockrell is her looks—grandma to the bone. She might even be mistaken for one of those silly matrons cartoonist Helen Hokinson used to draw for *The New Yorker.* In fact, she is a superb, consensus-building politician. Of all the big-city women mayors of Texas, she is probably the only one who could get elected anywhere—everybody likes her. Now in her second stint as mayor of San Antonio, Cockrell was the woman mayor of the largest city in the country until Jane Byrne was elected mayor of Chicago in 1979. One suspects she won the election in the first place precisely because she doesn't threaten anyone—grannies are always safe and reassuring.

Cockrell left office when her husband, Sid, became ill. He died four years ago, and she was drafted to run again last year. Cockrell has been overshadowed by the man who succeeded her and whom she in turn succeeded—the glamorous, sexy, handsome, articulate Mexican-American political star Henry Cisneros. Cisneros's political career has been brought to a temporary halt in the wake of an adulterous affair that became public. The bet, however, is that he will be back. Cockrell says without a trace of envy, "I don't feel overshadowed because I think I've been able to make a substantial contribution in my own way. Henry is just one of those superstar personalities. He was really a national Hispanic leader, a national figure. Besides, I always felt a lot of the publicity he received was good for the city."

Cisneros was a great builder and planner; unfortunately he left Cockrell with the bills for some of his grand schemes and she recently lost a tax rollback vote to the city's active antitax groups. She will cope. She gives much of the credit for her own career to the League of Women Voters, an estimable organization that has spawned many a political career, not to mention some of the most valuable citizens in the country. Cockrell thinks the struggle for acceptance by women in public life at the municipal level is over. "But when you look at the composition of the Legislature and the Congress, you know we still have a long way to go," she says.

Betty Turner, the mayor of Corpus Christi, is like someone everyone knew in school. She is an "awfully nice girl." She's peppy, kind, cheerful and she's always trying to please everyone. You can't *not* like her. It's as if Doris Day or June Allyson had grown up, become a grandma, and then become mayor. The word everyone uses to describe Turner is *cheerleader,* and she herself claims to be "an avid cheerleader for the city." She, like Strauss, has one of those mayorships with almost no constitutional power: She is practically limited by the charter to cheerleading, acting as a figurehead, and making folks feel better. She came up through the traditional Junior League-to-city council route.

The knock on Turner—the downside of her relentlessly upbeat style—is that she can't say no. This is an extremely common criticism of women politicians; because women are socialized to try to make everyone like them—a socialization further reinforced by politics itself—women pols tend to agree with everyone. Or at least to find some part of the case for all sides with which they can agree. But when an issue cannot be successfully compromised—and some can't—then the losers are apt to end up feeling betrayed by a mayor who has expressed sympathy for their point of view. The process is called waffling, lying, backing down, having no guts, and other less flattering names. All politicians are subject to this tendency, but only women politicians are subject to having it blamed on their sex.

Lynn Spruill, mayor of Addison, a suburb of Dallas, has, like Suzie Azar, a background in flying. Spruill is not only currently a pilot for Delta Airlines but also made naval history in the mid-1970s by qualifying as the first woman carrier pilot for the U.S. Navy. And like many of the other madam mayors of Texas, she worked her way to the top slot over several years of serving on the town council and the local planning and zoning commissions. Appointed mayor pro-tem in 1988 to fill out a remaining one-month term when the former mayor died, she discovered she liked the job a lot, ran on her own the next time around, and was elected the first woman mayor of largely upper-middle-class Addison.

Being mayor is, Spruill says, "probably the most frustrating and also the most wonderfully satisfying of any job I've had." Working in a "small town"—Addison has a population of 9,150—is what makes the work satisfying. "I like talking to people," Spruill says. "I touch people, I can make some difference in the quality of people's lives, make things better. Being mayor makes you feel you did good for the day." She has so thoroughly enjoyed it that some form of community service, she predicts, will always be part of her life.

Meanwhile, she still carries a full-time flying schedule—"I have to make a living before I can be mayor."

One of the shrewdest politicians in Texas is Ruth Nicholson, mayor of Garland from 1982 until her defeat in May 1990. In city government since 1975, Nicholson takes the long view on women in politics: "If you look at the five women among the mayors of the ten largest cities, you'll notice that all had previously served on the city council and that Kathy [Whitmire] had already been elected to citywide office. So we're talking experience and qualifications in every case. Second, notice that in the Southwest generally and in Texas almost exclusively—unlike other parts of the country—being mayor is a part-time or no-pay job." (Whitmire is the only one of the women mayors who makes an executive salary.)

"Now you can say, big deal, who are they going to find, except for a woman, to take a tough job that doesn't pay anything?" asks Nicholson. "But we're getting these jobs now and we didn't used to get these jobs. The fact is that this job does represent the acquisition of power, and it complements the financial gains of women working in the business and corporate worlds.

"But there is a catch-22. Precisely those women who would have previously become members of the city council and then moved on to be mayors are now working in big corporations for real money. But give them another five years, when they start to get to that point on the corporate ladder where men have traditionally done civic things, and you'll see what women with executive training can achieve in politics. I tell you that the women who are being elected now are already much more comfortable with the power aspect of this job than those of us who were elected back when 'women didn't do these things.' It required an adjustment, the idea that *we* had power. Now the women are thoroughly grounded, and they have a shorter learning curve. I'm glad I've been here while all these women were being elected. I can't tell you how much fun that is."

McCall's, August 1990

WHAT'S IN A NAME?

Shit the Dog finally croaked on December 9 after fourteen-and-a-half years of marplotting through life. Shit was the *Texas Observer*'s office dog in the early 1970s and, as such, did a lot to hold down the circulation of the magazine. Many who knew Shit consider her possibly the most worthless dog that ever lived, but they overlook her great talent—Shit had a genius for fouling things up.

As *Observer* dog, it was her invariable habit to greet all our readers who had faithfully climbed up three flights of stairs in order to renew their subscriptions by growling and snapping at them. Whereas, whenever some nut arrived at the office to scream about the communist propaganda we were publishing, she would frisk right up with her tail wagging to kiss him enthusiastically. She was also wont to contribute to the ambiance by going downstairs to pee on the landlord's rug. Our landlord was Judge Sam Houston Clinton, now on the court of Criminal Appeals: he tended to be a little humorless about those episodes.

Her politics weren't all bad: she once bit hell out of Col. Wilson Speir, head of the Texas Rangers. Shit never met another dog she didn't like and on the whole she liked people indiscriminately as well. She did have, however, strong prejudices against bicycle riders, uniformed law-enforcement personnel, and pregnant women. She spent much of her waking life getting into the neighbors' garbage and was fond of strewing it about generously. The acquisition of food was her major life interest and for this purpose she developed a fabulous impersonation of a starving dog. The fact that she was grossly fat much of her life only made the impersonation more impressive. Shit also liked to sleep a lot and never failed to sack out where she would cause maximum inconvenience, at the exact center of the traffic pattern, so people would either have to step over her or trip over her.

I never intended to name the dog Shit. Kaye Northcott foisted the little black puppy off on me with a heartless ploy—left her with me "just for the weekend" and then returned Monday threatening to take her to the pound and have her put to sleep. I was going to name her something lovely, like Athena, but reality intervened. She was the only dog I ever saw that could trip on the pattern in the linoleum, so we called her Shitface for a while, and then it got to be Shit for short and then it was too late.

In her younger years, Shit loved nothing so much as going on camping trips, where the opportunities for getting into trouble were almost limitless. Any trip on which she did not manage to fall into the cactus, steal the steaks, and turn over a few canoes, she considered a waste of time. I developed nerves of tungsten.

When I took Shit to New York in 1976, many people told me it was cruel to keep a ranch-raised dog in a big city. Of course she adored New York—so much garbage to get into, so many other dogs to meet, so little exercise. In a city full of Tsing Luck-poos and Shar-peis, people would look at Shit and say, "Oh, what breed is that one?"

"Purebred Texas blackhound," I always said, and they would nod knowingly and say they'd heard those Texas blackhounds were splendid dogs.

Shit once caused gridlock on the entire Upper West Side. I had found a parking space right in front of my building and so let Shit out of the car off her leash, as it was only a few steps to the door. Most unfortunately, a bicycle rider passed at that very moment. Shit charged into the street barking and snapping at the man, who had a baby in a small seat on the back of the bike. I tried not to call the dog in public, but I could see her knocking over the bike and the baby getting hurt. Clearly an emergency, so I let loose, "SHIT! SHIT!" This caused several neighborhood children to appear out of nowhere and to begin chanting in chorus while pointing at me, "She said a dirty word, she said a dirty word." The guy on the bike, justifiably upset about having been attacked by this beast, got off in the middle of the street and wheeled around yelling, "I'll have the law on you, lady. Letting your dog run loose without a leash is illegal in this city. That animal is a menace. I'm calling the cops."

In the meantime, a woman with an unrelated grievance over the parking space I had just occupied came marching down the block, arms akimbo, saying, "You have some nerve, you went right ahead and took that parking place, you saw us waiting there, but you went right ahead and took it, I can't believe your nerve, we were there first but you took that place. . . ." The kids kept chanting, the biker kept screaming, the lady kept bitching, Shit started running around everybody in circles, traffic came to a halt, then backed up through the red light, then two red lights, people got out of their cars to see what was going on, other people farther back started honking, Shit was delirious with the excitement of it all, the cops came, she attacked the cops, by this time traffic was backed up all the way up Amsterdam and down Columbus. A typical Shit performance.

I loved Shit, but she was quite wearing. I used to think wistfully that other dogs got dognapped or hit by cars. . . . Then one day, Shit did get hit by a car, but she didn't die: it just cost me $700 to get her leg fixed. She gimped around thereafter on this bionic leg, becoming more Shit-like by the year. The dog was a catalyst for trouble, disruption, uproar, consternation, confusion, and bedlam.

She went out with the style we had come to expect from her— hit by a car, but no mere dead dog by the side of the road. Nope, biggest mess you ever saw and it had to be cleared up by Northcott and myself. We got most of her remains into Kaye's plastic laundry basket and took her down to the pound, the two of us a pair of poorly matched pallbearers. The people at the pound were kind, but said they had to fill out a form. They needed my name. My address. And I waited one last time for the question I had answered a thousand times from bemused strangers, enraged neighbors, at kennels, veterinarians' offices, dog pounds, and police stations. "What is the dog's name?"

I had Shit for almost fifteen years. It seemed longer.

Texas Observer, February 1987

A SHORT STORY ABOUT THE VIETNAM WAR MEMORIAL

She had known, ever since she first read about the Vietnam War Memorial, that she would go there someday. Sometime she would be in Washington and would go and see his name and leave again.

So silly, all that fuss about the memorial. Whatever else Vietnam was, it was not the kind of war that calls for some *Raising the Flag at Iwo Jima* kind of statue. She was not prepared, though, for the impact of the memorial. To walk down into it in the pale winter sunshine was like the war itself, like going into a dark valley and damned if there was ever any light at the end of the tunnel. Just death. When you get closer to the two walls, the number of names start to stun you. It is terrible, there in the peace and the pale sunshine.

The names are listed by date of death.

There has never been a time, day or night, drunk or sober, for thirteen years she could not have told you the date. He was killed on August 13, 1969. It is near the middle of the left wall. She went toward it as though she had known beforehand where it would be. His name is near the bottom. She had to kneel to find it. Stupid clichés. His name leaped out at her. It was like being hit.

She stared at it and then reached out and gently ran her fingers over the letters in the cold black marble. The memory of him came back so strong, almost as if he were there on the other side of the stone, she could see his hand reaching out to touch her fingers. It had not hurt for years and suddenly, just for a moment, it hurt again so horribly that it twisted her face and made her gasp and left her with tears running down her face. Then it stopped hurting but she could not stop the tears. Could not stop them running and running down her face.

There had been a time, although she had been an otherwise sensible young woman, when she had believed she would never recover from the pain. She did, of course. But she is still determined never to sentimentalize him. He would have hated that. She had thought it was like an amputation, the severing of his life from hers, that you could live on afterward but it would be like having only one leg and one arm. But it was only a wound. It healed. If there is a scar, it is only faintly visible now at odd intervals.

He was a biologist, a t.a. at the university getting his Ph.D. They lived together for two years. He left the university to finish his thesis but before he lined up a public school job—teachers were safe in those years—the draft board got him. They had friends who had left the country, they had friends who had gone to prison, they had friends who had gone to Nam. There were no good choices in those years. She thinks now he unconsciously wanted to go even though he often said, said in one of his last letters, that it was a stupid, f---in' war. He felt some form of guilt about a friend of theirs who was killed during the Tet offensive. Hubert Humphrey called Tet a great victory. His compromise was to refuse officer's training school and go as an enlisted man. She had thought then it was a dumb gesture and they had a half-hearted quarrel about it.

He had been in Nam less than two months when he was killed, without heroics, during a firefight at night by a single bullet in the brain. No one saw it happen. There are some amazing statistics about money and tonnage from that war. Did you know that there were more tons of bombs dropped on Hanoi during the Christmas bombing of 1972 than in all of World War II? Did you know that the war in Vietnam cost the United States $123.3 billion? She has always wanted to know how much that one bullet cost. Sixty-three cents? $1.20? Someone must know.

The other bad part was the brain. Even at this late date, it seems to her that was quite a remarkable mind. Long before she read C. P. Snow, the ferociously honest young man who wanted to be a great biologist taught her a great deal about the difference between the way scientists think and the way humanists think. Only once has she been glad he was not with her. It was at one of those bizarre hearings about teaching "creation science." He would have gotten furious and been horribly rude. He had no patience with people who did not understand and respect the process of science.

She used to attribute his fierce honesty to the fact that he was a Yankee. She is still prone to tell "white" lies to make people feel better, to smooth things over, to prevent hard feelings. Surely there have been dumber things for lovers to quarrel over than the social utility of hypocrisy. But not many.

She stood up again, still staring at his name, stood for a long time. She said, "There it is," and turned to go. A man to her left was staring at her. She glared at him. The man had done nothing but make the mistake of seeing her weeping. She said, as though daring him to disagree, "It was a stupid, f---in' war," and stalked past him.

She turned again at the top of the slope to make sure where his name is, so whenever she sees a picture of the memorial she can put her finger where his name is. He never said goodbye, literally. Whenever he left he would say, "Take care, love." He could say it many different ways. He said it when he left for Vietnam. She stood at the top of the slope and found her hand half-raised in some silly gesture of farewell. She brought it down again. She considered thinking to him, "Hey, take care, love" but it seemed remarkably inappropriate. She walked away and was quite entertaining for the rest of the day, because it was expected of her.

She thinks he would have liked the memorial. He would have hated the editorials. He did not sacrifice his life for his country or for a just or noble cause. There just were no good choices in those years and he got killed.

Dallas Times-Herald, November 30, 1982

WORDS AND HEROES

★ ★

"Legislators do not merely mix metaphors:
they are the Waring blenders of metaphors,
the Cuisinarts of the field. By the time you let
the head of the camel into the tent, opening a
loophole big enough to drive a truck through,
you may have thrown the baby out with the
bathwater by putting a Band-Aid on an open
wound, and then you have to turn over the
first rock in order to find a sacred cow."

—MOLLY IVINS,
The New York Times Magazine

COPPEEEEE!

Gone. Forever. Gone. Nevermore shall we hear in the newsrooms of our nation that famous cry of yesteryear, "BOOOOOY!" Or even the genteel euphemism that succeeded it as blacks and women made their way into the ranks, "COPP-PEEEEE!" They are no more copyboys. They are one with the dodo bird and the linotypist. *Requiescant in pace.*

There is almost certainly a direct link between the current decline of American newspapers and the disappearance of the copyboy. It's a well-known fact, on the order of the-sun-rises-in-the-east, that newspapers are the most miserably managed of all human institutions. In the Olde Days, who were the only people at the paper who ever knew what was going on? The copyboys, of course. They knew who was sleeping with whom, where the booze was hidden, who made how much, who was on the Shit List, who was off the Shit List, who wrote the Shit List, how to get supplies, and everything else that matters in the management of a great metropolitan newspaper—or even a piddly provincial one.

So now we've gotten rid of copyboys and what's the result? Now *no one* knows what the hell is going on around the place. There is no reliable information anymore, and the upshot is this unappetizing succession of management consultants who keep arriving to introduce Management by Objective, or Zero-Based Budgeting, or the Z Theory, or the G Spot, or whatever nostrum is currently being peddled by the quacks of Harvard Business School. And none of it does any good; we remain hopelessly muddled because none of us can find a copyboy who will tell us, "What *gives*?"

What happened to copyboys was that we traded them in for computers, and it was a bad deal. When VDTs came into the newsroom, we no longer needed a corps of kids to ferry the copy from reporter to desk, book by book. (Books, children, is what we used to type our stories on—they consisted of several sheets of copy paper interlarded with carbons. The copyboys would take the dupes of the story and deliver them to appropriate editors. At Great Metropolitan Newspapers, the books came ready-made and all you had to do was tear off the top part to separate the sheets. Most papers were too cheap for such extravagance and reporters made their own books.) In addition to carrying copy, the boys were gofers with a thousand tasks and talents. They were sent to the morgue for information, to the supply room for equipment and to the composing room with edited copy. They were sent out of the building to get food and drink for those in great need or to fetch errant reporters and editors back from nearby bars. Most of them wanted to be newsmen when they grew up and functioned as an eager set of would-be reporter-trainees, keen to write anything from high school sports to weather boxes.

Some papers dropped copyboys when state laws required they be paid a living wage or put on the company pension plan. Interns and clerks have taken over many of their old chores, but it's not the same. The chief function of copyboys was to answer the cry, "BOY!" Their second most important function was to be ready and able to do absolutely anything else.

Called upon to memorialize and celebrate the late copyboy, newspaperpersons around the nation came up with an avalanche of stories that tend to divide neatly into categories, the first of which is:

The Worthless Copyboy: The *Minneapolis Tribune* once had a copyboy named Harold, who was so lazy and incompetent that when he went out and got himself a second job, working at the Post Office during the Christmas rush, no one noticed it until he showed up again after the holidays.

At the *Omaha World-Herald,* the copyboys were supposed to get the hourly temperature from the weather bureau: this gripping information was then set into a half-column table in six-point type and run on page one. One night a copyboy just got sick of it and stopped doing it. The table had the temperatures until 7 P.M. and then stopped: they were supposed to continue through 2 A.M. The executive editor in this unspecified era was a short, bombastic fellow who came into the newsroom next day to nail the culprit personally. "I want you to know, young man," he said, "that this is the first time since 1933 the *World-Herald* has not published a complete table of temperatures." The kid looked up and said, "What happened then?"

Fred Holley, now a copy editor at the *Los Angeles Times,* recalls that in his younger days on the *Virginian-Pilot,* there was no bridge across the river at Norfolk. The paper had a Portsmouth bureau with about fifteen people in it, and a squadron of copyboys was on duty at all hours to take the ferry over and back. One youth, unhappy with the progress of his career at the *Pilot,* was dispatched on a ferry mission one night and, like Charlie on the MTA, he never returned. Located quite some time later, the fellow was asked what the hell had happened. "When I got to the other side of the river," he reported, "I realized how tired I was, so I went home and went to bed."

Remonstrating with the Worthless Copyboy seems ever to have been a bootless task. Wally Allen, the gentle managing editor of the *Minneapolis Tribune,* was once trying to convince a copyboy who had lost the carbons from the Washington bureau, and who was guilty of other major derelictions, that his career in journalism was at stake. "Shouldn't the managing editor of a metropolitan newspaper have more important things to do?" inquired the kid.

The Copyboy Triumphant: At *The New York Times,* which specialized in improbably literate copyboys—according to Gay Talese, they were not only graduates of Ivy League colleges but many held master's degrees and Ph.D.'s as well—the lads were all keen on spotting errors in copy as they trotted with it from the reporter to the desk. The all-time champion in this field, whose name seems to be temporarily lost, was the copyboy who noticed the misattribution of a line of poetry in a speech by John F. Kennedy. Kennedy had either assigned Robert Lowell's work to someone else or vice versa: neither reporter nor editor had caught it, but the copyboy did.

According to Thomas Hardy of the *Chicago Tribune,* that paper once had a copyboy who was the last sentient human being left at the paper at 4:30 one morning when the City News Bureau sent out a bulletin about a sniper shooting at cars from a highway overpass. The police radios were full of it and the copyboy got more and more excited. The copyboy's superior in the chain of command, the night desk clerk, had taken off a few hours early that night, so on his own initiative the kid woke the slumbering night photographer and sent him to the scene. Alas, by the time the photographer arrived, the cops had taken care of the problem, there was no action, and the photographer returned demanding to know what right a pimply-faced kid had to send him out into the dark and stormy night. They had quite a fight about it, the copyboy maintaining that he was "the ranking editorial person on the floor and therefore the equivalent of the managing editor." The kid was thereafter known as "the deputy M.E."

For many years, *The New York Times*'s chief copyboy was Sammy Solovitz, an elderly gnome. The night of the 1977 blackout in New York City, Solovitz was in his glory. For twelve years, ever since the blackout of 1965, Solovitz had been preparing lest it ever happen again. In the darkened newsroom he went at once to a special supply cupboard and from thence began to pull out the damnedest collection of lighting you ever saw. With a *Times*ian sense of hierarchy, Solovitz gave the kerosene lanterns and best flashlights to the top editors. Lesser editors got the dinner candles and reporters got birthday-cake candles.

The most famous of all *Times* copyboy stories is told in innumerable versions, of which the most artistically satisfying follows:

It was election night in the era when Abe [Rosenthal] 'n' Arthur [Gelb] ran the metro desk. All hands were on deck, much bustle and bellowing. Far too busy to eat, the editors finally sent young John Kifner, the sockless copyboy, out for sandwiches around 11. Kif returned with a fine round of pastrami and hungry editors fell on it like starving dogs, except for Arthur Gelb, as ever, too engrossed in getting out the *Times* to attend to such mundane details as food. Kifner kept passing that perfectly good pastrami sandwich, sitting there getting cold on Gelb's desk. He was but a growing boy and had not been given a moment to eat himself. At last he could stand it no longer, grabbed half the pastrami and in two bites had swallowed the whole thing. Deirdre Carmody, then the city desk secretary, gasped in horror and said, "You have eaten Mr. Gelb's sandwich!"

As well hung for a sheep as a lamb, thought Kifner, and ate the other half. All stood around as though turned to stone by the *lèse-majesté* of it all. Right on cue, Gelb, ever frantic and distrait, windmilled up, looked at his desk, and said, "Who ate my sandwich?" Deafening silence. At last Kifner, with incomparable presence of mind, said, "You did, sir." "Oh," said Gelb. "That's right, I did," and went wheeling off again.

Deirdre Carmody reports that the tale has acquired several inaccuracies over the years. It was an afternoon event and even Kifner did not have the chutzpah to eat Mr. Gelb's sandwich—he wolfed it down under the mistaken impression that it was Carmody's. But Gelb's awful question and Kifner's response are gospel. She adds that Kifner was soon thereafter convinced that his career prospects at the *Times* would improve if he took up socks, and he has since risen steadily to his current eminence as a foreign correspondent.

Weird Copyboys or Copyboys with Weird Sidelines: Some papers, such as the *Times,* hired as copyboys only college graduates who wore three-piece suits, with the object of letting them compete for promotion to reporter. Other papers hired only students as copyboys, with the object of helping them get on in life. And some papers used the slots to fill their promise to the United Way to hire the handicapped. This led to some strange line-ups, with lots of missing parts and a sort of overall mix-and-match effect. The *Houston Chronicle* had one for a while who had seizures every now and then—people got used to it. A newsroom favorite at the Chronk was a copyboy named Brooks Smythe, who sang opera on his own time, had a fabulous voice, and, on occasions of sufficient state, could be persuaded to favor the newsroom with an aria.

The *St. Petersburg Times* had a copyboy/doper for a while at one of its bureaus. The bureau chief was a woman who could uncover a political scandal in a trice but suffered from a private life of appalling straightness. One day as the young man leaned over her desk, a shower of white powder came out of his pocket. "Gosh," said the bureau chief alertly, "why are you carrying baby powder around?"

The only murderer/copyboy I could find on record is of recent vintage. In the early 1980s, the *Milwaukee Journal* had an unusually weird copyboy. At a party at his house, he made a pass at a librarian in the basement, she rebuffed him, so he beat her to death with a hammer, then raped her, then smoked a couple of joints, went back upstairs, and rejoined the party.

The trade seems to have attracted any number of Milo Minderbinder characters, forever wheeling and dealing, copyboys who could get it for you wholesale, or for that matter, hot. Perhaps it was the supply-sergeant aspect of the calling that developed this trait, but it was not universal in the breed. Joe Barta, enterprising copyboy for the *Dallas Morning News* thirty years ago, had a nice sideline in cooking food on a hot plate he had in his locker. He could whip up hot dogs, fried chicken, or soup, and he sold it at a hefty markup, especially during Saturday and Sunday late shifts. This improved his salary of $32.50 a week. Unfortunately, one night Barta's hot plate burned a huge hole into the rubberized desk top of the night editor, Tom Simmons, who was not amused.

Zarko Franks, now retired from a picturesque career devoted to making Hildy Johnson look like a Boy Scout, himself started as a copyboy, "For Silas B. Ragsdale at the *Galveston Daily News* in 1937. I was a helluva copyboy. Got $18 a week and had to bargain with him to get it. I was such an outstanding copyboy that I wrote a piece for the *Quill,* called it, 'Why Can't Copyboys Get a Break in the Newspaper Business.' I was so goddamn good, I couldn't see what they were waiting for. 'Course I never saw the inside of a college until I was 50 years old and took my kid up to enroll him at UT. I used to pay all Mr. Ragsdale's bills, ran errands for him and one of the main things was to get an assignment out of Virginia Gwin, the city editor, a doll. She was one of the few in town who recognized the sleeping genius."

Some who did not start as copyboys were pressed into service. David Nimmer, now with WCCO-TV in Minneapolis, was hired as a reporter on the *Minneapolis Star* with the ink still smudgy on his college degree. "I think I was twenty-three, but I looked like I was thirteen," says Nimmer. "I was wearing my only suit, had a butch haircut. Lee Canning, the city editor, was not enamored of having me there. I was supposed to write zone shorts and obits. That first day I walked past Bev Mindrum's desk, she'd been there about six years, and as I went by, she said, 'Boy, would you run this copy up to the city desk.' I thought, what the hell, I'd better do it. I was ready to salute anything that moved at that point. So I dropped it on Canning's desk and he said, 'What-the-hell-are-you-doing?' Then took me by the sleeve and dragged me over to Bev's desk and said, 'I know he doesn't look like one, but goddammit, he's a reporter.' " (Canning's favorite line, cherished by all who worked for him, was "Slug it Death and move it in takes.")

Many former copyboys made pejorative mention of the copyboy scene in the memorably bad newspaper movie *-30-,* starring Jack Webb. In this improbable confection of clichés, the copyboys are found huddled around bongo drums, singing a calypso tune about the copyboy's life. It's not that far off. Larry Batson of the *Minneapolis Star and Tribune* tells the following story concerning Daryle Feldmeier, later of the *Chicago Daily News,* who was managing editor of the *Minneapolis Tribune* in the mid-1960s. "Once or twice a year, he would take off his robes of state and sit in on the news desk for a night. Everybody hated this. You couldn't go out and get a drink, you had to pretend to be interested in everything. Feldmeier would be bored stiff by seven and he got on the nerves of the copyboys something awful. He was always asking them to go look up something in the library. Well, it was a sports night, so we had four or five extras around, plus the regulars, so there should have been a great cadre, but by 10, they'd all disappeared. There were none. Feldmeier got redder and redder and he kept sending people out to look for them. Finally, he went himself. Checked everywhere. At last he tried the main men's room, a big place with ten or twelve stalls, no one there, he looked round, not a sign, so he turned to leave. Just as the door was closing, he heard a guitar string quietly go, 'Boing.' He stayed by the door, the copyboys came down off the toilets one by one and then gathered around the guitar to smoke and sing softly, 'Hang down your head, Tom Dooley.' "

Girls first started showing up as copyboys in the era of the miniskirt, causing no end of distraction. Blacks came along a little earlier in the North. Roger Witherspoon recalls a famous case at the New York *Daily News*: no one had warned a new black copyboy about the traditional form of address. At his first summons, this son of Harlem decked an editor. "As I understand it, he got canned," says Witherspoon.

A good squad of eager-beaver copyboys could spark a whole newsroom. The *Arizona Republic* had a complement of them fifteen years ago. They hired high school students and Dan Hansen, now head of AP's Boston photo bureau, became head copyboy at eighteen. He proudly recounts the current professional standings of the kids he hired—one is a columnist for the *Orange County Register,* another is photo editor for AP's Los Angeles bureau, another is doing well in public relations in Phoenix, one is a successful freelancer in San Francisco, one is still at the *Gazette.* He says diplomacy was a key part of the job. "We were the liaison between the news department and composing. An editor would say to me, 'You go downstairs and tell that son of a bitch to move his ass.' I'd go downstairs and say, 'Mr. Cobb, Mr. Franks requests that you please. . . .' The guy in composing would say, 'You go back upstairs and tell that bastard to go to hell.' So I'd go upstairs and say, 'Mr. Franks, Mr. Cobb said to tell you they're not quite ready yet.' " Hansen started work the day Patty Hearst was kidnapped and followed the story with such passionate intensity that it almost broke his heart that she was finally caught on the P.M.'s time. He also became fascinated by the Don Bolles murder case and volunteered to run errands and do research for the Investigative Reporters & Editors team that came to Phoenix to work on it. He was the kind of copyboy who would turn out anytime, day or night, with cables to jumpstart a reporter's cranky Volkswagen.

They are all gone now—all the eager beavers and the goof-offs and the weird ones. Copyboys were, above all, wise to things, they knew. If an editor was in a foul mood, they would warn reporters. If a deskman came in drunk, they would warn an editor. If a reporter was in a bar about to miss a deadline, they'd call the barkeep and have him sent home. But they only did it if they liked you. Copyboys punished the grumpy, the rude, and the arrogant by never telling them anything. Without them, our internal communication has gone to hell and our manners have gotten worse. And no one even knows where or when the last copyboy disappeared to or who was the last newspaper reporter to shout, "COPP-PEEE!" Even for a craft frequently accused of having no sense of history, this is a lamentable failure of documentation. It can only be hoped for the sake of their eccentric tradition that the last copyboy was canned for insubordination.

THE LEGISLATIVE MANGLE

L egislative language is governed by a law of etymology that is also the ancient code of the bureaucracy. It doesn't have to be right, it just has to be close enough for government work. If they understand what you mean, it doesn't matter what you say or how you say it. In most legislatures, punctilious attention to correct usage is considered elitist. The word *government,* for example, is normally pronounced "gummint"; *bureaucracy* is "bureaucacy"; *fiscal* comes out "physical," and one moves not to suspend the rules, but to "suppend."

These are not malapropisms or mispronunciations—which is "mispronounceciations" in legislative circles. Nor are they the result of ignorance, bad diction, poor enunciation, or the regional speech deformity called a

Texas accent, or a Maine accent, or a New York accent. Graduates of Harvard do the same things to these words as lawmakers who flunked out of Texas A & I do, no matter where they serve.

The universality of odd legislative pronunciations, particularly of the words most commonly used in the course of parliamentary business (pronounced "bidness" in Texas) stems from the very frequency of their use.

"Mr. Speaker?" "For what purpose, Mr. Doaks?" "Will the gentleman yield for a question?" "Mr. Pitts, will you yield to Mr. Doaks for a question?" "I yield, Mr. Speaker." "Mr. Doaks, the gentleman yields."

This exchange may occur 100 or more times a day. Little wonder it gets boiled down to the interrogatory "Gennlemunyiel?," followed by the affirmative "Gennlemunyiels."

Anyone who has ever spent time listening to a legislature knows the astonishing speed at which all presiding officers and reading clerks can spit out the formulaic incantations of parliamentary procedure.

Another influence on the odd things that happen to words in a legislature is the elementary political principle that it's dumb to make people think you think you're smarter than they are. It's not just bad manners, it's bad politics. The result is a kind of linguistic populism, a mad rush to identify with the common man, in which everybody picks up everybody else's errors of speech, and over time many of them become institutionalized.

All the entering freshmen pick them up, because God forbid anyone should mistake them for the kind of fancy-pants, smarty-pants, snot-nosed snob who would point out to a Chevy dealer from Lubbock that the name of the nineteenth-century poet is Lord Byron, not "Lard Barn"—and then sit back and think he has scored a point. This is particularly true if the presiding officer of a chamber is given to the mangling of a word; no one wants to make the speaker feel dumb, so the speaker's mistakes become part of the institutional heritage of a given chamber.

If you listen long enough, you can trace linguistic oddities back to their originators years after those distinguished former members have gone to glory. Certain mistakes have such charm and originality that they are adopted as improvements on the original—especially if they come up often and will relieve the tedium of a verbal formula.

Good presiding officers are gifted at this kind of thing. Billy

Wayne Clayton, a former Speaker of the Texas House, contributed "intimate domain," which is much nicer than "eminent domain"; "the sediment of the House" (as in, "It's the sediment of the House that we adjourn for dinner"); "Let's do this in one foul sweep"; "quid pro crow"; "ominous courts bill" for "omnibus courts bill"; "Let me give you an analogous," or "I've got an analogous for you." That last is a variation on the familiar, "Lemme give ya' a hypothetic," which I believe can be traced to Renal B. Rosson of Snyder, who served in the Texas Legislature in the 1960s.

The incumbent Speaker of the Texas House, Gib Lewis of Fort Worth, is such a gifted malapropist that his speech is called Gibberish, and his best efforts—known as Gibberisms—are prized and imitated even in the Senate:

"Disperse with the objections" and get on with the vote. "This is unparalyzed in the state's history." "I want to thank each and every one of you for having extinguished yourselves this session." "I cannot tell you how grateful I am—I am filled with humidity." "This legislation has far-reaching ramifistations." "It could have bad ramifistations in the hilterlands." "This problem is a two-headed sword: it could grow like a mushing room." "We don't want to skim the cream off the crop here." "We'll run it up the flagpole and see who salutes that booger."

If something is unusual, it's "adnormal." If he's confused, "There's a lot of uncertainty that's not clear in my mind." "Economic diversity" becomes "economic versatility." If you need to cut the budget, you should not fire people but do it through "employee nutrition."

Stanley Steingut, former Speaker of the New York Assembly, was a master of the mixed metaphor, having contributed the immortal "Dis bill, if passed, will derail da ship of state." My favorite was his explanation of a slow-starting session: "Dis session has been hit by an avalanche of creepin' paralysis."

The New York City Council was the cradle of two splendid contributions in this field: "What is being scattered to the winds here is just a drop in the bucket." And, "As we debate dis bill, da sword of Damocles is hangin' over Pandora's box."

Anyone left befuddled by the language, not to mention the logic, of a legislative presentation is apt to be greeted with the old stopper, "I can 'splain it to you, but I can't understand it for you."

In Congress, there are some who are unashamed to aspire to

eloquence, even to scholarship, but the only state legislator I ever knew who would not join in the mispronounceciation of a word for the sake of camaraderie with her fellows was former State Senator and Congresswoman Barbara Jordan. But then, as the first and only black woman ever to serve in the Texas Senate, Jordan knew she would never be one of the boys.

The New York Times Magazine, September 17, 1989

KILLING THE
MESSENGER

A few years ago, Jules Feiffer drew an Everyman who offered, in serial panels, these observations about the state of the nation:

1. Truth hurts.
2. Before truth, this was a happy country.
3. But look what truth did to us in Vietnam.
4. Look how the truth fouled us up in the 1960s *and* the 1970s.
5. Truth has changed us from a nation of optimists to a nation of pessimists.
6. So when the president makes it a crime for Government workers to go public with truth, I say, "Hoorah!"
7. And when he bars the press from reporting our wars, I say, "About time!"
8. America doesn't need any more truth.
9. It needs to feel better.

Ronald Reagan, Feiffer observed elsewhere, represented "a return to innocence; a new moral, ethical, and political Victorianism. Reagan's Victorianism transcends truth. It circumvents politics. It gives America what it demands in a time of insoluble crisis: fairy tales."

Lately, through no initiative of its own, the American press has been debunking fairy tales and once more telling depressing, pessimistic, hurtful, unhappy truth. With predictable results. "The nation's news organizations have lost substantial public esteem and credibility as a result of the Iran-Nicaragua affair . . . according to a new Gallup Poll for the Times Mirror Company," said a front-page story in *The New York Times* on January 4.

What we have really lost is popularity. People don't like being roused from the rosy Reagan dream that it's morning in America, so they turn on the messenger who brings the bad news.

Here is a sample—a letter to the editor of my local paper, the *Austin American-Statesman*: "Like sharks circling, the news media are in a feeding frenzy. They would love to bring down a very popular President. From the beginning, President Reagan's foreign policy has been under attack. First it was Grenada, but that turned out to be a triumph; next it was the bombing of Libya. During that attack we were deluged with quotes from *Pravda* and TASS, but, alas, that too was a triumph for Reagan."

The letter writer, Jean Whitman, continued: "The media are delighted that irresponsible and traitorous Congressmen are leaking top-secret information to them. . . . Consider the media score: They loved Castro, hated the Shah; they champion the leaders in Zimbabwe and Angola, where tribal murder is now common; they champion the African National Congress, a communistic party, in South Africa. They ignore the plight of Afghanistan. They so divided the country, making heroes out of the SDS and Jane Fonda, that the real heroes came home to hostility after fighting a horrible war in Vietnam."

Whitman is as serious as a stroke, and while there may not be many citizens who hold her detailed agenda of grudges, the 17 percent drop in confidence in the television news and the 23 percent drop in confidence in the credibility of newspapers uncovered by the *Times-Mirror* poll do represent a kill-the-messenger response.

The reaction is predictable, of course, but that isn't helping the press deal with it. Like the Supreme Court, the press follows the election returns. And the press, like politicians, wants to be popular.

The trouble with waking up America so rudely, after six years of letting it slumber happily in dreamland, is that we're now being greeted with all the enthusiasm reserved for a loud alarm clock that goes off much too soon. "Ah, shaddap!" "Turn it off!" "Throw it at the cat!"

And when the going gets tough for the press in America, the press fudges, the press jellies. That's what we're doing now. We are retreating to a fine old American press cop-out we like to call objectivity. Russell Baker once described it: "In the classic example, a refugee from Nazi Germany who appears on television saying monstrous things are happening in his homeland must be followed by a Nazi spokesman saying Adolf Hitler is the greatest boon to humanity since pasteurized milk. *Real* objectivity would require not only hard work by news people to determine which report was accurate, but also a willingness to put up with the abuse certain to follow publication of an objectively formed judgment. To escape the hard work or the abuse, if one man says Hitler is an ogre, we instantly give you another to say Hitler is a prince. A man says the rockets won't work? We give you another who says they will.

"The public may not learn much about these fairly sensitive matters, but neither does it get another excuse to denounce the media for unfairness and lack of objectivity. In brief, society is teeming with people who become furious if told what the score is."

The American press has always had a tendency to assume that the truth must lie exactly halfway between any two opposing points of view. Thus, if the press presents the man who says Hitler is an ogre and the man who says Hitler is a prince, it believes it has done the full measure of its journalistic duty.

This tendency has been aggravated in recent years by a noticeable trend to substitute people who speak from a right-wing ideological perspective for those who know something about a given subject. Thus we see, night after night, on *MacNeil/Lehrer* or *Nightline,* people who don't know jack-shit about Iran or Nicaragua or arms control, but who are ready to tear up the peapatch in defense of the proposition that Ronald Reagan is a Great Leader beset by comsymps. They have nothing to offer in the way of facts or insight; they are presented as a way of keeping the networks from being charged with bias by people who are themselves replete with bias and resistant to fact. The justification for putting them on the air is that "they represent a point of view."

The odd thing about these television discussions designed to "get all sides of the issue" is that they do not feature a spectrum of people with different views on reality: Rather, they frequently give us a face-off between those who see reality and those who have missed it entirely. In the name of objectivity, we are getting fantasyland.

The Progressive, March 1987

THE PERILS AND PITFALLS OF REPORTING IN THE LONE STAR STATE

The *Houston Journalism Review,* may it rest in peace, once got me to set down my beliefs about being a reporter. Reading it now, I conclude that I was quite an idealistic young thing. Even odder, I still believe it all.

I think the reason the editors of this publication asked me to write an article on the pitfalls of being a reporter is because it's clear to them that I have fallen into every pit possible. I'm not insulted: I see it as an opportunity to practice participatory journalism. And a little advocacy journalism as well: there are a lot of pits out of which you should stay.

I have yet to enter into sexual congress with any of my news sources (which probably reflects as unfavorably on their appeal as it does favorably on my good sense), but apart from that, I believe I've hit all the pits. The first was cynicism. As a fledgling female reporter I had two splendid models to choose from—Brenda Starr and Poteet Canyon. But I hadda go and choose Hildy Johnson to imitate. Bogey in a trench coat figures in there somewhere, too. It is my considered opinion that Hildy has done more harm to American journalism than Frank Munsey, Spiro Agnew, and Everett Collier, combined. Generation after generation of pimply-faced kids have come staggering out of J schools and into city rooms pretending to be characters out of *The Front Page*. At least young reporters just pretend to be cynical. With most older reporters, cynicism is a habit. A stupid, vitiating habit sustained by sloth.

During a discussion of corruption in Texas politics not long ago, one of Houston's finest remarked, "Look, baby, that's the way it always has been and that's the way it always will be." Whereupon he took a particularly worldly toke off his Pall Mall. He should only get lung cancer. Failing that, he should get his ass out of journalism.

Being a cynic is so contemptibly easy. If you let yourself think that nothing you're working on is ever going to make any difference, why bust your tail over it? Why care? If you're a cynic, you don't have to invest anything in your work. No effort, no pride, no compassion, no sense of excellence, nothing. You can sit around on your butt for most of the day, because, as has been proved time and again on Houston newspapers, you don't really have to produce much of anything to pull down $160 a week. The rest of your time you can spend in bars impressing young reporters with your worldly wisdom.

Best get yourself straight early on about why you're in this business. Not for the money, we trust. Some people are in it because it's so seldom boring, which I regard as an acceptable excuse. This next part is extremely sticky because it's a damn sight simpler to criticize other people's ideas than it is to set forth your own. One is never in so much danger of making an ass of one's self as when one is engaged in saying, "This I believe . . ."

Having adequately prefaced my credo, I'm ready to fire. I believe that ignorance is the root of all evil. And that no one knows the truth. I believe that the people is not dumb. Ignorant, bigoted, and mean-minded, maybe, but not stupid. I just think it helps, anything and everything, if the people know. Know what the hell is going on. What they do about it once they know is not my problem.

The discerning reader will have noticed several pitfalls in the preceding paragraph. For example, the people pit. I have meditated on the people pit and have come to the conclusion that it has always been there and always will be. Reporters are constrained to think of readers and viewers and listeners abstractly, a great, gray blob, out there. But what amazes me is the ubiquitous reportorial attitude which holds that the masses *out* there are the masses *down* there. Every newspaper I've ever worked on has had a Mythical Average Reader. In Minneapolis, our MAR was the retarded wife of a North Dakota farmer. In Houston, I am told, the MAR is an Aggie sophomore.

Any good teacher will tell you that aiming at the lowest common denominator is poor practice. In communicating anything, you do better if you aim slightly above the heads of your audience. If you make them stretch a little, they respond better. If you keep aiming at the dumb ones, you never challenge them and you bore the hell out of the bright ones. You also commit the grievous and pernicious error of thinking that the people is dumb. One of the most horrific results is that the people start to think so themselves.

If in fact you hold that the people is dumb, if that attitude is not a pose, you're in the wrong business. Go join an ad agency.

The people pit cannot be cured, but it can be ameliorated by knowledge. Every reporter in Houston should know and know well Bellaire, Pasadena, The Fifth Ward, River Oaks/Memorial. You should know those areas and the people in them on a good-or-better basis. You should have friends in those areas and you should know the areas geographically, sociologically, historically, economically, and culturally. S'funny, once you know people you tend to care about them.

Also, in cultivating your regard for the people, the readers, it helps if you don't read the letters-to-the-editor column.

The kind of contempt for readers represented by the MAR concept is what leads reporters into the Great Pit, the most absurd perversion in our business. In-ism has become so acute that a reporter can be generally defined as a person who knows, but doesn't tell. You can find out more about what's going on at the state capitol by spending one night drinking with the capitol press corps than you can in months of reading the papers those reporters write for. The same is true of city hall reporters, court reporters, police reporters, education writers—any of us. In city rooms and in the bars where newspeople drink, you can find out what's going on. You can't find it in the papers.

There is a degree to which the structure and values of the

Establishment press are responsible for this phenomenon. Reporters learn early on that there are certain central truths they cannot tell readers—for example, the governor of Texas is definitely a dimwit. Such truths are invariably denounced as subjective or even subversive observation and are edited out forthwith.

But reporters, in general, tend to fall in with the Establishment's limitations on truth with alarming complaisance. It is as though we had internalized the restraints. Despite the fact that most of us object to them intellectually, we obey them unconsciously after a while. There's not a major newspaper I know of in this country that's going to let you tell it like you find it. But that's no excuse for giving up. You have no business sitting around with your friends over beers telling them what *really* happened at today's city council meeting. The very least you owe yourself and your readers is to try to get out what you know. Playing the get-the-facts-straight-and-let-the-truth-go-hang-itself game is management's bag. Your obligation, your responsibility is not to the management of the *Houston Post,* the *Houston Chronicle,* or the *Houston Whatever.* It is to yourself, to your own standards of excellence, and to your readers. If your readers don't know as much as you know about your beat, you're a failure. So damn many of us write about the surface and save the juicy stuff for our friends; we can dine out on what we don't put in our stories.

You know and I know that it's not easy to get the truth into newspapers—so much of it is not family fare. But you can't have been in this business for a year without learning at least the basics of all the gimmicks there are for getting the stuff through. The curve ball, the slideroo, the old put-it-in-the-17th-graf trick. Tell your editor the opposition will have the story in its next edition. Show 'em where *The New York Times,* or better yet, the *Dallas Morning News,* has already done this story. If you haven't got enough points with management to pull off a strong story on your own, give it to one of your colleagues. Find another angle on it. Localize the hell out of it. Disguise it as a feature.

Or, you can use the Janis Joplin-Zarko Franks take-another-little-chunk-of-their-ass-out technique. The inimitable Zarko, the Chronk's city editor, was grousing one day about all these g.d. kids he's got working for him who want to tell the Truth allatime, fer Chrissakes. "I tell 'em," said Zark, "you can't tell the *truth*, honey, this is a *daily newspaper.* Every day these kids wanna write "War and

Peace." I tell 'em, look, baby, today you just tell the readers a little bit of the truth. That's all we got room for. Then tomorrow you go back and you pick up another little piece of the truth. And the day after that, another piece. You'll get it all eventually, but you ain't never gonna get none of it if you shoot for the whole wad every day."

If all else fails, pass your story along to the *Texas Observer.*

Whatever you do, don't give up. Because all you can do once you've given up is bitch. I've known some great bitchers in my time. With some it's a passion, with others an art. With all of them, it is a dissipation of the energy they should be putting into reporting. I know, I know, the reason why newspeople bitch so much is because they've got a lot to bitch about. It's still a waste of time. Think Pollyanna. Read George Bernard Shaw or go listen to Ralph Yarborough. Anything but full-time bitching.

One of the most depressing aspects of reporters-as-a-group is that they tend to be fairly ignorant themselves. There is no excuse for it and there is a complete cure for it. Read, read, read. At least one good paper every day. It's kind of fun to switch them around: Monday, the *Christian Science Monitor*; Tuesday, the *Louisville Courier-Journal*; Wednesday, the *Washington Post*; Thursday, *Le Monde*; Friday, the *L.A. Times*; Saturday, *Manchester Guardian*; Sunday, *The New York Times.* Better yet, all of them every day, plus the major papers in Texas. You should be reading every good magazine you've ever heard of and most of the bad ones. Concentrate on opening your mind. If you're 55 and straight, read *Rolling Stone.* If you're 25 and hip, *Reader's Digest.* If you're liberal, read the *National Review*; conservative, read *New Republic.* You should be reading at least one good book a week—history, anthropology, sociology, politics, urban problems. If you were a fine arts major, read about economics. If you were a business major, find out about ballet. I'm not joking about any of this. You have got to stretch your mind, further and further. The alternative is letting it congeal, harden, and contract. You must be able to see more and understand more than most folks or you're never going to be able to explain what you do see to most folks. This isn't elitist; it's just part of the basic job requirement—the same way a pianist has to keep his hands limber or a mechanic will start boning up on the Wankel. It's your job, that's all.

George Orwell wrote a preface to *Animal Farm* concerning freedom of the press, which was published for the first time a few months ago. In it he speaks of the phenomenon of voluntary censorship, of the orthodoxies of fashionable thought and how subtly we censor ourselves. In order to be able to resist intellectual fashions, you have to be well informed. Very well informed. I sometimes think that reporters should be required to go through an experience analogous to that required of psychiatrists, who must themselves be analyzed before they are allowed to practice. We need to be aware of our own biases in order to compensate for them, aware of our own vanities and weaknesses.

Reporters need to be people people. It helps if you're an extrovert, but it's not necessary. I have frequently been amazed, when taking a colleague along to a meeting of radicals or blacks, to find my colleague actually afraid of such people. I find it absurd and wrong when reporters are ill at ease with people, just plain people, who happen not to be like them. There are reporters who simply can't deal with anyone who's not white, college-educated, middle class. I'm not sure whether that's sad or funny, but I know it doesn't make for good journalism. I don't know how you learn to relate to people—listen to them, I suppose. Spend enough time around very different kinds of people so that they don't strike you as odd. Maybe read some of the *I'm O.K., You're O.K.* genre of interpersonal relations. Dale Carnegie, anyone?

As a final thought about job qualifications, I'd like to suggest to you that it's racist for any Texas reporter south of Lubbock not to be able to speak Spanish.

One of the happy side effects of doing a lot of reading is that it will improve your writing, which needs it. Would you like to know why people don't read newspapers anymore? Because newspapers are boring. Dull. Tedious. Unreadable. No fun. I don't need your excuses: I read both Houston papers every day and I'd rather listen to local television news myself.

An editor once told me, "Adjectives and adverbs are dangerous words." There went half the English language. "Facts," Norman Mailer said to Judge Julius Hoffman, "mean nothing, sir, without their nuance." Nuances, I grant you, are very damned hard to get by the copy desk. Every desk has someone on it who is convinced that both *whispered* and *screamed* mean the same thing as *said.* I dare say, we have all seen our fair share of murmurs, croaks, rasps, shouts, and gasps bite the dust, not to mention all the adjectives and adverbs of our lives. Nevertheless, recalling previous pits, you will be neither cynical, discouraged, or bitchy about this. Right? Right. You will try. And try again. And again. And you will smile. Because it's so much healthier than crying or throwing up.

Be comforted, good writing is the wave of the future. *The New York Times* gets more readable every day: it's hard to find a pure-fact pyramid story in a good paper anymore. They throw in little hints now about what the facts mean. If you do get discouraged about trying to bring a little humanity into your writing in the face of constant desk opposition, think of yourself as part of the anti-anomie brigade. Fight alienation. Get on John Donne's side. There are too damn many lonely people in the world who just can't handle it, who are afraid of other people, who don't understand what's going on, who fear change. It doesn't help them to get a newspaper plopped on their front stoops every day that reduces the whole rich, human, comic, tragic, absurd, exasperating, and exciting parade of one day's events into a dehydrated lifeless set of unrelated facts. We keep writing about events as though they were pictures on a wall, something we could stand off and look at, when in fact they are the stuff of our lives. The news gets sanitized, homogenized, pasteurized, dehumanized, and wrapped in cellophane. No wonder people forget they're human. Fight it. Use adjectives.

Which brings us to the serious pitfall. That is, taking one's self seriously. In a way, I'm afraid to broach this one, since there's no shortage of cynics to remind us that the product only costs 10 cents and most people use it to wrap their fish.

How easily we come to accept the power, such as it is, that we carry around with us. I imagine most of you have had the experience, on an investigation, of walking up to some crook and saying, "I'm Joe Smith from the *Daily Hallelujah*" and watching the poor beggar start to sweat. Now there's a power trip. So is watching a pol, as you whip out your notebook, shift out of his normal style, get glassy-eyed, take on a fake heartiness, and say, "Well now Joe, let me tell you about my stand on that issue. . . ." The mayor calls you by your first name. So does the superintendent of schools and the head of the black power movement in town. Not to mention the bartender at the Press Club. You're in with the big people, all right. With any luck at all, Ben Barnes not only remembers your name but stops to josh with you about the time you asked him a tough one in Amarillo. Preston and Sissy never remember anybody's name, but it's In to know that, too. You got people you can drop in on. Big people in this town. Developers, bankers, lawyers, judges. They all know you. Hell no, you never have been asked to join the Cap Club, but you drink there a lot. Mecom, Mischer, Moody. Been in a few poker games with the judge. . . . Remember the time the mayor asked me, he said, Joe . . . Talked to Herman about that the other day . . . Wortham, Welch, Wyatt, Winchester . . . Ike Arnold says . . . Hell, ol' Percy hisself told me she was guilty . . . Guy I know knows Connally real well and . . . Saw George Brown at the Petroleum Club with . . . Heard the latest 'bout Gertrude . . . Stumpf, Cummings, L.C. . . . Roy's real sick . . . Palm's craziern a loon . . . Barbara'll take Curtis with no sweat.

Sure we talk about the biggies among ourselves with our best Hildy Johnson sneers on. And we all have our Genuines for comfort—those Real People we discovered all by ourselves, usually on feature assignments. The lady in Baytown with twelve kids who got her engineering degree when she was forty-seven; the woman in the Heights with kidney disease who won't take charity; the black dentist who thinks he's got the answer on biodegradable cans; and we all have our favorite welfare case, don't we? And we all keep going back to the Cap Club, don't we? Dugger once said of John Connally, "He never messes with the top waters." In the Cap Club, that's a compliment. Look, we know the movers and the shakers because they make news and that's what we write about. But watch your ass, reporter, or you'll wind up like most of your brethren—a power groupie. Power is an insidious commodity. It's fascinating. Once you get into who's doing what to whom for why, it's as addictive as smack. And it works the same way: you need more and more of it and you produce less and less. You start to identify with your sources and then you're gone. You spend so much time with those people that you can't imagine the city being run in any other way. "That's the way it always has been and that's the way it always will be, baby." That's why it's called Establishment journalism. You concentrate on the people at the top, the people with power; you watch, you study how they make their moves, you get fascinated by it, and pretty soon you can't see anything else—just the top, just the power. And the others, the people, the readers, matter so little that you don't even bother to let them know what's going on. You start to think like the people you cover. It can happen on any beat—business, police, politics, education. The stuff you want is from the top—you want to quote the chief, the superintendent, the chairman of the board. There are no reliable sources who earn less than $10,000 a year.

There are ways to kick the habit. Institutional reporting (Haynes Johnson on labor), human reporting (Ernie Pyle on a war) investigative reporting (Sy Hersh isn't talking to General Lavelle about that illegal bombing—he's talking to the pilots who did it.)

Cultivate clerks and secretaries. They haven't got as big a stake as their bosses in covering up what's going on. There's no point in asking Herman Short about police brutality. Go look at Johnny Coward's foot and eye and chest. Don't listen to the president of Armco tell you about ship channel pollution: go look at the ship channel.

Do not go to press conferences. An abomination. A manipulative device. Stop letting sources get away with lies because they hold high positions and titles. The *Chronicle* ran a front-page story not long ago about some astronaut blasting the government for cutting back the space program. The astronaut was quoted as saying that 80 percent of the federal budget went for welfare programs. Don't let him get away with that just because he's an astronaut. Right after that quote, the *Chronicle* should have run the actual percentage of the budget that goes for welfare programs. There's no excuse for spreading misinformation just because it comes from someone in a high place.

I am told that a Houston editor is fond of reminding his reporters, "This is not a crusading newspaper." I think that's too bad myself, but I could live with it. Us crusaders screw up with alarming frequency, too. Don Rottenberg, late of the *Chicago Journalism Review,* declared in his farewell article, "There are still places where people think the function of the media is to provide information." I'd settle for that. And I don't think you should settle for anything less.

Houston Journalism Review, January 1973

ROBERT SHERRILL

I meant to start by claiming that Robert Sherrill is the Last Free Journalist in America, but he'd spot that for meretricious merchandising. The evidence for the claim is that Sherrill works for himself, thinks for himself, and never has given a damn who he pissed off. That doesn't make him unique. But you must admit, the combination is precious rare in our craft nowadays.

Sherrill prefers to be called an "independent writer" because, he says, many people think a freelance is the equivalent of a Buddhist monk out begging with his bowl. Okay, but calling Sherrill independent is like calling a dwarf short. As morals-to-the-story go, it's a pleasure to report that Sherrill is actually sort of mildly rich and famous these days. Quick, tell a Yuppie: cantankerousness pays. He appears to be obstreperously healthy, but we can rest assured he will die someday. I move the following epitaph for his tombstone: HERE LIES A MAN WHO NEVER KISSED ASS. Then we might add: P.S. AND HE NEVER DRESSED FOR SUCCESS EITHER. (Sherrill generally wears clothes about the level of formality of blue jean cut-offs and a shirt that seems to have survived use by most of the Navy through World War II. He has one of those strong Scotch-Irish faces that sort of wobble between ugly-strong and handsome-strong. Actually, what he looks like is a more rugged, solid version of John Connally, a description that will doubtlessly disgust him.)

There's always the danger Sherrill will be mistaken for some journalistic manifestation of a Clint Eastwood character—particularly given his notorious pugilistic exploits. Actually, he's an unusually civilized man. Willie Morris, in his book *North Toward Home,* described the Bob Sherrill of twenty-five years ago thus:

> He was already a veteran reporter who had written, in the old tradition, for some twenty-five papers all over America. When he grew tired of one town, or began to hate an editor's guts too much for his own sense of balance, he would simply depart for another, usually in the dead of night. Sherrill was a painter and a poet, and had once worked briefly on a Ph.D. at an Ivy League graduate school before concluding that the city room of any middle-sized daily was more civilized and usually more literate. He was also a cynic, but with a soft underspot he almost never showed, and he joined the *Texas Observer,* as he told me at the time, to see if idealism existed, and if so whether it was worth the effort.

Sherrill is chagrined by what he refers to as "Willie's romanticism." This is gentle of Sherrill, whose normal reaction to anything he finds saccharine is, "It makes me puke." Sherrill says he had worked on more than a dozen papers, "but certainly not twenty-five." His other quibbles are equally self-deprecating. There is one pained note: "I certainly did not tell him that I joined the *Observer* to see if idealism existed. I would never make such a private observation, even to a friend of twenty years, much less to a stranger, as Willie was to me then." That's consistent with Sherrill's extraordinary personal reticence. His friend W. E. (Ned) Chilton III, publisher of the *Charleston* (West Virginia) *Gazette,* says, "He is a very private person and a very shy person." Sherrill is a mean writer, but a modest and gentle man. Usually. He says he "jumped like Nijinsky" at the chance to join the *Observer* because he wanted the freedom that makes that paper attractive.

Sherrill is the son of an itinerant newspaperman; mother a Texan, father a Georgian. His first newspaper job, straight out of high school in 1942, was as a copyboy on the late, largely unlamented *Fort Worth Press*. From 1948 until 1960, Sherrill worked on small and medium-sized dailies in California, Arizona, Texas, and Tennessee. In between newspaper jobs he got a master's in English from the University of Texas, another from the University of Minnesota and dropped out of a doctoral program at Cornell. He also taught English at the University of Texas, Texas A & M, and the University of Missouri during those years. His opinion of academia is even lower than his opinion of newspapers:

> When I started there weren't more than half a dozen newspapers worth a damn. I never worked on any of the good ones. And I didn't improve the lousy ones I worked on. Here and there I worked on the copydesk, though I can't spell for beans. Once I was a sports editor, but I could never remember which teams were in the National and which in the American League. I was a farm reporter for awhile but never wrote about anything memorable. Except cattle bloat.

Sherrill denies that he used to quit because he hated editors. "I found them mostly just a boring lot who sat around with their thumbs in their ears trying to second-guess the publishers' wishes, little realizing that the publishers never thought of anything but the cash register. Occasionally I even worked for an editor who was charming, either in a serenely simple-minded or a serenely grubby fashion." Of the former, he recalls a West Texas editor, "a really likeable guy in his way, who went around the newsroom whistling hymns, and occasionally stopping to give a reporter a friendly lecture about how 'every thing in West Texas is news,' a theme that would prompt him to send us chasing off hundreds of miles to interview some half-drunk sheriff about some diddly situation." Sherrill remembers one sheriff who insisted on being photographed while kissing the barrel of his six-shooter.

When accused of poetry, Sherrill is apt to produce some astonishing verse to refute the accusation ("Nun On An Analyst's Couch" has to be read to be believed). Perhaps Sherrill's most famous oeuvre is an ode to Charles E. Greene, a memorably bad editor of the *Austin American-Statesman* in the 1950s. Greene wrote a weekly column, full of dreadful stuff. (Ironically, Texas' most prestigious journalism awards are named after Charlie Greene.) One day Greene held forth on how delightful it was to hear the sonic booms made by hotdog pilots from Bergstrom AFB. "Every time I hear a boom, I feel more secure," wrote Greene, ever a man to favor our country's peace forces. The booms were knocking the rest of the citizens of Austin off their chairs, causing no small degree of annoyance. The Austin paper also ran a Poetry Corner in those days, which printed offerings by local poets. The week after Charlie Greene's moving tribute to sonic booms, the following pastoral, "A Barrier Broken" by Mrs. T. U. Merde, appeared in the Poetry Corner:

Sound of our warriors
Hovering High!
Invincible guardians
Threading the sky!
Only for freedom
Never for conquest!
Crashing in speed, come
Eaglets of splendid zest!
Greet us with bombast!

The message in the left margin was spotted that afternoon by a deskman. There was unanimous agreement around the rim that the culprit must be that s.o.b. Sherrill, except for the dissenting opinion of a guy who'd known Sherrill since they were copyboys together. "If it was Sherrill," claimed this old pal, "he'd've spelled shit with two *t*'s."

Sherrill the painter stays equally hard to dig out from behind Sherrill's obdurate refusal to put himself forward. He paints well enough so that Chilton, who doesn't appear to be blinded by friendship, keeps a portrait of himself done by Sherrill in his office along with a Thomas Eakins.

There are a lot of great Sherrill stories from the newspaper years, but let's leave it that, whether you agree with him or not, Bob

Sherrill earned his right to his opinions about American journalism in the trenches:

> Daily newspapers out in the boonies are, or were, better than working in a textile mill, but not because they required much more intelligence. But even if they have improved in quality, dailies of all sizes still seem to have been produced on the same assembly line, if you judge them by their attitude and their degree of sophistication. [*New York Times* reporter] Clyde Haberman recently wrote from Tokyo, "Journalism in Japan, although practiced by highly trained, dedicated people, has a way of appearing to be an exercise in sameness." My God, could he possibly have been implying that U.S. journalism *isn't*? Whether you pick up the *Chico Register* or the *New York Times,* the menu is going to be pretty much the same. They are all journalistic Howard Johnsons. No, worse than Ho-Jos. They advertise twenty-eight flavors but serve only vanilla. Maybe a little weak strawberry now and then. The reason is obvious: money. I saw the other day the New York Times Co. earned more than a billion dollars last year, and the Washington Post Co. earned nearly a billion. Shit, you think the czars of those outfits—and the same goes for the *L.A. Times* and the *Chicago Tribune* and all the rest—are newspaper people? Don't be silly. Their view of "news" is absolutely the same as Iacocca's view of cars or Calvin Klein's of pants. It's just an item of commerce.
>
> To say that the people who run news corporations are part of the establishment is obvious. . . . Ben Bagdikian likes to remind people that Hearst, Pulitzer and E. W. Scripps, at least when they started out, were protectors of the masses—when was the last time you heard that word used?—against the oppression of big corporations. They were arousers. The corporate descendants of those men would be embarrassed to run the stories and editorials those guys did because they were so radically hostile to big business.

Like all press critics, Sherrill likes to pick on *The New York Times* and the *Washington Post* because they are supposed to be the best:

> But they're grossly overrated. They are timid, pompous, often shallow and soggy with self-interest. This isn't the fault of their

reporters. They have some great reporters. It's the fault of the top brass. Neither paper has anyone near the top with one-tenth the guts of Ned Chilton. He loves to do battle with the establishment. He loves to call corporate crooks and political crooks just that—crooks. He's always being sued and you know what he does? Sues 'em right back. He'll fight something right up to the U.S. Supreme Court, and you won't hear him complain—as you hear the owners of the bigger papers—about the cost. His motto is—"Sustained Outrage." I think he is the most refreshing publisher in the business.

Chilton likewise loves and admires Sherrill, but points out, "Yeah, I have adopted 'Sustained Outrage' as my motto, but guess who gave it to me, who suggested it? Sherrill. But he wouldn't tell you that. He's too shy. Same way he won't go out and plug his books. He won't do any radio or television shows to sell his books. Me, I'm a ham, I'd love to go out and do it for him—hell, no one knows what he looks like, I could show up and say I'm him."

One other publisher has earned Sherrill's approval over the years, even though he considered the guy's politics gaga. Sherrill once worked for the Hoiles chain, a group that was and still is of Libertarian conviction. Old Man Hoiles was fond of saying, "Any publisher who has more than three cars in his funeral procession is a failure."

There are a couple of ways to be a free journalist in America. One is to have enough money to tell the world to go to hell. Sherrill is free in that way. Another way is not to fear being poor. Sherrill is free like that, too. He observes that one great advantage of having worked for the *Texas Observer,* that fragile outpost of liberalism, is that one learns to live off the land. In my own days at the *Observer,* the business manager lived under the Addressograph and the reporters stole pencils from the governor. "It breeds a kind of coyote craftiness," says Sherrill, who has slightly more ennobling recollections of how we covered an entire state on no money.

Among other things, working on the *Observer* will teach a body that all the griping reporters do about not having enough time or enough money or enough horses to do the Big Story is mostly so much eyewash. It doesn't usually take that much time or that much money or that many horses. What you need more than anything else is to get up off your butt and go do it. Another reason Sherrill is free is that the man works. Good Lord, does he.

After three years on the *Observer,* Sherrill moved along to the *Miami Herald* as a political reporter. During this time he researched and wrote much of what became *Gothic Politics in the Deep South.* The book is a classic. You shouldn't cover Southern politics unless you've read it. Sherrill next managed to get himself fired by the *St. Pete Times* for spending too much of their time writing for magazines, so he started doing it full time. "My next total immersion in poverty" is how he describes his move to Washington, D.C., a place not notably in need of another journalist. He and his wife, Mary, had just under $500 in the bank and that remained their "cushion." "Boy oh boy, we worked our ass off," says Sherrill. It should be explained that Mary Sherrill does much of the research for her husband and also knows how to spell. Theirs is an exceptional partnership, but since this is not about her, that's all you get to know. Except that she's musical and smokes cigars.

"One year I wrote seven pieces for *The New York Times Magazine.* We worked constantly. All in all, I did thirty-nine pieces for the *Times Magazine.* At first it was just the *Nation* and the *Times* that kept me alive, but just barely. Then I began picking up assignments from *Playboy* and *Esquire* and a whole raft of others. Meanwhile, we were shoveling out books. We've done seven trade and two college texts."

Sherrill says of his literary offspring: "If they weren't the highest quality, at least they were biodegradable." Actually, most of the books got excellent reviews—four were praised on the front page of *The New York Times Book Review* and *Saturday Night Special* was nominated for a National Book Award. It is still the definitive work on handguns in America. One of Sherrill's textbooks, *Why They Call It Politics,* has now reached its fourth edition. Sherrill observes dispassionately that none of his books was a "red-hot seller." He also regards almost all publishers as thieves and rotters: I understand this opinion has wide currency amongst authors. (Sherrill has a penchant for elaborate titles or subtitles, *Military Justice Is to Justice as Military Music Is to Music* [1970] being an example.)

Ronnie Dugger, himself an independent journalist and publisher of the *Texas Observer,* says, "Sherrill's greatest pleasure is in detonating quasi-liberal Democrats, like Kennedy." His first book was a natural for a Texan in Washington in the mid-sixties: *The Accidental President* (1967) about Lyndon Johnson. It was probably the meanest thing written about LBJ until Robert Caro's book came out, and it's more readable than Caro. Sherrill is always readable. His style is literate, sardonic, mordant, periodically punctuated by some truth stated so bluntly it sort of makes your teeth hurt. *The Drugstore Liberal* (1968) about Hubert Humphrey and *The Last Kennedy* (1976) about Senator Edward Kennedy both follow Sherrill's liberal-bashing tradition. Sherrill both dislikes liberals and is one—he dislikes especially those liberals too gutless to admit that's what they are.

Sherrill's last book, *The Oil Follies, 1970–1980,* did not get particularly good reviews. He is currently working on a biography of Jimmy Carter, who probably deserves it, and another college textbook.

Sherrill believes his chief accomplishment in life is having survived as an independent writer. He attributes his survival to "fortuitous circumstance—I was lucky enough to be thrown out on the street when Lyndon Johnson was president. The *Observer*'s reputation as the scrappiest paper in Texas helped me a lot in Washington. Everything I wrote about Johnson was read as though it had a special sting, when in fact my way of calling him a vicious horse's ass was no better than the way used by many non-Texan reporters."

Sherrill claims another advantage in those early days in D.C.— he was banned from the White House. The Secret Service refused to grant him a press pass on grounds that he was "a physical threat to the president." They wouldn't tell him why and they wouldn't let him appeal, so he sued them. The ACLU took the case and it required nine years to rehabilitate Sherrill's reputation. "By that time I didn't give a shit whether I got into the White House or not. In fact, by that time I had come to the conclusion that it was the *last* place in Washington to get anything remotely resembling news. But after the court victory, just for a joke, I had Victor [Navasky] list me on the *Nation's* masthead as 'White House correspondent.' "

Well of course Sherrill wouldn't whine about being shut out, though he admits, "I would have liked to attend some of Nixon's press conferences, just to see up close if he looked like the sweaty little rat we knew him to be." Sherrill dwells happily on the glamour of being banned. He claims that, next to being remembered by your high school classmates as the big football hero who made the last-minute touchdown, the best thing is being remembered as the guy who got kicked off the team for pouring sugar in the coach's gas tank.

It's nice that Sherrill thinks he got noticed in Washington because he'd been with the *Observer* and because he was the kid who got chucked off the team. He does not attribute his success to the fact that he is an exceptionally fine journalist. Others do. He would also point out that his "success" shines like a mere candle compared with the sun of some titan of the trade like, say, ABC's Geraldo Rivera.

Sherrill wound up on the Secret Service blacklist because he duked out two guys who thoroughly deserved it, runs the short, objective version. His first trip to Fist City took place in Texas: Sherrill fell afoul of a coach/principal in the Panhandle who didn't want him gathering information about the schooling of migrant laborer kids. "We fell into a vigorous discussion which left him with slightly fewer teeth," recalls Sherrill. According to *Observer* lore, Sherrill had left the town and was driving back to Austin when he got so mad thinking about this dork that he turned around and drove back 200 miles just to have this discussion.

The second case occurred in Florida. The governor's ex-press secretary had been set up with a witch-hunting committee to investigate homosexuality among teachers and other such fine topics. Sherrill wrote several stories for the *Miami Herald* concentrating on the more humorous aspects of the proceedings. So the fellow in question sent a letter to every member of the legislature calling Sherrill a liar. This made Sherrill quite angry: "I wasn't a liar." So when the fellow next passed through the press room, Sherrill called upon him to apologize, and when he didn't, "I struck him with righteous wrath. He got a very sore jaw out of it and I got a fine, but my colleagues at the *Herald* passed the hat to pay it." I have heard this gladiatorial passage described in Washington as "the time Sherrill decked the governor of Florida."

These are the only two times on record that Sherrill ever hit anyone, but he does have a lousy temper and a short fuse. He is prone to quarrel, even with dear friends. They just wait until he gets over it. Sherrill and Dugger once didn't speak for an entire year, which wouldn't have been so silly except they lived across the street from each other. Mary Sherrill and Jean Dugger thought it incredibly stupid and went right on being close friends. Sherrill sets extremely high standards, for both himself and others. He quarrels with friends on matters of high principle. He quarrels with publishers and editors about money and editing. Simple and compound stupidity and inefficiency can also set him off. He is not a tolerant man. When he loses his temper he yells and roars and can be rather frightening. Why he lived in Washington for so long passeth all understanding: he cannot abide bullshit and Washington is the bullshit center of the universe. The one thing that will touch off Sherrill's deepest, unremitting anger is injustice. He does not forgive those who do real harm: the long piece he did for Ned Chilton's paper on the tenth anniversary of Richard Nixon's resignation from the presidency is a masterpiece of sustained outrage. I believe the only honor Sherrill has ever earned that he would want mentioned in a profile like this is that he made Richard Nixon's first White House Enemies List.

Sherrill doesn't think a freelancer thrown loose in Washington today could survive. "In the first place, you have to earn so much more money. We never paid more than $200 a month for rent or house payments. More important, there were more outlets for my kind of stuff then. *Playboy* was still very much into social issues. Today it's mostly interested in pieces about how to change a flat tire on a Mercedes without messing up your Guccis. 'Life-style' is now the thing at some magazines that used to be looking for scrappy political pieces. Some of the magazines I used to write for are dead. *Ramparts* gone, *Scanlan's* gone, *Pageant* gone, *Saturday Review* gone." Also with the wind is *Lithopinion,* "the most beautiful magazine you ever saw," according to Sherrill. Put out as a showpiece by Local One of the Lithographer's Union in New York City, Sherrill edited it in his spare time for a spell. You couldn't buy it: they gave it away. It cost $6 an issue to produce and it was, truly, beautiful.

"When the *Nation* was run by Carey McWilliams, I felt it was the greatest magazine in the world," says Sherrill. "It's spirit was the spirit of Western populism, prairie populism because it reflected the spirit of Carey, who was a Westerner through and through. Under Victor Navasky, it is an Eastern magazine, not populist, but New York liberal. I don't fit into that crowd. Don't get me wrong: I admire Victor greatly. I've never met anyone kinder or gutsier. But he sees the world differently and he is more of a showman than Carey. Even the *Nation* is affected by the same ailment that afflicts all the other opinion magazines and certainly the daily press. Gene McCarthy once said that every presidential candidate talks about what he's going to do domestically, but when he is elected and gets to the White House he discovers he doesn't have the kind of power that can change things much domestically. So he plunges into foreign affairs and forgets domestic problems. For whatever reason, the press these days seems to have done the same thing:

It seems to have grown tired and dispirited when it comes to reporting domestic problems. Foreign affairs is the big thing now. Consumer issues that used to be so big hardly get a mention these days. The press used to love to tear the ass off specific politicians. Now the tearing is comparatively perfunctory. I don't have a good guess as to why this is. But I think it is because so many of the reforms have gone sour, in whole or in part, that there is a general suspicion that under the present system of government the United States is ungovernable and lasting reform unachievable, but they are afraid to suggest radical changes. Now, when conservatives—and some liberals, like Teddy—have sold the public on the sport of kicking regulation, is when the *Nation* should be crusading for the return of regulations. I mean *crusading.*

Sure, labor unions are generously loaded with bums and cheats, which is exactly why the *Nation* should be talking about them as a living force and one that is worth cleaning up and reviving. If anything has silenced the voice of the left wing, I think it is the minorities. For years, the welfare of the minorities was the number-one theme of us do-gooders. But now the problem isn't so much lifting them up as it is knowing what the hell to do with them. My answer is that the liberal press, and the press in general, should stop treating the minorities as special citizens. They should criticize the hell out of them when they get out of line.

We kicked this around happily, sitting by his swimming pool like a couple of reactionaries grousing about the cost of yard-help. So how do you dump on the minorities for repellent behavior without setting off the bigots? Sherrill was not so long in Washington that he has forgotten the real world: Despite the peculiar delusions of the neo-whatsits on the East Coast, the country does not suffer from the excesses of liberal governance. Conservatives have always run the Real World and they still do (the R.W. being everywhere in America except Manhattan, D.C., and Minnesota). Sherrill thinks we need a sort of liberal suicide squad to dump on our own sacred cows—black and brown folk who act like pigs, gays who harass merchants, unqualified minority teachers who think they're entitled to special protection. "I wouldn't mind being called a racist as long as I had a chance to get some debate going," says Sherrill. He's also looking for some magazine that'll let him propose that we tax hell out of the churches if they open their holy yaps one more time about abortion, prayer in the schools, or anything else. No one really thought Sherrill was going to spend his golden years playing shuffleboard, but what a relief to know he gets more cantankerous as he gets older.

Sherrill and Mary live on several acres of pine forest out on Old Dirt Road outside Tallahassee. Old Dirt Road is, in fact, an old red dirt road, running through country that reminds you that "perfumed air" is not just a cliché of romance fiction. Martin and Melba, the poodles, love it out there in the woods. (Martin of the *Times,* so registered with the A.K.C., is named after the late Martin Waldron, who was one of Sherrill's closest friends.) The house is lovely, jammed with art and books and Mary's musical instruments; they have a real studio for painting. Sherrill seems a bit restive here, but one of the better things about the Real World is that someone with Sherrill's passion can make a big difference. No sooner had he arrived to take up residence once more in the Sunshine State than he was pitchforked into a topic that stirs up enough bile and decibels to satisfy even Sherrill. The problem is that the state of Florida is executing people who are hopelessly insane, or, as Sherrill so elegantly put it, "frying whackos." After Sherrill had published a particularly Sherrillian account of this barbarity, the governor sent one whacko to the state nuthouse and the state supreme court ruled that another condemned man had the mind of a moron and couldn't possibly have aided in his own defense.

Dugger believes Sherrill left Washington out of disgust with politicians and American politics. Dugger calls him an "outrigger journalist," like the great canoes that can sail across oceans alone. "Everything in journalism today is institutional," says Dugger. "Sherrill is not a person who's against affiliating with institutions, but a person who doesn't stay with them or identify with them. He keeps whole his sense of himself. His celebrated truculence is part of being that kind of inviolable journalist, I think.

There is also a great humility about Sherrill. It is easy, because of the aggressiveness of his work, to underestimate his humility and tentativeness. He's damn sure what shouldn't be done, but part of the puzzle of Sherrill is that he's not more assertive about what he believes to be the good. He is always somewhat in proximity to the precipice. I think there is a poetic idealist working at his center. That active anger over injustice, that boiling of idealism from the red-hot bottom of the pan. He is really generous with his colleagues: that's the other side of his 'cut 'em off at the knees' style. He is a complex man. I think he's one of the most important journalists in the country and that people in journalism schools ought to be studying him.

Ned Chilton says, "He's *sui generis.* I think both he and Mary are kind and simple. Simple in the sense that they don't want much except honesty and decency. They are honest and decent with each other and with their friends. I think he's a beautiful man."

Washington Journalism Review, November 1985

BEULAH MAE DONALD

Some heroes are not swift or strong and they do not look like Sir Lancelot. This one is old and tired and overweight: the height of her worldly achievement was to work as a hotel chambermaid. She has "the sugar," diabetes, which leaves her weak; ironic that someone with her strength should be so frail. Tragedy can strike anyone, but only heroes face it with the grace and courage shown by Beulah Mae Donald.

The Ku Klux Klan murdered her youngest son, lynched him, and after a long struggle to get justice, Beulah Mae Donald finally sued the Klan herself. A poor, uneducated black woman, raised in Mississippi more than a half century ago to fear the Klan, she sued them, and won. She won a $7 million judgment and now owns Klan headquarters in Alabama, but the money is of no interest to her except to help others.

They found his body hanging from the tree like a strange fruit on a cold Mobile morning in August of 1989. A nineteen-year-old black man-child named Michael Donald, shy outside his family, a student at the state technical school who worked part time at the local newspaper. Michael Donald loved to play basketball and to watch football on TV and he was just crazy about music. He was a sweet young man, the much-loved baby of a large family, and would do anything his mama told him to—mop a floor, hang out the clothes, cook the supper. It was a family joke the way Michael would wait on his mama. "Some childrens gots to prove they are grown by the way they don't mind you anymore," says Beulah Mae Donald, who has forgotten more about children than most of us will ever learn, "but Michael was not that way."

They had taken him off the street at gunpoint the night before, dragged him into the woods, and hit him more than a hundred times with a heavy tree limb while he begged them over and over, "Please don't kill me." They finally did it by putting a noose around his neck and pulling it while they beat him until he collapsed, and then they slit his throat three times just to make sure. Then the murderers took his body back to town and strung it up in a tree in a vacant lot across the street from their own house. The next morning they called a television station. The television crew arrived before the police did.

Then came squad cars all over the place and neighbors and crowds of curiosity seekers. Members of the Mobile Unit 900 Klavern of the United Klans of America sat on the front steps across the street and watched it all and sniggered. Bennie Hays, the Great Titan of the Klan, second highest ranking Klan official in Alabama, walked around the scene and said: "That's a pretty sight. Gonna look good on the news. Gonna look good for the Klan."

Mobile district attorney Chris Galanos announced that race did not appear to have been a motive in the killing. Mobile police said the fact that a cross had been burned on the courthouse lawn that same night had nothing to do with the case. When black leaders objected and called the murder a lynching, white politicians said they were "fanning the flames of racism." The cops thought Michael might have been dating a white woman he worked with at the *Mobile Press Register* or perhaps he was involved in drug dealing. Beulah

Donald let them search his room and they tore it apart but they found no drugs.

The local authorities couldn't catch anyone, the FBI couldn't find anything during its investigation on grounds of possible civil rights violations, and finally it all just came to a halt. In 1981, Mobile had one of the highest per capita murder rates in the country—and a police force that didn't even have a homicide squad. The D.A.'s office was understaffed, underpaid, and overwhelmed. Mobile's white establishment thought they were doing the best that they could. In Mobile's black community, people were convinced the authorities didn't give a damn who had killed Michael Donald. As far as they were concerned, the lynching was part of a pattern of violence against blacks ignored by or even instigated by authorities. And for Beulah Mae Donald, this was the time of anguish; she knew what had happened to Michael but she didn't know why. She knew her son and all she wanted proved was that "Michael did no wrong."

The way the proof came about is this: Beulah Mae Donald had been in the first class of foster grandparents ever operated by the Mobile Community Action Program and she took the toughest kids, working at the school for retarded children. She loved it and still misses them and would like to go back if "the sugar" would let her. Those pioneer foster grandparents became especially fond of a beautiful young social worker Vivian Davis, the director of the CAP agency. Vivian was engaged to a young lawyer and rising political star, State Senator Michael Figures. The day Michael Donald's body was discovered, Vivian brought Figures with her on a visit of condolence to Ms. Donald. He offered to do whatever he could to help, and ever since he has acted as her attorney and friend.

Michael Figures was one of the main organizers of a march in Mobile in August of 1981 to demand that something be done about Michael's murder. But it did no good. Cynthia Donald Mitchell, one of Beulah's daughters, picketed the courthouse, hoping to stir the police into action. It did no good, either.

"We could push from the outside, but we had no one on the inside," said Michael Figures. "No one on the police force or in the D.A.'s office or on the city commission." Although 36.2 percent of the people in Mobile are black, according to the 1980 census, no black was elected to the city council until 1985. Robert Eddington, a white Mobile lawyer, observed that every single public entity in Mobile, every agency, board, commission, and council, has been under federal court order in recent years because of segregation. "It's not just racism," he said. "They're also butt-headed. Butt-headedness is an old Southern sin. People here don't like being told what to do and so they get butt-headed about it." This is true, but not very consoling if you are black.

There was one Mobile black man who was an insider. Michael Figures's brother, Thomas Figures, had been named Assistant United States Attorney in 1978 and he made it his highest priority to get the Justice Department to authorize a second FBI investigation. The first reaction of the new FBI agent on the case, James Bodman, was, "Why the hell do you want to reopen this can of worms?" But the two of them, working together, cracked the case, playing one Klansman off against another. Once they had an informant, they had plenty of evidence from the Mobile medical examiner to convict the men. James (Tiger) Knowles confessed in exchange for a reduced sentence, was given life in prison, and put in the federal witness protection program. Henry Hays, the son of Bennie Hays, received the death penalty. Beulah Mae Donald did not go to the trial; she could not bear to look at them.

The two men who had actually murdered Michael Donald were in prison by January 1985. But the morning Michael Donald's body was found, Henry Hays had made one call from the house across the street even before he called the television station. He called his daddy. "He did it for his daddy," said Morris Dees of the Southern Poverty Law Center. There was evidence all over the case that more Klansmen than just Henry Hays and Tiger Knowles were involved. There was evidence of prior knowledge, conspiracy, aiding and abetting.

Morris Dees and the Southern Poverty Law Center have been keeping track of the KKK since 1971. They had filed lawsuits that so infuriated the Klan that Klansmen burned the center's office in Montgomery. The organization has since built a new building. Dees approached Ms. Donald and Michael Figures about the possibility of bringing a civil case against the Klan. The idea was to prove that Knowles and Hays had acted as agents of the United Klans of America, the most consistently violent of all the Klan groups. It took eighteen months to prepare the case and everyone involved was in some danger the entire time. (In 1984, a right-wing fanatic murdered the Denver talk-show host Alan Berg; Morris Dees was the next person on his hit list. Dees is also under a death threat from Louis

Beam, a paramilitary nut and Klansman now on the loose.) Step by step, by carefully turning former Klansmen, Dees built up the chain of evidence, not against the individual Klansmen but against the Klan itself.

"Ms. Donald didn't have to go along with the lawsuit," said Dees. "I will never know how painful it was for her, but I do know her persistence was critical to the case. At the end of the first day of trial, the Klan lawyer came to me and offered to settle out of court for $100,000. I took that offer to Ms. Donald and she turned it down. She wanted to see it through. This is a woman who lived in a public housing project, below the poverty level, a hardworking woman who has been extremely poor all her life. She was doing this for Michael."

The case Dees presented—proving the Klan was responsible for Michael Donald's death because his murderers had acted as agents of the Klan—was a legal tour de force. It has been written up in the *American Lawyer* and other legal journals. The case has more potential to break the Klan than criminal prosecution of individual members because it makes the Klan financially responsible for the misdeeds of any member. There is no question where the emotional heart of the case lay. Ms. Donald sat at the plaintiff's table throughout the long trial; she never testified, but rocked back and forth when the testimony brought her too much pain. On the stand, Tiger Knowles at first testified unemotionally about how he and Henry Hays "went out looking for a black person," any black person, to kill that night. Beulah Mae Donald wept silently as he stepped out of the witness box to demonstrate how he had killed Michael.

When the defense got a chance to give summations, Tiger Knowles spoke directly to the jury. He began crying. "I've lost my family. I've got people after me now. . . . I was acting as a Klansman when I done this. And I hope that people learn from my history. I do hope you decide a judgment against me and against everyone else involved. Because we are guilty."

His body began shaking as he turned to Beulah Mae Donald and said, "I can't bring your son back. God knows if I could trade places with him, I would. I can't. Whatever it takes—I have nothing. But I will have to do it. And if it takes me the rest of my life to pay it, any comfort it may bring, I hope it will."

Ms. Donald rocked back and forth and then said to him, "Son, I forgave you a long time ago. From the day I found out who y'all was, I asked God to take care of y'all, and He has. I turned it over to the Lord." The jurors wept. The judge wiped away tears. After only four hours of deliberation, the jury announced its $7 million judgment.

Of course the Klan doesn't have any money. Its only real asset is the headquarters building worth perhaps $113,000, now for sale. Ms. Donald, sitting in her apartment in the projects in Mobile, said, "If I end my days right here, it's all right with me. I don't mind. I wouldn't use the money but to help someone else anyway." The reason you know that's true is because that's how Beulah Mae Donald uses her money now, to help others.

In some ways, Beulah Mae Donald is like the stereotype of the kind, black woman that white Southerners like to empathize with. She is religious, hardworking, wronged but without bitterness, unprotesting about her place in the world, fatalistic. She shows such strength and such cheer in the face of a rather grim life that it's almost awesome. "Life is a mystery, and it's just what you make out of it," she says. It has been observed that you cannot change an established order with good manners, great charm, or Christian resignation, all traditional virtues of women. "There is no progress without struggle," said Frederick Douglass.

But it would be a mistake to think that women like Beulah Mae Donald do not fight the world's injustice. She would not fight for herself. She did not protest in the 1960s: although she admired Martin Luther King, Jr., she did not march to Selma or anywhere else—she was working as a maid to make a living for eight children. It is those children she sent out to fight the world's injustice. And when one of them was victimized by it, then she fought for her child. She not only beat the Klan; she may have broken it. Her major source of strength is her faith. When she says, "I turn it over to the Lord," she means just that. God cannot cure the pain those problems cause her—she still weeps for Michael—but God can take away the anger and the bitterness, so she can look at his killers and pray for them. Henry Hays is now on death row for Michael's murder. Beulah Mae Donald does not favor execution. "We cannot make life, so we have no right to take it away," she says.

Beulah Mae Donald is no plaster saint. All her sorrows cannot kill her sense of humor. She and Pat Clark, the director of Klanwatch, a project of the Southern Poverty Law Center, get together to go out to dinner and giggle like a couple of teenagers. She knows that "the old Devil will get so busy" and get into all of us. Her judgments of others are not so cushioned by charity that she can't call a no-good bum a no-good bum. She can be crashingly frank—about her ex-husbands, among others.

Beulah Mae Gregory Donald is sixty-seven years old, born in 1920 in De Lisle, Mississippi, the baby of a large family. Her daddy Marion was a sawmill worker and her mama Mary took in washing and ironing. Of that family, only Beulah Mae and her oldest brother Clancy are now left to remember how it was when two dollars was all the money in the world and they all helped their mama so she could make that. "She was a sweet mama and was the one taught us right from wrong, taught us prayer and blessings. I got all my faith from my mama."

Cynthia Mitchell, Beulah Mae Donald's own daughter, said, "My mother protected us from all kinds of discrimination and even knowing about discrimination. It was not until after Michael was killed that she called us together and started talking to us about the Klan. About Emmett Till, who was killed by them, and John Kennedy and Martin Luther King, Jr., and the civil rights movement." For children not born until the 1960s, it was all history, not everyday life. Beulah Mae Donald said, "I never told them because I thought them days was gone, I thought it was all past, old times."

The Gregory family moved to Mobile when Beulah Mae was seven. She dropped out of school in the tenth grade because she got married and pregnant at fifteen by William Miller, a boy not much older than she, who still lived at home with his mama and daddy. They had two children, but never lived together. Beulah Mae continued to live with her mother, who never reproached her, but just accepted what life brought. "In those times, you couldn't get on state welfare, so I went on to work."

She has worked ever since. First at St. Andrew's Hotel, then at Le Clade Hotel, and later for Ms. Hall, who had four children. "Two things I know and that's children and cleaning up."

Beulah Mae was on her own with her two girls for ten years, but shortly after World War II she met David Donald of Bay Minette, Alabama, who had been in the service. "He came along and looked after them, too, there's not many men will do that. After I met him, I sat down. I commenced to have children behind children. Leo, Stanley, Cecilia, and Cynthia." There was a baby girl between Stanley and Cecilia who died at six months. "And then here come

Michael, and that was a surprise." The greatest tragedy of her life, until Michael's murder, was the horrifying death of her oldest sister in the early 1940s. "She had separated from her husband and he came back one night and shot her five times, killed her at my mama's door. I never did get over the hurt of that, it was for no reason."

In the early 1960s, David Donald went to New York City and got a good job at Barnard College. She went up there intending to stay just a few months, just to see what it was like in the North, but stayed more than two years. "Then I got homesick. I didn't have anything to do but cook and eat, so I came back and went to work. My mama had lost her strength for the work and my daddy got sick and went blind and they needed me here."

Her son Leo lives in Detroit, works for General Motors, has three children, and still comes to visit his mama. Stanley is in Biloxi, works at Kessler Field, has a wife and one baby; Cecilia is a secretary at the CAP agency in Mobile, has three children; Cynthia works at Carver State Technical School and has one baby. Cecilia and Cynthia both graduated from Carver. Michael was in college when he was killed. They are all the children of a woman who never finished tenth grade and who worked as a maid all her life. She is so proud of those children. There are grandkids and even "great-grands" for Beulah Mae Donald to take care of, which she loves to do. It is a home-centered life.

"She has always been open with us, talked to us about everything and so we feel very close to her," said Cynthia. "She still tells us right from wrong, even if it's against what we're thinking; she will stand up to us even though we're grown now. She is a firm-loving person and we all enjoy her."

"My life?" asked Beulah Mae Donald with some surprise. "Well, it don't take long to tell."

Ms., January 1988

ONE LONE MAN

John Henry Faulk died on April 9, 1990. I miss him terribly.

O n a blazing hot summer day last year, the director of the Central Texas chapter of the American Civil Liberties Union was frantically phoning members to announce that the First Amendment was in dire peril from the Austin City Plan Commission. The First Amendment tends to be under steady fire in the Great State, but the Austin Plan Commission is rarely found on the side of jackbooted fascism. What happened was, the Reverend Mark Weaver, a fundamentalist divine with a strong local following, hell-bent on driving all the dirty bookstores out of town—he had come up with a zoning scheme by which this was to be accomplished. The Plan

Commission held a hearing that night attended by over three hundred members of Weaver's group, Citizens Against Pornography, and by six members of the Civil Liberties Union. The Libertarians flocked together. Nothing like sitting in the midst of a sea of Citizens Against Pornography to make you notice that your friends all look like perverts.

The Reverend Weaver rose to address the commission. An eloquent preacher, he took right off into the tale of a woman who lives directly behind the pornography theater on South Congress Avenue. The very day before, she had watched a man come out of that theater after the five-o'clock show, go into the alley behind the theater, right behind her house, and . . . masturbate. Three hundred Citizens Against and the members of the Plan Commission all sucked in their breath in horror. Made a very odd sound. *"Yes,"* continued the Reverend Weaver, "that man *masturbated* right in the alley, right *behind* that lady's house. And she has two little girls who might have *seen* it—if it weren't for the wooden fence around her yard." And with that the Reverend Weaver jerked the stopper and cussed sin up a storm. It looked bad for the First Amendment.

When it came their turn, the Libertarians huddled together and decided to send up their oldest living member. He shuffled to the mike, gray hair thin on top, a face marked with age spots and old skin cancers, one eye useless long since. He spoke with a courtly Southern accent. "Members of the Plan Commission, Reverend Weaver, Citizens Against, ladies and gentlemen. My name is John Henry Faulk. I am seventy-four years old. I was born and raised in South Austin, not a quarter of a mile from where that pornography theater stands today. I think y'all know that there was a *lot* of masturbation in South Austin before there was ever a pornography theater there." Even the Citizens Against laughed, and the First was saved for another day.

Thirty years ago John Henry Faulk destroyed the blacklisting system that had terrified the entertainment industry during the McCarthy era. His was one of the most spectacular show trials of that sorry time; he won the largest libel award that had yet been granted in the United States ($3.5 million) and was honored up to his eyebrows by freedom lovers everywhere. Then he went back to Texas—broke, his career still ruined—never saw any of the money, and learned you can't eat honor. This is the story of John Henry Faulk's life since Louis Nizer won out over Roy Cohn in their courtroom battle about whether the man called the Will Rogers of his generation was actually a communist.

Been so long since Texas freedom fighters couldn't count on Johnny Faulk almost no one can remember the time. He is a folklorist and humorist by profession, a storyteller, and a scholar of the Constitution. He's also a good man to have around when guerrilla tactics are called for.

Back in 1975, there was an unholy uproar in the state over another preacher, Brother Lester Roloff of Corpus Christi, since gone to glory. Brother Roloff ran a home for "wayward girls" without a state license; claimed he didn't need permission from the State of Texas to beat the Devil out of those girls and the Lord into them. At one point the state was forced to throw him into the slammer for contempt of court, and this caused his followers to swear vengeance on every godless politician and every godless licensing law in Texas.

Safe in Austin was State Senator Ron Clower of Garland, a cheerful fellow who followed the old legislative precept "Vote conservative, party liberal." Clower had done a substantial amount of beer-drinking, river-running, and good-timin' with a crowd of Austin liberals, of whom Johnny Faulk is one. Vast was the surprise of the Senator's friends when an item appeared in the papers saying Clower had introduced a tiny amendment to exempt Brother Roloff from state supervision. It was felt he should have known better.

The day of the hearing on his amendment, Clower's office received a call from a Reverend Billy Joe Bridges of Lovelady, leader of the White Christian Children's Army, a full-immersion, footwashing fundamentalist sect headed toward Austin to help Brother Clower hold off the forces of Satan. "We're bringin' three busloads of children. Red-white-and-blue buses," crooned Bridges. "We'll take those Christian children right up into the Senate gallery, and they'll float little paper airplanes with the words of Jesus written on them onto the Senate floor. We'll be the Christian Children's Air Force for the day, you see. Heh, heh."

Clower had been hoping to avoid publicity on this misbegotten amendment, but Cactus Pryor, a television newsman at KLBJ in Austin, called to say he'd heard the White Christian Children's Army was coming and the station wanted to have its cameras on the capitol steps to catch the "charge." Could Senator Clower's office tell him what time the buses were expected? "Oh God, television!"

groaned Clower. The liberal *Texas Observer* called: "We've just received a press release from some outfit called the White Christian Children's Army. What the hell is going on?"

"They've put out a press release!" screamed Clower's aide.

Came a call from Belton, the voice low and threatening. "This is Officer Joe Don Billups with the Department of Public Safety. We've just stopped three red-white-and-blue buses for speeding. They said your office could explain."

Clower, no idiot, took only a few more hours to realize it was all a put-on. The culprits never confessed, but a few months later, when Johnny Faulk received a call at 3 A.M. from the Democratic Telethon to verify his pledge of five hundred thousand dollars, Senator Clower was the chief suspect.

In the ugly, angry time of "Lyndon's War" against the communist Vietnamese, which all good Texans felt called upon to support, John Henry Faulk was making a slim living as an after-dinner speaker—and, for that matter, after-lunch—in front of such prestigious and high-paying organizations as the Grimes County Taxpayers Association and the Madisonville Kiwanis. He was never fool enough to come out against the war. But he would recount conversations he'd had with his cousin Ed Snodgrass, an old geezer so retrograde he has a sign over his mantelpiece that says, ROBERT E. LEE MIGHT HAVE GIVE UP, BUT I AIN'T. Cousin Ed would get to fussin' about all the dirty, long-haired peaceniks. "Don't you believe in the right to dissent, Cousin Ed?" Faulk would ask.

"Dissent? Oh hell yes, I believe in dissent. H'it's in the Constitution. What I can't stand is all this criticism. Criticize, criticize, criticize. Why can't they leave ol' Lyndon alone and let him fight his war in peace? Lookit this war. We send our best boys over there, in broad daylight, in million-dollar airplanes, wearin' pressed uniforms, to bomb them Veetnamese, and what do they do? Come out at night. On their bicycles. Wearin' pyjamas. Not even Christian. I tell you what, if we wasn't bombin' 'em, they would not be able to bomb theirselves. If they don't like what we're doing for 'em, they ought to go back where they come from." Johnny Faulk could get laughs out of Republicans with this routine, and no one ever got mad at him. They did, however, go away with the notion that there was something, well, ludicrous about the war.

"I never attack people for what they think," explains Faulk. "That's crucial. If I want to say something I know will stir folks up,

I make one of my characters say it. Then I disagree with my character, chide him for being foolish." Which is why the man once accused of being a Red is now asked to speak everywhere in Texas.

Johnny Faulk got branded a communist when he ran for union office in New York in 1955. At the time, Faulk remembers, "I was choppin' in the tall cotton." He was starring in his own five-day-a-week network radio show on CBS, called *Johnny's Front Porch,* and also appearing twice weekly on television on two panel quiz programs and in a variety of other slots as a guest panelist or guest host. Faulk ran as part of an anti-blacklisting slate for the board of AFTRA, the American Federation of Television and Radio Artists. Other members of the ticket included the CBS News reporter Charles Collingwood and the performers Orson Bean, Faye Emerson, Garry Moore, and Janice Rule. The anti-blacklisters won twenty-seven of the thirty-five seats on the board. A month after the new officers took over, AWARE, Inc.—"An Organization to Combat the Communist Conspiracy in Entertainment-Communications" —issued this bulletin about the group: "The term 'blacklisting' is losing its plain meaning and becoming a Communist jargon-term for hard opposition to the exposure of Communism." The newsletter then presented a number of allegations against Faulk. He once appeared on a program with Paul Robeson. He helped the Henry Wallace campaign in 1948. He sent second-anniversary greetings to a record company that sold "people's folk songs." Item No. 4 said, "A program dated April 25, 1946, named 'John Faulk' as a scheduled entertainer (with identified Communist Earl Robinson and two non-Communists) under the auspices of the Independent Citizens Committee of the Arts, Sciences, and Professions (officially designated a Communist front, and predecessor of the Progressive Citizens of America)."

It turned out that "officially designated a Communist front" meant some witness of indeterminate reliability had once mentioned the group in front of a congressional committee. It also turned out that John Henry Faulk did sure as a by-God have an intimate supper on the night of April 25, 1946, at the Astor Hotel with a known agent of the Soviet Union. And not just any agent—he dined with Andrei Gromyko, the Soviet ambassador to the United Nations. The dinner celebrated the first anniversary of the United Nations, and several hundred other people also showed up. Eleanor Roosevelt and Harold Ickes, the former Secretary of the Interior, were cochairmen of the event—presumably the "two non-Communists" mentioned in the AWARE bulletin—and Secretary of State Edward Stettinius was the main speaker. Johnny Faulk, fresh up from Texas, never did get to howdy or shake with the Big Red, but his career was destroyed anyway.

CBS fired Faulk a few months after the AWARE bulletin came out. "They didn't want to do it, and felt terrible about it," Faulk says. He was told that his ratings were slipping and that Arthur Godfrey was being given his time slot on radio. His lawyer, Louis Nizer, later proved in the trial that Faulk's ratings were going up at the time he was fired. But AWARE operated by putting pressure on advertisers, invoking the threat of a boycott by the American Legion if companies bought time on programs that employed suspected Reds. The system blacklisted, among others, an eight-year-old actress who was to have played Helen Keller in *The Miracle Worker*. AWARE itself was on retainer from the networks to sniff out subversives, so it had financial incentives to keep doing so.

Faulk filed a suit for libel against AWARE in 1956, but it didn't come to trial for six years, until the spring of 1962. In the meantime, he was out of show business and down to small odd jobs like selling encyclopedias. In his book *The Jury Returns* Louis Nizer wrote of John Faulk's case:

> One lone man had challenged the monstrously powerful forces of vigilantism cloaked in superpatriotism.
>
> One lone man with virtually no resources had dragged the defendants into the courts, and although outrageously outnumbered, had withstood starvation and disgrace, and summoned enough strength to battle them into submission.
>
> One lone man was so naive in his profound patriotism that he did not conceive of himself as fighting a heroic battle, but simply as doing what any American would do—defy the bully, spit at his pretension, and preserve his faith in his country's Constitution and principles.

This is Nizer at his most magniloquent, a style Faulk adores to imitate. In sorry truth, though, the "lone man" wasn't all that lone. He had the support of family and friends (from Edward R. Murrow to the beloved Texas historian, folklorist, and naturalist J. Frank Dobie), and Nizer was probably the finest trial lawyer in the country. In fact, Johnny Faulk had a wonderful time filing that lawsuit. "It required no courage to fight," he says, "because I never doubted I would win. I never thought of doing anything else."

One legacy of his seven years on the blacklist is that Faulk almost never publicly criticizes the Soviet Union or communism. He has no use for communists: "I knew a number of 'em on the University of Texas campus back in the thirties, well-intentioned but kind of pitiful people. And off-putting, like all true believers, like anyone who thinks he has The Truth and has no questions, no doubts, just wants to proselytize." But Faulk also believes that Americans hear so much anti-communist propaganda already there's no point in adding another scintilla to it. It galls him that to this good day a person is still expected to profess anti-communism as a way of proving his loyalty. "He must manifest it, say it, swear it, and pledge it," as Nicholas von Hoffman writes in his biography of Roy Cohn, "not once but . . . head covered, hand over heart, in the classroom, the ballpark, at the testimonial dinner."

During preparation for the trial Nizer kept pushing Faulk for proof that he'd done something actively anti-communist. It was fine that he was such a patriot he'd enlisted in the merchant marine at the start of World War II, then managed to get a job overseas with the Red Cross, and finally finagled his way into the Army despite being one-eyed. But what had he done *against* communists? After weeks of listening to Nizer press this issue, Faulk launched into a splendid extemporaneous tale of finding his dear old crippled grandmother one day reading the *Daily Worker*. No sooner had he said, "But Granny, that's a *communist* newspaper!" than the oil lamp in her tar-paper shack tumped over, setting the place ablaze. Faulk grabbed her wheelchair and started toward the porch and safety, but "as I wheeled her out, I looked down and saw that *Daily Worker* in her lap, realized she was just a *communist* pawn, and was so filled with loathing I turned her chair and pushed the old lady back into the flames!" Nizer listened to this entire faradiddle without expression and then snapped, "We can't use it." Nizer had so little humor he introduced into evidence Faulk's boyhood award for perfect attendance—seventy-two consecutive Sundays—at the Fred Allen Memorial Methodist Church in South Austin. Faulk is not much of a Methodist, but his mother sure was.

South Austin was then the city's black neighborhood, and Johnny's father was Judge John Henry Faulk, Sr., a man of progressive principles, whose hero was Clarence Darrow. The elder Faulk had served

as Eugene V. Debs' state campaign manager in the days when Socialists got a sight more votes than Republicans in Texas. As an attorney
he had often represented poor black people, so he moved his family
to a beautiful old home in South Austin called Green Pastures, now
one of the city's best restaurants, run by Johnny Faulk's nephew Ken
Kooch. Johnny grew up among blacks, and they were his childhood
friends.

John Henry Faulk's great natural gift is an almost freakish aural
memory. One day last year, as he walked in South Austin, he began
reminiscing about his childhood neighbors. One was an elderly black
woman whose only child, a retarded son, had died years earlier.
When she got to missing that child too bad she would call to him
as though he were still alive, and the neighborhood children made
fun of her for it. Suddenly, across a distance of sixty-five years or
more, the voice of an old black woman came out of Faulk's throat,
a crackled call of love: "Come on, son. Come on, son. Mama's
waitin'." The voice hung like a ghost along the dirt lane.

Because the Faulk family had progressive opinions on "colored
people" for that time, John Henry did not recognize his own racism
until he was at college. He and his mentor, Frank Dobie, so loathed
Hitler that they studied his speeches, and it slowly dawned on them
that racism could apply to blacks as well as to Jews. Talk about a
couple of Texas boys in a quandary—now what to do? They con-
sulted Faulk's childhood chum Alan Lomax, who had not only gone
off to prep school and Harvard but was also the son of John A.
Lomax, who had started the folklore collection at the Smithsonian
Institution. They felt Lomax was wise in the ways of the great world.
He advised that amongst the intelligentsia the word was pronounced
"Negro" rather than "Nigra," and that this was the sure sign by
which black people could tell you weren't prejudiced against their
kind. Johnny Faulk and Frank Dobie sat around solemnly practicing
the word—*"Kneee-grow, Kneee-grow"*—to get it right. Faulk's gift
for mimicry made it easy for him, but poor Dobie, a full generation
older and with a Texan accent, had to rehearse for ages.

In order to get a master's degree in folklore, Faulk traveled
around East Texas in the late thirties with a recorder taping what
was then called "colored folklore." In 1941, he was working for his
doctorate and teaching at the university when he got a Rosenwald
grant to collect more material. "Rural blacks in those days were so
isolated. They were too poor to have electricity, so even the radio was

unknown to them," Faulk says now. "Many of their cultural traditions have since been so thoroughly wiped out not even many black people know about them." These days Faulk rarely does black characters, but one still in his repertoire is the Reverend Tanner Franklin, who preaches a sermon on David and Goliath in the wondrous, ancient sing-preaching of Afro-Americans that is virtually gone. You can hear it now only on old records and in the voice of Johnny Faulk replicating the Reverend Franklin as he sings:

> *Go down angel, consume the flood.*
> *Snuff out the sun, turn de moon to blood.*
> *Go down angel, close de door.*
> *Time have been, shan't be no more.*

Faulk's yarns about Texas frequently have a bizarre flavor. Long before anyone had heard of Lenny Bruce, Johnny Faulk was doing black humor in the form of country stories. Strange deaths, weird funerals, matrons complacently rocking as people go mad around them. It's possible that Faulk's career never would have blossomed on television, because what storytellers need above all else is time. It is an art born of leisure, and a story well told can pause for any number of interesting sidetracks. From 1975 to 1981, Faulk was employed on "Hee Haw," the corn-pone country version of "Laugh-In." He was the resident cracker-barrel philosopher, commenting on politics in thirty-second skits. ("Why, the trouble with Jerry Ford is, he played center for so long he looks at the world backward and upside down." HEE-HAW.) Faulk's humor is not suited to one-liners. The show was pretty awful, but it was steady work, and Faulk delighted in it. In addition to his congenital optimism, he has that show-business habit of thinking everything's coming up roses—whatever project he's doing is fabulous, the director is wonderful, he's met the loveliest people.

His "Hee Haw" fame has been useful to him at some odd points. Although he makes a living as an after-dinner speaker, ever since his trial Faulk has considered his real work educating Americans about the First Amendment, and to that end he donates his time and talent without stint. One day, in March 1979, he got a call from a lawyer representing the pornographer Larry Flynt. Flynt was on trial in Atlanta for obscenity, and his goose was pretty well cooked. Georgians have no use for Yankee pornographers, even those who have been shot, crippled, and brought to Jesus by President Carter's sister. The judge had turned down almost every expert Flynt's lawyers had tried to call—scholars from Harvard and Yale. Faulk remembers the attorneys implying they were down to the bottom of the barrel, and if Faulk would come over to Atlanta they'd pay him to testify as an authority on the First Amendment.

Faulk doesn't take money for testifying about the First Amendment, but he agreed to stop by Atlanta on his way to a "Hee Haw" taping in Nashville. Thinking he should know what he was about to defend, he bought his first copy of Flynt's *Hustler* magazine at the Houston airport. Slipped off the plain brown wrapper and like to had a stroke. "H'it was a picture of a nekkid lady with her finger stuck up herself and her tongue out like this. . . ." Faulk arrived for a conference of the Flynt defense team that opened with the newly born-again defendant insisting they all form a circle, join hands, and pray. Faulk silently addressed the Lord with a strong sense of grievance over being there at all. The lawyers warned Faulk that security at the courthouse was tight, because of the earlier shooting; the Georgia lawmen hated the Flynt team and daily threw them up against the wall, searched them, emptied their briefcases on the ground, and verbally harassed them.

Next morning the defense team headed into the courthouse and met the first line of the law—Georgia State Troopers. "They wore shiny mirror silver sunglasses, big guns on one hip, big billy clubs on the other," Faulk remembers, "and they were *mean* lookin'." He braced himself for the search, but the troopers parted before him, whispering as they fell back, "H'it's John Henry Faulk, from 'Hee Haw'! H'it's John Henry Faulk, from 'Hee Haw'!" And the dreaded sheriff's men, said to be even meaner than the troopers, they, too, turned out to be fans, and, instead of throwing Faulk up against the wall, asked for his autograph. Danged if the judge didn't watch "Hee Haw," and the jurors, who beamed at him. Even the prosecutor told the court he was proud to have Mr. Faulk of "Hee Haw" testify in his case.

Faulk started by talking about growing up in South Austin without indoor plumbing. His family had an outhouse and, being on the poor side, never could afford toilet paper, so his mama used to put the Sears, Roebuck catalog out there for that purpose. But being a good Methodist Sunday-school teacher, she always cut out the pages with the corset ads on them, lest the boys get excited in the outhouse. The judge and the jury were chuckling along at this story, and Faulk had already made points about changing community standards.

The prosecutor, no fool, leaped up, shoved a copy of *Hustler* under Faulk's nose, and roared, "*Mr. Faulk*! Would you have wanted your mother, the Methodist Sunday-school teacher, to have seen *this*?" Sure enough, Faulk reports, there was another nekkid lady with her finger stuck up herself and her tongue hangin' out. "*Shut your mouth, boy!*" he replied. "You want lightnin' to strike this courthouse? God will call it down at the very *idea* of my sainted mother seeing such a thing!" He continued in a far quieter vein. "Of course I would not have wanted my mother to see such a thing. Nor do I want my wife to see it, nor my son. That's ugly. That's so ugly. But let me tell you about why the Founding Fathers wrote what they did in our Constitution where it says, 'Congress shall make no law. . . .' " Faulk was eloquent in the cause, but notes, "Didn't do him a damn bit of good. They found his ass good and guilty."

Faulk has recently recovered from cancer. Although he admits that having cancer nearly scared him to death, he also loves being the center of attention and reveled in all the concern. Doctors in Houston managed to rid him of a lemon-size tumor in the middle of his head solely by using radiation. His salivary glands were damaged in the process, and that makes his stage work more difficult, but he appears to have regained most of his energy. Right now he's working on a one-man show he already tried successfully in Houston last year. The play, called *Deep in the Heart*, involves a collection of Faulk's characters all placed loosely in some mythical Texas town, and will be in New York this fall under the direction of Albert Marre, who did *Man of La Mancha*, among other productions. It will be the first time Faulk has performed in New York since he was blacklisted. He is so excited he practically dances when he talks about it: he has the capacity for delight of an eight-year-old at Christmas.

No tragedy here, no life destroyed by McCarthyism. He has a close family—three sisters and a brother—and Faulk family gatherings tend to look like county conventions. He had messed up two marriages before he met Elizabeth Peake, a British nurse, in 1964, and struck it lucky. They have one son, Yohann, who is nineteen. Faulk claims he is "the only kid ever born on Medicare." Among Liz

Faulk's outstanding qualities is her immense common sense, a commodity for which her husband is not noted—imagine Maggie Thatcher with a heart. She keeps track of his schedule, his money, and his health, while he wanders around blithely being funny about politics and serious about the Constitution. What fun, what joy, thinks he, and wades once more into the battle. It infuriates him to see this country betray its best, basic principles, and he sometimes concludes that most of his fellow-citizens are nincompoops. But Faulk is always confident that the genius of the Founders will triumph in the end. He speaks of them with a reverence, love, and depth of knowledge all the flag-waving patriots down to the V.F.W. Hall recognize and respect.

Wigwag, Summer 1988

HOW ANN RICHARDS GOT TO BE GOVERNOR OF TEXAS

The way Ann Richards got to be governor of Texas started back when Bill Hobby decided not to run. Hobby had been lieutenant governor since the memory of man runneth not to the contrary. Lite-Guv-for-Life, we used to call him, and during eighteen years in office, the quiet, studious Houston millionaire had earned the esteem of almost everyone in Texas.

But he'd just come off some killer special sessions in 1989, about workers' comp, for pity's sake, and the man was tarred. Plumb tuckered. His advisers told him he couldn't even take a vacation—no fox-hunting in Ireland, which is what Hobby actually does for fun. Who the hell ever heard of a governor of Texas who fox-hunts? No vacation, they said, you've got to face Jim Mattox right now. If he was going to make the race, he'd have to poop or get off the pot right then.

No wonder Hobby got off the pot.

Mattox, then the attorney general, is the pit bull of Texas politics. Mattox is so mean he wouldn't spit in your ear if your brains were on fire. He is such a fearsomely vile campaigner that he got elected as a liberal out of Dallas for twenty years. Aside from that, he's a pretty decent public servant.

So that left no one but Richards to run against the Dick Nixon of Texas Democrats. "Lite Guv," all her friends said. "Go for Lite Guv." Trouble with Lite Guv is, it pays squat: $7,200 a year, just like the members of the Legislature. You have to be as rich as Hobby to hold that job. Richards got some money out of her divorce, but she used it to buy a house and then she had to earn a living. Fifty-four years old, single, recovering alcoholic—hell, what the woman needed was a pension. Governor of Texas makes $94,000 a year. Don't ever let anyone tell you giving politicians a raise won't attract better candidates.

It all seemed fairly simple at the start: Richards had been state treasurer for eight years; she had a genuinely terrific record in that office; she had national name recognition from her funny keynote address to the Democratic Convention of 1988; and she had a negative rating of 4 percent. Six months later, she won the Democratic nomination for governor with her negatives at 50 percent and half the people in the state under the impression that she was a lesbian drug addict. That's politics in our time.

Yo, well, it was a doozy, start to finish. In addition to the formidable attorney general, Richards faced former Governor Mark White (1982–86), who, as these things go, had been quite a decent governor. (In Texas, we do not hold high expectations from the office; it's mostly been occupied by crooks, dorks, and the comatose.) White would have been counted one of our more successful chief executives, had not the price of oil—indeed, the entire economy of the state—not crashed to ruin on his watch. It wasn't his fault that the price of oil slid from $30 to $9 a barrel; on the other hand, who else could we blame?

So here are these three Democratic candidates—Richards, Mattox, and White—putting on a primary so ugly it became a national joke. Incidentally, the state was in crisis. State governments have four basic areas of responsibility: roads, schools, prisons, and what

Governor Allan Shivers used to call "your eleemosynary institutions." In Texas, three of the four were so bad they'd been declared unconstitutional. The schools, the prisons, and the state homes for the mentally retarded and mentally ill were all under court order. On top of that, the state faced a huge deficit and clearly needed to restructure its entire tax system, an utterly regressive, jerry-built, patched-up fiscal disaster area designed to encourage "a healthy bidness climate." So what was the big issue in the primary? The death penalty.

They held a Fry-Off. Mattox got on television and announced he couldn't wait to pull that old death-penalty lever; when he was A.G. he used to go up to the state pen and watch guys get fried for the fun of it. Mark White got on television and actually strolled through a gallery of baddies who'd been fried when he was governor while he talked about how keen he is on frying people. Richards kept saying, "Me too." Mattox found some prison newsletter that had endorsed Richards and put up an ad that said, "Vote for Jim Mattox: *He* hasn't been endorsed by anyone on death row." You'd have thought they were all running for State Executioner. "Saturday Night Live" did a satirical skit on the primary in which the candidates wore black hoods and carried axes.

Mark White was the first casualty, knocked off by a third-place finish in the March primary that left Richards and Mattox in a run-off. Everyone thought the primary race was pitiful—the run-off was just flat ugly. White stomped off in a huge huff, swearing he'd never vote for Richards, who had run an attack-ad on him he thought was below the belt. Below hell, there was no belt in that race. Then Mattox showed the world how to be really crass. Richards had discussed her alcoholism openly; at the end of a televised debate, she was asked if she had ever used illegal drugs and she refused to answer the question. All hell broke loose. It was widely known that in the crowd of writers, country singers, liberal politicos, and freelance fun and funny people Ann Richards went around with in Austin in the late sixties and early seventies, almost everyone tried marijuana. Richards's position was that if she answered the drug question, everyone around the state who was still out there drinking and doping would be discouraged from coming in for help, because if they could still beat you over the head with it after ten years of sobriety, there was no point in sobering up.

The Texas political world went bonkers. Why doesn't she answer the question? Why won't she answer the question? Half her supporters thought she should just 'fess up; the other half warned that it would finish her candidacy. Some thought she should say, "I was too drunk to remember." Everybody had a scenario, everybody thought they knew what she should do. None of it had anything to do with roads, schools, prisons, or taxes, but it was the only issue in the run-off. She was asked "the question" again at the second televised debate and again refused to answer. After that debate she was surrounded by a mob of screaming reporters, all demanding that she answer the question. By the time her staff waded into the scum and dragged her out, Richards was white and shaking. I never saw her enjoy a single day of the campaign from then on. She became tight and guarded with reporters, answering every question as though it were booby-trapped.

Mattox put up an ad posing the new question: "Did Ann Richards use cocaine?" More flap. The issue just would not go away. Everybody started running ads saying the other guy's ads were unfair. It got wonkier and wonkier. Some guy showed up claiming he had seen Mattox, who is a teetotal Baptist, smoke dope. This citizen was put on television making this claim in both Houston and Dallas before anyone could even check out whether he'd just been released from the state nuthouse. Someone else popped up to say he'd seen Richards use cocaine ten years before, at a Jim Mattox fund-raiser. The press did not cover itself with glory. The citizenry was disgusted. Richards limped through the run-off in April with 54 percent. And there stood Clayton Williams.

He had a thirty-point lead. He had $10 million ($8 million of it his own money). He had the best television ads anyone had ever seen. And he was a likeable guy. He wasn't a politician, he had no record to attack. His big issue was drugs. He, Clayton Williams, proposed to stop drug use in the state of Texas. (This also has nothing to do with roads, schools, prisons, or taxes, but whatthehey?) His announced plan was to take young drug-users and "teach 'em the joys of busting rocks."

Claytie Williams is in truth a perfect representative of a vanishing Texas. He's white, he's macho, he's rich (oil, cattle, banking, and communications). He really does wear cowboy boots and a cowboy hat all the time. He worships John Wayne, has a statue of Wayne in the lobby of his bank in Midland. Williams is open-hearted, sentimental, and gregarious. He's not only an Aggie (a graduate of Texas

A & M University), he still gets tears in his eyes whenever he hears the Aggie fight song. He's got a trophy-wife named Modesta. He hunts. He drinks. He occasionally gets into fistfights. And he believes the world simple.

One of his most brilliant ad series would give some simple-minded, tough-talk answer to a complex problem and then close with, "And if they tell you it can't be done, you tell them they haven't met Clayton Williams yet." If they'd just shut him up in a box for the duration of the campaign, he'd be governor today.

In late March, he invited the press corps out to his ranch for roundup. They got bad weather. Sitting around the campfire with three male reporters, Williams opined, "Bad weather's like rape: as long as it's inevitable, you might as well lie back and enjoy it." Bubba, the shorthand we use to denote the average, stereotypical Texan, has been using that line for years. But it was Williams's fate in the campaign to keep unerringly finding that fault line between the way things have always been in Texas and the way things are getting to be. Richards shrewdly picked up on the difference with her end-lessly reiterated slogan about "the New Texas." Claytie Williams is Old Texas to the bone.

Later, a bizarre rumor about "honey hunts" out at Williams's ranch began circulating. I don't know who started it, but I do know it was ably spread by George Shipley, a campaign consultant known to the press corps as "Dr. Dirt," who was then working for Richards. According to this rumor, to reward his top employees, Williams would hire a bunch of whores and then take everyone out to the ranch and let the boys hunt down the whore ladies. Apparently in an effort to address this rumor, Williams publicly allowed as how the only truck he'd ever had with prostitutes was when he was a student at A & M and would go to Mexico because it was the only way you could "get serviced" in those days. (Technically speaking, it is the bull that services the cow, not vice versa.) Texas Hispanics naturally do not enjoy being reminded that Anglo Texans have been using Mexico as a whorehouse for generations. And Texas women don't like being reminded that Bubba thinks of them as a service station.

This touched off a new round of bad Claytie Williams jokes: "How many Republicans does it take to screw in a lightbulb?" "Republicans don't screw in lightbulbs: They screw in Mexico."

Polls showed the gender gap in support for Richards or Williams getting wider all summer. Williams had enough money to keep his ads on during the hot season, Richards didn't. Unfortunately for Williams, three of his ads were so full of egregious errors and misstatements they had to be pulled down. This lent incentive to the press's "ad police" efforts: most of the state's major newspapers took to dissecting new political ads to see how their content measured up to the truth. This was done most effectively by television stations, notably WFAA in Dallas and KVUE in Austin, which were better able to show how the pictures used in ads can be misleading.

Interestingly enough, one of Williams's ads showed Ann Richards at the political highlight of her career, making the keynote address to the Democratic Convention in 1988, specifically, the famous line on President Bush: "Poor George. He can't help it. He was born with a silver foot in his mouth." The ad ran in August, at the start of the Persian Gulf crisis, when patriotism was at flood tide and criticizing the president was tantamount to treason. But I was astonished at how many people objected to that line and held it against Richards throughout the campaign. The line itself is already classic and will be used in every anthology of political humor published hereafter. Yet a surprising number of men are alarmed by the thought of a witty woman. They think of women's wit as sarcastic, cutting, "ball-busting": it was one of the unstated themes of the campaign and one reason why Ann Richards didn't say a single funny thing during the whole show. Margaret Atwood, the Canadian novelist, once asked a group of women at a university why they felt threatened by men. The women said they were afraid of being beaten, raped, or killed by men. She then asked a group of men why they felt threatened by women. They said they were afraid women would laugh at them.

Williams blooped again on October 11, not a slip of the tongue, but a carefully planned confrontation that just didn't work. The press had been gnawing on a story about Williams's bank, Claydesta National (that's a combination of Clayton and Modesta, you see; very Texan) illegally selling credit insurance, particularly to poor black people applying for auto loans. Richards's campaign planted that story (Dr. Dirt again), but since it was a legitimate story, the press ran with it. All Richards herself ever said about it was that she only knew what she read in the papers. Richards was to appear before Williams at a forum in Dallas. Television cameras caught Williams just before he went up on the dais, saying to a friend, "Watch what I'm going to do to her now, watch this." As Williams moved behind the seated line of dignitaries on the dais, Richards, who had already spoken and was fixing to leave, got out of her chair, put out her hand, and said, "Hello, Claytie." Williams feigned surprise, then indignation. "I'm not going to shake hands with you," he says, "I won't shake hands with a liar." And he moved past leaving Richards to say after him with commendable self-possession, "Well, I'm sorry you feel that way about it, Clayton."

Bubba didn't mind the rape joke or Claytie's shooting an endangered species of mountain sheep or ripping off black folks, but Bubba did not like that scene. It played over and over on television and Bubba thought it was tacky. Bubba may screw Mexican whores, but Bubba is not rude to a lady. Williams then managed to observe within hearing of the press that he planned to "head her, hoof her, and drag her through the dirt." When Richards predicted she would win the race, Williams giggled on camera and said, "I hope she hasn't started drinking again," a line so tacky Richards used it in one of her own ads. A spoof of the Williams' tagline became popular: "If you think Texas doesn't have a village idiot, you haven't met Clayton Williams yet."

But the polls still showed Williams ten points ahead, then seven points ahead. The Richards campaign was praying for Williams to screw up again, and he cheerfully obliged. Williams's people had sagely dodged all requests for a debate, since Williams knew almost zip about state government, but two Dallas television stations, KERA and WFAA, managed to rope him in to "in-depth" interviews. He gave a shaky performance, his ignorance more visible than usual. Then one interviewer asked, almost as a throwaway, "What's your stand on Proposition One?"

"Which one is that?" Williams inquired.

"The only one on the ballot."

He was still lost, so the interviewer told him what the proposition was about—concerning the governor's power to make late-term "midnight" appointments. Williams still didn't know if he was for it or against it.

"But haven't you already voted?" inquired the interviewer. "You told us you voted absentee. Don't you remember how you voted?"

"I just voted on that the way my wife told me to; she knew what it was," Williams explained.

He was so clearly a candidate in a world of trouble, the clip made the national news. The polls now showed her within three points. All Richards had to do was stay out there plugging away, not make any mistakes, and keep drawing that line about the difference between the Old Texas and the New Texas. There were Richards yard signs all over upper-class Republican neighborhoods in Dallas and Houston, thanks to the women. Texas politics features an astonishingly dedicated corps of Republican women who woman the famous Republican phone banks—notoriously more effective than anything Texas Democrats have ever been able to pull together. Republican women not only weren't working the phone banks, they were lying about who they were going to vote for. It wasn't just the abortion issue: many upper-class Republican women are pro-choice, but they were also wincing over how it would look to the rest of the world to have Claytie as governor of Texas. He's such a throwback, like a character out of *Giant*. The old Texas stereotypes, which these women have been struggling to bury for years by their good works for art museums and symphony orchestras and ballet companies, would be so reinforced by Governor Clayton Williams they could hardly bear to think about it. And let's face it, Modesta is a tacky name.

The candidates went into the last weekend dead even, but Williams got President Bush down to work for him nonstop. Bush pretended he was running hard against Saddam Hussein and might have pulled it off, had not Williams blooped again. The Richards campaign, which had been trying hard to get Williams to reveal his tax returns (Richards had already made hers public), kept faxing tax questions to reporters wherever Williams went. On the Friday before election, asked again about taxes during a small-town television interview, Williams replied as he always did, "I have paid millions of dollars in taxes." Then he added, "Except in 1986, when I didn't pay anything." The press almost missed it. The throwaway line made it into one wire story, but was buried. Richards's campaign people saw it and went ballistic. Bill Crier, Richards's press secretary, had a hard time getting her to pick it up and use it. She was in Houston that night, but it hadn't made the Houston newscasts, it wasn't on the wires, she was tired, she couldn't see it. But Crier insisted she bring it up in front of a union audience. The audience went nuts. Clayton Williams, a multimillionaire, paid no taxes in 1986. Perfectly legal, of course. Like everyone else in oil, he lost a lot of money that year. But it reminded everyone one more time what they don't like about rich Republicans—the guy is sitting on a bank account with at least $10 million in it, he had enough money that year to make thousands of dollars in political contributions to Republican candidates, but he didn't pay any taxes. Everyone else in Texas had a bad year in 1986, too. Unemployment was almost 13 percent. But the rest of us had to pay taxes. It's not fair. The rich get all the breaks.

A subsidiary theme was, "Can you believe he was dumb enough to say that?" The half of the press corps traveling with Williams missed the whole thing. First of all, they got into a fight with the pilot of the press plane, who wouldn't let them drink. When they got to Laredo, they were told their rooms at La Posada were not available. Actually, the Williams's campaign had cancelled the reservations and then shipped the reporters across the border to a Mexican hotel with no telephones. Editors trying to find their reporters that night to check out the story were S.O.L. The ploy backfired: Several papers did miss the story Saturday, but that meant it hit the Sunday papers, with a much larger readership. Richards's campaign people stayed up all night making a radio commercial about Williams's failure to pay taxes. Monte Williams did the voiceover and volunteers drove hundreds of miles all over the state to get it to radio stations, where it aired Sunday and Monday. It was the last impression voters got of Clayton Williams before the election. His campaign was in free-fall.

Richards won with 52 percent of the vote. We knew it was over at 7 P.M. election night, before any official returns, when Clayton Williams's press secretary, Bill Kenyon, started berating the press. Williams was exceptionally gracious in defeat, reminding everyone of why they'd ever liked him in the first place.

The scene at Richards's headquarters hotel on election night, the Hyatt in Austin, was like nothing ever seen before in Texas politics. It's true Ann Richards had some heavy-hitters give money to her campaign—some wealthy trial lawyers, the Jewish socialist insurance millionaire from Waco (a class of one) Bernard Rapoport, and a few Texas women with their own money. But by and large Richards had done something unprecedented in state politics. She raised almost $8 million in $25 contributions—it was the great bulk of her money. When Texas lobbyists back the wrong candidate, they say among themselves that they have to catch "the late train" over to the winner. With Richards, it was a Midnight Special. The lobbyists started pouring into her hotel around 9 P.M. and it looked like

a conga line—oil, insurance, timber, chemicals. Upstairs, there was
no one "insider" party for the big givers, as there usually is. Instead
there were at least ten different parties for people, most of them
women, who had raised big money in small chunks. There was an
intensity of celebration normally felt only by the family and staff of
a victorious politician. Perhaps because women show emotion more
easily than men, the intensity factor was formidable. People were
packed into the main ballroom like sardines. They sang and laughed
and greeted one another with that peculiar female Texan greeting
call that sounds like calling pigs, "OOOOOOOooooo, honeee, how
good to see yew again!" Finally Ann spoke and everyone laughed and
wept some more, and then she reminded them to drive home safely.

PERMISSIONS ACKNOWLEDGMENTS

Some of the essays in this book were originally published in *The Atlantic Monthly*, *The Dallas Times-Herald*, *Houston Journalism Review*, *McCall's*, *Mother Jones*, *Ms.*, *The New York Times Magazine*, *Savvy*, *The Texas Monthly*, *Texas Observer*, and *Washington Journalism Review*.

Grateful acknowledgment is made to the following for permission to reprint previously published material: THE NATION: Five articles by Molly Ivins that appeared in *The Nation:* "H. Ross Went Seven Bubbles off Plumb" (October 14, 1984); "The Gibber Wins One and Other News" (November 23, 1985); "Tough as Bob War and Other Stuff" (June 7, 1986); "Practicing Nuance Down at Luby's" (November 8, 1986); "Dumb Bankers, Mavericks Too" (January 23, 1989). Copyright © 1984, 1985, 1986, 1989 by *The Nation* magazine/The Nation Company, Inc. Reprinted by permission. THE PROGRESSIVE: Twenty-one articles by Molly Ivins that appeared in *The Progressive:* "How to Survive Reagan" (March 1986); "The Front Line" (May 1986); "As Thousands Cheer" (September 1986); "Oil on the Rocks" (November 1986); "The Great International Blink-Off" (December 1986); "Persian Diversion" (January 1987); "Killing the Messenger" (March 1987); "Grab the Salt" (September 1987); "Running on His Rims" (October 1987); "Soap Opera" (February 1988); "The Word's the Thing" (August 1988); "Texas-Style Ethics" (September 1988); "Too Wussy for Texas" (November 1988); "Dallas Does It Again" (February 1989); "State of the States" (April 1989); "Kindler and Gentler Already" (December 1989); "Post-Election Gloating" (January 1990); "The Czar Is Hooked" (February 1990); "Post-Invasion Pacification" (March 1990); "The Golf . . . er, Gulf . . . Crisis" (October 1990); "Season of Drear" (February 1991). All articles are reprinted by permission of *The Progressive*, 409 East Main Street, Madison, Wisconsin 53703. TEXAS MONTHLY: "Lubbock, Seat of the Rebellion" by Molly Ivins, from the May 1989 edition of *Texas Monthly*. Reprinted by permission of *Texas Monthly*.

"One Lone Man" was originally published in the Summer 1988 issue of *Wigwag*.